CRE▲TIVE
HOMEOWNER®

VACATION
HOME PLANS

CREATIVE HOMEOWNER®, Upper Saddle River, New Jersey

COPYRIGHT © 2006

CRE▲TIVE
HOMEOWNER®

A Division of Federal Marketing Corp.
Upper Saddle River, NJ

VP/Publisher: Brian H. Toolan
VP/Editorial Director: Timothy O. Bakke
Production Manager: Kimberly H. Vivas

Home Plans Editor: Kenneth D. Stuts
Home Plans Designer Liaison: Maureen Mulligan

Design and Layout: Arrowhead Direct (David Kroha, Cindy DiPierdomenico, Judith Kroha)

Cover Design: David Geer

Printed In China

Current Printing (last digit)
10 9 8 7 6 5 4 3 2 1

Vacation Home Plans
Library of Congress Control Number: 2005909253
ISBN-10: 1-58011-308-7
ISBN-13: 978-1-58011-308-3

CREATIVE HOMEOWNER®
A Division of Federal Marketing Corp.
24 Park Way
Upper Saddle River, NJ 07458
www.creativehomeowner.com

Note: The homes as shown in the photographs and renderings in this book may differ from the actual blueprints. When studying the house of your choice, please check the floor plans carefully.

Photo Credits
All landscape illustrations by: Steve Buchanan (Portfolio of Designs), Michelle Angle Farrar, Lee Hov, Robert LaPointe, Rick Dasham and Teresa Nicole Green (Guide to Installation)

Front Cover: *main* plan 291015, page 233; *insets left to right* plan 391056, pages 224–225; plan 131056, pages 8–9; plan 291015, page 233; plan 291015, page 233 **page 1:** plan 121190, page 190 **page 3:** *top to bottom* plan 111049, page 186; plan 191001, page 160; plan 291015, page 233 **page 4:** plan 111003, **page 5:** plan 331005 **page 6:** *top* plan 141028; *bottom* plan 161002 **page 7:** plan 221022, page 252 **pages 48–49:** *both* courtesy of Kraftmaid Cabinetry, Inc. **page 50:** *both* courtesy of Wellborn Cabinets **page 51:** courtesy of Kraftmaid Cabinetry, Inc. page 52: courtesy of Wellborn Cabinets **page 53:** *top right* courtesy of Wellborn Cabinets; *top & bottom left* courtesy of Merillat Industries **pages 106–107:** *both* courtesy of Kraftmaid Cabinetry, Inc. **page 108:** courtesy of Osram-Sylvania **pages 109–110:** *both* courtesy of Kraftmaid Cabinetry, Inc. **page 111:** courtesy of IKEA **page 147:** *top* courtesy of Weber; *bottom right* courtesy of Frontgate; *bottom left* courtesy of Broilmaster **page 148:** courtesy of Sub-Zero **page 149:** *both* courtesy of Malibu Lighting/Intermatic **pages 150–151:** *top right* Marvin Slobin/courtesy of California Redwood Association; *bottom* courtesy of Southern Forest Products Association; *top left* courtesy of Malibu Lighting/Intermatic **pages 170–171:** Bradsimmons.com **page 172:** *top* Bradsimmons.com; *bottom* Tony Giammarino/Giammarino & Dworkin **page 173:** courtesy of California Redwood Association **page 174:** John Parsekian **page 175:** *top* John Glover; *center* courtesy of California Redwood Association; *bottom* Raven Bussolini/Positive Images **page 277:** plan 121036, page 23 **page 287:** plan 291015, page 233 **back cover:** *top main* plan 131056, pages 8–9; *bottom main* plan 391056, pages 224–225; *insets left to right* plan 291015, page 233; plan 441024, pages 262–263; plan 441015, pages 274–275

Contents

Getting Started

Maybe you can't wait to bang the first nail. Or you may be just as happy leaving town until the windows are cleaned. The extent of your involvement with the construction phase is up to you. Your time, interests, and abilities can help you decide how to get the project from lines on paper to reality. But building a house requires more than putting pieces together. Whoever is in charge of the process must competently manage people as well as supplies, materials, and construction. He or she will have to

- Make a project schedule to plan the orderly progress of the work. This can be a bar chart that shows the time period of activity by each trade.
- Establish a budget for each category of work, such as foundation, framing, and finish carpentry.
- Arrange for a source of construction financing.
- Get a building permit and post it conspicuously at the construction site.
- Line up supply sources and order materials.
- Find subcontractors and negotiate their contracts.
- Coordinate the work so that it progresses smoothly with the fewest conflicts.
- Notify inspectors at the appropriate milestones.
- Make payments to suppliers and subcontractors.

You as the Builder

You'll have to take care of every logistical detail yourself if you decide to act as your own builder or general contractor. But along with the responsibilities of managing the project, you gain the flexibility to do as much of your own work as you want and subcontract out the rest. Before taking this path, however, be sure you have the time and capabilities. Do you also have the

time and ability to schedule the work, hire and coordinate subs, order materials, and keep ahead of the accounting required to manage the project successfully? If you do, you stand to save the amount that a general contractor would charge to take on these responsibilities, normally 15 to 30 percent of the construction cost. If you take this responsibility on but mismanage the project, the potential savings will erode and may even cost you more than if you had hired a builder in the first place. A subcontractor might charge extra for hav-

Acting as the builder, above, requires the ability to hire and manage subcontractors.

Building a home, opposite, includes the need to schedule building inspections at the appropriate milestones.

ing to return to the site to complete work that was originally scheduled for an earlier date. Or perhaps because you didn't order the windows at the beginning, you now have to pay for a recent cost increase. (If you had hired a builder in the first place he or she would absorb the increase.)

Hiring a Builder to Handle Construction

A builder or general contractor will manage every aspect of the construction process. Your role after signing the construction contract will be to make regular progress payments and ensure that the work for which you are paying has been completed. You will also consult with the builder and agree to any changes that may have to be made along the way.

Leads for finding builders might come from friends or neighbors who have had contractors build, remodel, or add to their homes. Real-estate agents and bankers may have some names handy but are more likely familiar with the builder's ability to complete projects on time and budget than the quality of the work itself.

The next step is to narrow your list of candidates to three or four who you think can do a quality job and work harmoniously with you. Phone each builder to see whether he or she is interested in being considered for your project. If so, invite the builder to an interview at your home. The meeting will serve two purposes. You'll be able to ask the candidate about his or her experience, and you'll be able to see whether or not your personalities are compatible. Go over the plans with the builder to make certain that he or she understands the scope of the project. Ask if they have constructed similar houses. Get references, and check the builder's standing with the Better Business Bureau. Develop a short list of builders, say three, and ask them to submit bids for the project.

Contracts

Lump-Sum Contracts

A lump-sum, or fixed-fee, contract lets you know from the beginning just what the project will cost, barring any changes made because of your requests or unforeseen conditions. This form works well for projects that promise few surprises and are well defined from the outset by a complete set of contract documents. You can enter into a fixed-price contract by negotiating with a single builder on your short list or by obtaining bids from three or four builders. If you go the latter route, give each bidder a set of documents and allow at least two weeks for them to submit their bids. When you get the bids, decide who you want and call the others to thank them for their efforts. You don't have to accept the lowest bid, but it probably makes sense to do so since you have already honed the list to builders you trust. Inform this builder of your intentions to finalize a contract.

Cost-Plus-Fee Contracts

Under a cost-plus-fee contract, you agree to pay the builder for the costs of labor and materials, as verified by receipts, plus a fee that represents the builder's overhead and profit. This arrangement is sometimes referred to as "time and materials." The fee can range between 15 and 30 percent of the incurred costs. Because you ultimately pick up the tab—whatever the costs—the contractor is never at risk, as he is with a lump-sum contract. You won't know the final total cost of a cost-plus-fee contract until the project is built and paid for. If you can live with that uncertainty, there are offsetting advantages. First, this form allows you to accommodate unknown conditions much more easily than does a lump-sum contract. And rather than being tied down by the project documents, you will be free to make changes at any point along the way. This can be a trap, though. Watching the project take shape will spark the desire to add something or do something differently. Each change costs more, and the accumulation can easily exceed your budget. Because of the uncertainty of the final tab and the built-in advantage to the contractor, you should think twice before entering into this form of contract.

Contract Content

The conditions of your agreement should be spelled out thoroughly in writing and signed by both parties, whatever contractual arrangement you make with your builder. Your contract should include provisions for the following:

- The names and addresses of the owner and builder.
- A description of the work to be included ("As described in the plans and specifications dated . . .").
- The date that the work will be completed if time is of the essence.
- The contract price for lump-sum contracts and the builder's allowed profit and overhead costs for changes.
- The builder's fee for cost-plus-fee contracts and the method of accounting and requesting payment.
- The criteria for progress payments (monthly, by project milestones) and the conditions of final payment.
- A list of each drawing and specification section that is to be included as part of the contract.
- Requirements for guarantees. (One year is the standard period for which contractors guarantee the entire project, but you may require specific guarantees on

When submitting bids, all of the builders should base their estimates on the same specifications. Once the work begins, communicate with your builder to keep the work proceeding smoothly.

Inspect your newly built home, if possible, before the builder closes it up and finishes it.

certain parts of the project, such as a 20-year guarantee on the roofing.)
- Provisions for insurance.
- A description of how changes in the work orders will be handled.

The builder may have a standard contract that you can tailor to the specifics of your project. These contain complete specific conditions with blanks that you can fill in to fit your project and a set of "general conditions" that cover a host of issues from insurance to termination provisions. It's always a good idea to have an attorney review the draft of your completed contract before signing it.

Working with Your Builder

The construction phase officially begins when you have a signed copy of the contract and copies of any insurance required from the builder. It's not unheard of for a builder to request an initial payment of 10 to 20 percent of the total cost to cover mobilization costs, those costs associated with obtaining permits and getting set up to begin the actual construction. If you agree to this, keep a careful eye on the progress of the work to ensure that the total paid out at any one time doesn't get too far out of sync with the actual work completed.

What about changes? From here on, it's up to you and your builder to proceed in good faith and to keep the channels of communication open. Even so, changes of one sort or another beset every project, and they usually add to its cost.

Light at the End of the Tunnel.

The builder's request for a final inspection marks the end of the construction phase—almost. At the final inspection meeting, you and the builder will inspect the work, noting any defects or incomplete items on a "punch list." When the builder tidies up the punch list items, you should reinspect. Sometimes, builders go on to another job and take forever to clean up the last few details, so only after all items on the list have been completed satisfactorily should you release the final payment, which often accounts for the builder's profit.

Some Final Words

Having a positive attitude is important when undertaking a project as large as building a home. A positive attitude can help you ride out the rigors and stress of the construction process.

Stay Flexible. Expect problems, because they certainly will occur. Weather can upset the schedule you have established for subcontractors. A supplier may get behind on deliveries, which also affects the schedule. An unexpected pipe may surprise you during excavation. Just as certain, every problem that comes along has a solution if you are open to it.

Be Patient. The extra days it may take to resolve a construction problem will be forgotten once the project is completed.

Express Yourself. If what you see isn't exactly what you thought you were getting, don't be afraid to look into changing it. Or you may spot an unforeseen opportunity for an improvement. Changes usually cost more money, though, so don't make frivolous decisions.

Finally, watching your home go up is exciting, so stay upbeat. Get away from your project from time to time. Dine out. Take time to relax. A positive attitude will make for smoother relations with your builder. An optimistic outlook will yield better-quality work if you are doing your own construction. And though the project might seem endless while it is under way, keep in mind that all the planning and construction will fade to a faint memory at some time in the future, and you will be getting a lifetime of pleasure from a home that is just right for you.

Plan #131056

Dimensions: 40' W x 54' D
Levels: 1.5
Square Footage: 1,396
Main Level Sq. Ft.: 964
Upper Level Sq. Ft.: 432
Bedrooms: 3
Bathrooms: 2
Foundation: Slab or basement
Materials List Available: Yes
Price Category: B

This ruggedly handsome home is a true A-frame. The elegance of the roof virtually meeting the ground and the use of rugged stone veneer and log-cabin siding make it stand out.

Features:

• **Living Room:** This area is the interior highlight of the home. The large, exciting space features a soaring ceiling, a massive fireplace, and a magnificent window wall to capture a view.

• **Side Porch:** The secondary entry from this side porch leads to a center hall that provides direct access to the first floor's two bedrooms, bathroom, kitchen, and living room.

• **Kitchen:** This kitchen is extremely efficient and includes a snack bar and access to the screened porch.

• **Loft Area:** A spiral stairway leads from the living room to this second-floor loft, which overlooks the living room. The area can also double as an extra sleeping room.

Main Level Floor Plan

Copyright by designer/architect

Great Room

Upper Level Floor Plan

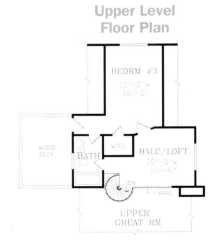

Right Side View

Rear View

Kitchen

Dining Room/Great Room

Plan #271053

Dimensions: 70' W x 34' D

Levels: 2

Square Footage: 2,458

Main Level Sq. Ft.: 1,067

Upper Level Sq. Ft.: 346

Bedrooms: 3

Bathrooms: 2½

Foundation: Crawl space or daylight basement

Materials List Available: No

Price Category: E

The octagonal shape and window-filled walls of this home create a powerful interior packed with panoramic views.

Features:

- **Great Room:** Straight back from the angled entry, this room is brightened by sunlight through windows and sliding glass doors. Beyond the doors, a huge wraparound deck offers plenty of space for tanning or relaxing. A spiral staircase adds visual interest.

- **Kitchen:** This efficient space includes a convenient pantry.

- **Master Suite:** On the upper level, this romantic master suite overlooks the great room below. Several windows provide scenic outdoor views. A walk-in closet and a private bath round out this secluded haven.

- **Basement:** The optional basement includes a recreation room, as well as an extra bedroom and bath.

Images provided by designer/architect.

CAD FILE AVAILABLE

Copyright by designer/architect.

Main Level Floor Plan

Upper Level Floor Plan

Optional Basement Level Floor Plan

order direct: 1-800-523-6789

Plan #391036

Dimensions: 28' W x 32' D
Levels: 2
Square Footage: 1,301
Main Level Sq. Ft.: 728
Upper Level Sq. Ft.: 573
Bedrooms: 3
Bathrooms: 2
Foundation: Basement
Materials List Available: Yes
Price Category: B

Images provided by designer/architect.

This home, as shown in the photograph, may differ from the actual blueprints. For more detailed information, please check the floor plans carefully.

This home is a vacation haven, with views from every room, whether it is situated on a lake or a mountaintop.

Features:

- Main Floor: A fireplace splits the living and dining rooms in this area.
- Kitchen: This kitchen flows into the dining room and is gracefully separated by a bar.

- Master Suite: A large walk-in closet, full bathroom, and deck make this private area special.
- Bedroom or Loft: The second floor has this bedroom or library loft, with clerestory windows, which opens above the living room.
- Lower Level: This lower floor has a large recreation room with a whirlpool tub, bar, laundry room, and garage.

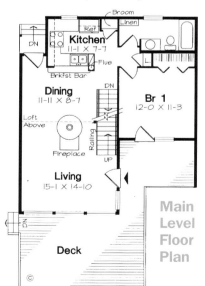

Main Level Floor Plan

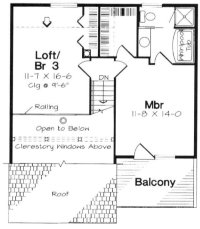

Upper Level Floor Plan

Copyright by designer/architect.

Lower Level Floor Plan

Plan #151747

Dimensions: 39' W x 36'10" D

Levels: 2

Square Footage: 1,477

Main Level Sq. Ft.: 1,131

Upper Level Sq. Ft.: 346

Bedrooms: 3

Bathrooms: 2

Foundation: Crawl space

CompleteCost List Available: Yes

Price Category: B

Images provided by designer/architect.

You'll step back into time when you come home to this simple log home with three bedrooms and a full covered porch.

Features:

- **Great Room:** This room with fireplace opens to the kitchen and dining area with a door to the rear yard.

- **Kitchen:** This U-shaped work area has an abundance of cabinets and counter space.

Enjoy the open feeling as you look into the great room.

- **Master Bedroom:** This main-level bedroom has two closets and a nearby bathroom and convenient laundry closet.

- **Upper Level:** The upper level has a bathroom with a corner shower and a large bedroom with attic-space access for seasonal storage.

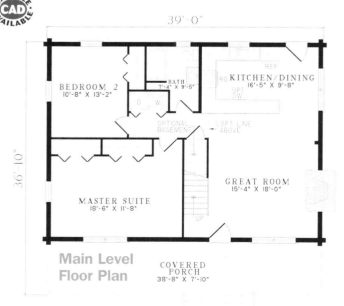

Main Level Floor Plan

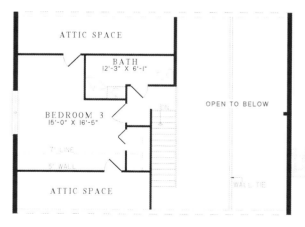

Upper Level Floor Plan

Copyright by designer/architect.

Plan #391026

Dimensions: 35' W x 42' D
Levels: 2
Square Footage: 1,470
Main Level Sq. Ft.: 1,035
Upper Level Sq. Ft.: 435
Bedrooms: 3
Bathrooms: 2
Foundation: Crawl space, slab, or basement
Materials List Available: Yes
Price Category: B

Images provided by designer/architect.

A charming front and dormer with arched window are telltale signs this home is the proverbial home sweet home.

Features:

- **Living Room:** The cozy fireplace calls out, "Sit and relax," as this large gathering area welcomes you home.

- **Kitchen:** This island kitchen is open to the breakfast area, which has a sloped ceiling.

- **Master Bedroom:** This secluded room is located upstairs, with easy access to a large bathroom.

- **Bedrooms:** Two almost-equal-sized bedrooms are located on the main floor and share a common full bathroom.

Main Level Floor Plan

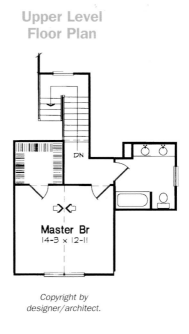

Upper Level Floor Plan

Copyright by designer/architect.

Plan #151748

Dimensions: 38' W x 42' D
Levels: 1.5
Square Footage: 1,382
Main Level Sq. Ft.: 1,040
Upper Level Sq. Ft.: 342
Bedrooms: 2
Bathrooms: 2
Foundation: Crawl space
CompleteCost List Available: Yes
Price Category: B

This log home lends itself a romantic feel with its front covered porch.

Features:

- Great Room: This room with cozy fireplace has access to the rear deck and is open to the loft above. The skylights flood this area with natural light.

- Kitchen: This kitchen with a range island and washer-dryer closet opens to the dining room.

- Master Suite: You ascend the stairs to this retreat, with its walk-in closet, private deck, and full bathroom with linen closet.

- Bedroom: Located on the main floor, this secondary bedroom has a large closet.

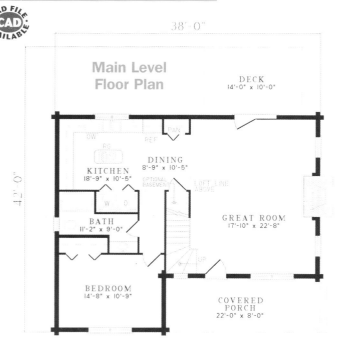

Upper Level Floor Plan
Copyright by designer/architect.

Images provided by designer/architect.

Plan #151529

Dimensions: 43' W x 66'6" D
Levels: 1
Square Footage: 1,474
Bedrooms: 2
Bathrooms: 2
Foundation: Crawl space or slab
CompleteCost List Available: Yes
Price Category: B

This elegant design is reflective of the Arts and Crafts era. Copper roofing and carriage style garage doors warmly welcome guests into this split-bedroom plan.

Features:

• Great Room: With access to the grilling porch as a bonus, this large gathering area features a 10-ft.-high ceiling and a beautiful fireplace.

• Kitchen: This fully equipped island kitchen has a raised bar and a built-in pantry. The area is open to the great room and dining room, giving an open and airy feeling to the home.

• Master Suite: Located on the opposite side of the home from the secondary bedroom, this retreat offers a large sleeping area and two large closets. The master bath features a spa tub, a separate shower, and dual vanities.

• Bedroom: This secondary bedroom has a large closet and access to the full bathroom in the hallway.

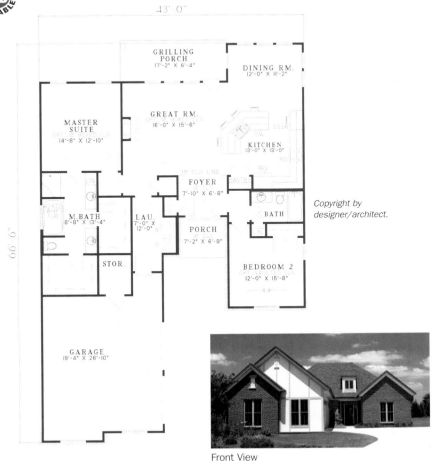

Copyright by designer/architect.

Front View

Plan #131003

Dimensions: 60' W x 39'10" D
Levels: 1
Square Footage: 1,466
Bedrooms: 3
Bathrooms: 2
Foundation: Crawl space, slab, or basement
Materials List Available: Yes
Price Category: B

Victorian styling adds elegance to this compact and easy-to-maintain ranch design.

Features:

- Ceiling Height: 8 ft.

- Foyer: Bridging between the front door and the great room, this foyer is a surprise feature.

- Great Room: A 10-ft. ceiling adds to the spacious feeling of this room, while the corner fireplace gives it an intimate feeling. Sliding glass doors at the rear of the room open to the backyard.

- Dining Room: This formal room adjoins the great room, allowing guests and family to flow between the rooms.

- Breakfast Room: Turrets add a Victorian feeling to this room that's just off the kitchen and overlooks the front porch.

- Master Suite: Privacy is assured in this suite, which is separated from the main part of the house. A compartmented bath and large walk-in closet add convenience to its beauty.

Images provided by designer/architect.

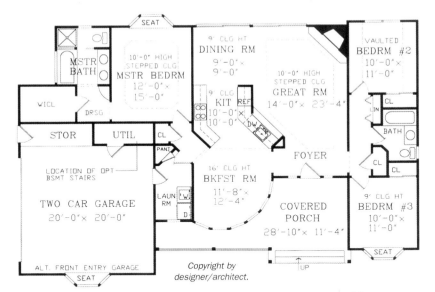

Copyright by designer/architect.

Breakfast Room

Plan #151010

Dimensions: 38'4" W x 68'6" D
Levels: 1
Square Footage: 1,379
Bedrooms: 3
Bathrooms: 2
Foundation: Crawl space, slab
CompleteCost List Available: Yes
Price Category: B

Images provided by designer/architect.

This French Country home has a spacious great room for friends and family to gather, but you can sneak away to the covered rear porch or patio off the master suite for cozy tête-à-têtes.

Features:

- Entry: Take advantage of the marvelous 10-ft. ceilings to hang groups of potted flowering plants.

- Great Room: This spacious room, with an optional 10-ft. boxed ceiling, is the place to curl up by the gas fireplace on a cold winter night.

- Kitchen: The kitchen includes a bar for casual meals, and is open to the breakfast room.

- Rear Porch: Enjoy leisurely meals on the covered rear porch that you can access from both the master suite and the breakfast room.

- Master Suite: The 10-ft. boxed ceiling in the bedroom and the master bath with a whirlpool tub and separate shower make this suite a luxurious place to end a long day.

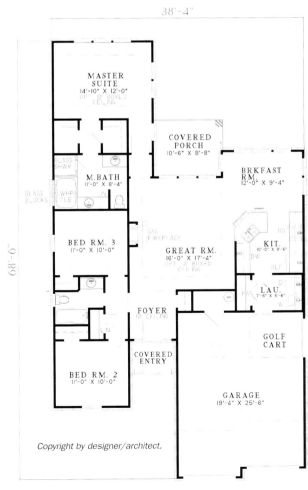

Copyright by designer/architect.

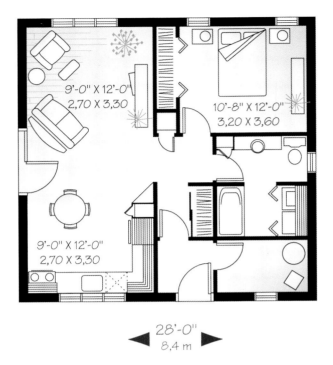

Plan #181014

Dimensions: 28' W x 28' D
Levels: 1
Square Footage: 784
Bedrooms: 1
Bathrooms: 1
Foundation: Monolithic slab
Materials List Available: Yes
Price Category: A

Images provided by designer/architect.

CAD FILE AVAILABLE

9'-0" X 12'-0"
2,70 X 3,30

10'-8" X 12'-0"
3,20 X 3,60

9'-0" X 12'-0"
2,70 X 3,30

◄ 28'-0" ►
8,4 m

Copyright by designer/architect.

Plan #181145

Dimensions: 33' W x 31' D
Levels: 1
Square Footage: 840
Bedrooms: 1
Bathrooms: 1
Foundation: Full basement with walkout
Materials List Available: Yes
Price Category: A

Images provided by designer/architect.

CAD FILE AVAILABLE

16'-0" X 16'-0"
4,80 X 4,80

14'-8" X 11'-0"
4,40 X 3,30

9'-0" X 13'-0"
2,70 X 3,90

8'-0" X 13'-0"
2,40 X 3,90

12'-0" X 11'-8"
3,60 X 3,50

31'-0"
9,3 m

◄ 33'-0" ►
9,9 m

Copyright by designer/architect.

Plan #181005

Dimensions: 30' W x 30' D
Levels: 1
Square Footage: 869
Bedrooms: 2
Bathrooms: 1
Foundation: Full basement
Materials List Available: Yes
Price Category: A

Images provided by designer/architect.

CAD FILE AVAILABLE

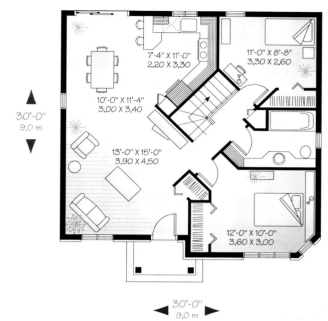

7'-4" X 11'-0"
2,20 X 3,30

11'-0" X 8'-8"
3,30 X 2,60

10'-0" X 11'-4"
3,00 X 3,40

13'-0" X 15'-0"
3,90 X 4,50

12'-0" X 10'-0"
3,60 X 3,00

30'-0"
9,0 m

30'-0"
9,0 m

Copyright by designer/architect.

Plan #281010

Dimensions: 34' W x 31' D
Levels: 1
Square Footage: 884
Bedrooms: 2
Bathrooms: 1
Foundation: Crawl space
Materials List Available: Yes
Price Category: A

Images provided by designer/architect.

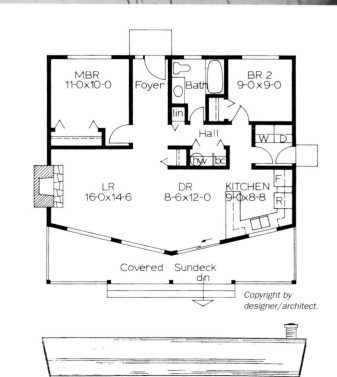

MBR
11-0x10-0

Foyer

Bath

BR 2
9-0x9-0

lin

Hall

W D

LR
16-0x14-6

DR
8-6x12-0

KITCHEN
9-0x8-8

hw bc

F R

Covered Sundeck
d/n

Copyright by designer/architect.

Rear Elevation

Plan #181126

Dimensions: 35' W x 30' D
Levels: 2
Square Footage: 1,468
Main Level Sq. Ft.: 958
Upper Level Sq. Ft.: 510
Bedrooms: 3
Bathrooms: 2
Foundation: Basement
Materials List Available: Yes
Price Category: B

Images provided by designer/architect.
This home, as shown in the photograph, may differ from the actual blueprints.
For more detailed information, please check the floor plans carefully.

A multiple-gabled roof and a covered entry give this home a charming appearance.

Features:

• Entry: You'll keep heating and cooling costs down with this air-lock entry. There is also a large closet here.

• Kitchen: This efficient L-shaped eat-in kitchen has access to the rear deck.

• Great Room: This two-story space has a cozy fireplace and is open to the kitchen.

• Master Bedroom: Located on the main level, this area has access to the main bathroom, which has an oversized tub and a compartmentalized lavatory.

• Bedrooms: The two secondary bedrooms are located on the upper level and share a common bathroom.

Great Room

Main Level Floor Plan

30'-0"
9,0 m

12'-0" X 12'-0"
3,60 X 3,60

19'-8" X 14'-0"
5,90 X 4,20

14'-0" X 13'-0"
4,20 X 3,90

13'-0" X 9'-0"
3,90 X 2,70

35'-0"
10,5 m

10'-0" X 11'-0"
3,00 X 3,30

15'-0" X 11'-0"
4,50 X 3,30

Upper Level Floor Plan

Copyright by designer/architect.

Rear View

Dining Room

Kitchen

Stairs

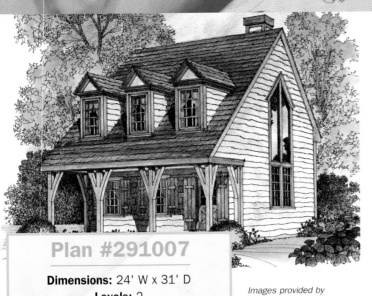

Upper Level
Floor Plan

24'-0"

5'-0" KNEEWALL
CEILING CLIP
LOFT
12'-4" x 8'-0"
DN
BATH
WOOD RAIL
CEILING
EXPOSED BEAM
VAULTED
MASTER BED
13'-2" x 11'-0"
CEILING CLIP
5'-0" KNEEWALL
W.I.C.

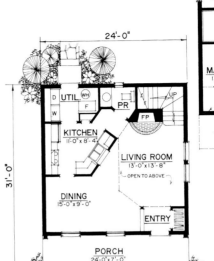

31'-0"

D UTIL WH
W F
PR
UP
KITCHEN
11'-0" x 8'-4"
FP
LIVING ROOM
13'-0" x 13'-8"
OPEN TO ABOVE
DINING
15'-0" x 9'-0"
ENTRY

PORCH
24'-0" x 7'-0"

Main Level
Floor Plan

*Copyright by
designer/architect.*

Plan #291007

Dimensions: 24' W x 31' D
Levels: 2
Square Footage: 1,065
Main Level Sq. Ft.: 576
Upper Level Sq. Ft.: 489
Bedrooms: 1
Bathrooms: 1½
Foundation: Crawl space
Materials List Available: No
Price Category: B

*Images provided by
designer/architect.*

Plan #181010

Dimensions: 34' W x 30' D
Levels: 1
Square Footage: 947
Bedrooms: 2
Bathrooms: 1
Foundation: Full basement
Materials List Available: Yes
Price Category: A

*Images provided by
designer/architect.*

CAD FILE
CAD
AVAILABLE

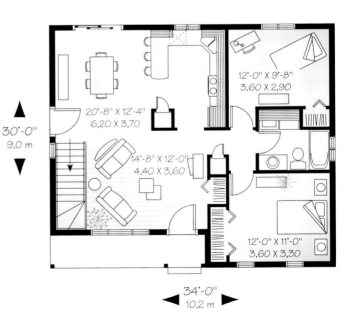

30'-0"
9,0 m

20'-8" X 12'-4"
6,20 X 3,70

12'-0" X 9'-8"
3,60 X 2,90

14'-8" X 12'-0"
4,40 X 3,60

12'-0" X 11'-0"
3,60 X 3,30

34'-0"
10,2 m

Copyright by designer/architect.

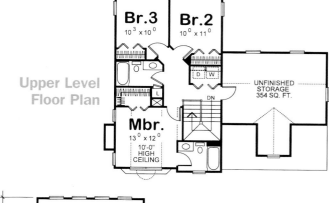

Upper Level Floor Plan

Br.3
10³ x 10⁰

Br.2
10⁰ x 11⁰

UNFINISHED STORAGE 354 SQ. FT.

Mbr.
13⁰ x 12⁰

10'-0" HIGH CEILING

DN

D W

L

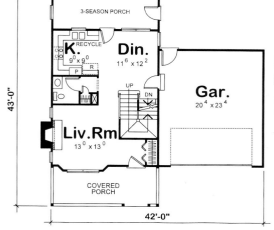

Main Level Floor Plan

Copyright by designer/architect.

3-SEASON PORCH

K.
9⁰ x 9⁰

RECYCLE

P

R

Din.
11⁶ x 12²

Gar.
20⁴ x 23⁴

UP

DN

Liv.Rm
13⁰ x 13⁰

COVERED PORCH

43'-0"

42'-0"

Plan #121036

Dimensions: 42' W x 43' D
Levels: 2
Square Footage: 1,297
Main Level Sq. Ft.: 603
Upper Level Sq. Ft.: 694
Bedrooms: 3
Bathrooms: 2½
Foundation: Basement
Materials List Available: Yes
Price Category: B

Images provided by designer/architect.

CAD FILE AVAILABLE

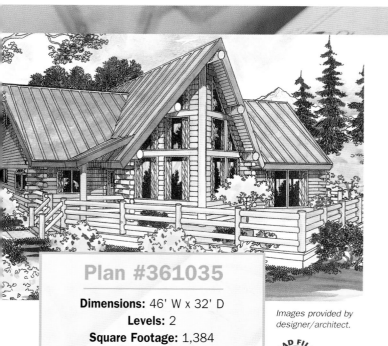

Utility

Kitchen
12'8" x 12'

Dn to Bsmt

Up

Master Suite
12'8" x 12'

Living
20'4" x 30'2"

Deck

Main Level Floor Plan

Storage

Dn

Vaulted Loft
15' x 19'2"

Storage

Open to Living Below

Upper Level Floor Plan

Copyright by designer/architect.

Plan #361035

Dimensions: 46' W x 32' D
Levels: 2
Square Footage: 1,384
Main Level Sq. Ft.: 1,119
Upper Level Sq. Ft.: 265
Bedrooms: 2
Bathrooms: 2
Foundation: Basement
Material List Available: No
Price Category: B

Images provided by designer/architect.

CAD FILE AVAILABLE

Plan #401019

Dimensions: 34' W x 32' D
Levels: 1½
Square Footage: 1,256
Main Level Sq. Ft.: 898
Upper Level Sq. Ft.: 358
Bedrooms: 3
Bathrooms: 1½
Foundation: Crawl space
Materials List Available: Yes
Price Category: B

Images provided by designer/architect.

A surrounding sun deck and expansive window wall capitalize on vacation-home views in this design. The full-height windows flood the living and dining rooms with abundant natural light and bring attention to the high vaulted ceilings.

CAD FILE AVAILABLE

Features:

• Living Room: A woodstove in this room warms cold winter nights.

• Kitchen: This efficient U-shaped kitchen has ample counter and cupboard space. Behind it is a laundry room and rear entrance.

• Master Bedroom: Located on the first floor, this main bedroom has a large wall closet.

• Bedrooms: Two family bedrooms are on the second floor and have use of a half-bath.

Main Level Floor Plan

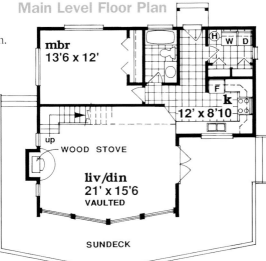

Upper Level Floor Plan

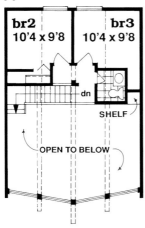

Copyright by designer/architect.

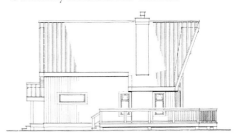

Left Side Elevation

Rear Elevation

Right Side Elevation

Images provided by designer/architect.

Plan #121009

Dimensions: 50' W x 58' D
Levels: 1
Square Footage: 1,422
Bedrooms: 3
Bathrooms: 2
Foundation: Basement
Materials List Available: Yes
Price Category: B

This amenity-filled home is perfect for the growing family or as a retirement retreat.

Features:

• Ceiling Height: 8 ft. unless otherwise noted.

• Great Room: This inviting space is the perfect place for gatherings of all sizes. It shares 12-ft. ceilings with the dining room and kitchen.

• Dining Room: In addition to the 12-ft. ceiling, arched openings, and built-in book cases make this an elegant place to dine.

• Private Porch: After dinner, step through a door in the dining room to enjoy a summer breeze in this inviting porch.

• Master Suite: The boxed ceiling lends drama to this suite and a walk-in closet adds convenience. Luxury comes from the whirlpool bath.

• Garage: You won't be short of parking and storage space in this two-bay garage. As a bonus there is space for a workbench.

Copyright by designer/architect.

Plan #401005

Dimensions: 24' W x 28' D
Levels: 2
Square Footage: 1,073
Main Level Sq. Ft.: 672
Upper Level Sq. Ft.: 401
Bedrooms: 3
Bathrooms: 1½
Foundation: Basement
Materials List Available: Yes
Price Category: B

Scalloped fascia boards in the steep gable roof and the fieldstone chimney detail enhance this chalet.

Features:

- **Outdoor Living:** The front-facing deck and covered balcony are ideal outdoor living spaces.

- **Living Room:** The fireplace is the main focus in this living room, separating it from the dining room.

- **Bedrooms:** One bedroom is found on the first floor; two additional bedrooms and a full bath are upstairs.

- **Storage:** You'll find three large storage areas on the second floor.

Images provided by designer/architect.

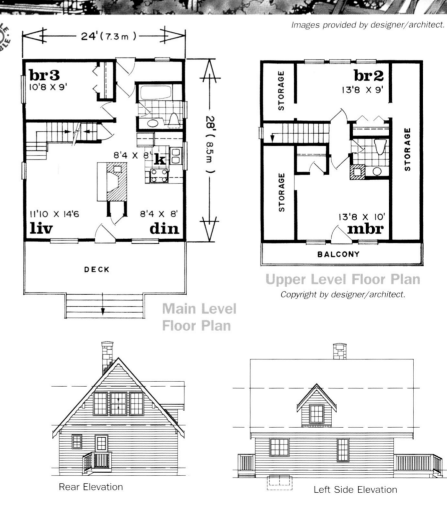

CAD FILE AVAILABLE

Main Level Floor Plan

Upper Level Floor Plan
Copyright by designer/architect.

Rear Elevation

Left Side Elevation

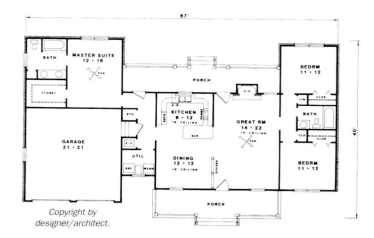

Plan #171002

Dimensions: 67' W x 40' D
Levels: 1
Square Footage: 1,458
Bedrooms: 3
Bathrooms: 2
Foundation: Slab, crawl space
Materials List Available: Yes
Price Category: B

Copyright by designer/architect.

SMARTtip
Accent Landscape Lighting

Accent highlights elements in your landscape. It creates ambiance and helps integrate the garden with the deck. Conventional low-voltage floodlights are excellent for creating effects such as wall grazing, silhouetting, and uplighting.

Plan #131004

Dimensions: 59'4" W x 35'8" D
Levels: 1
Square Footage: 1,097
Bedrooms: 3
Bathrooms: 2
Foundation: Crawl space, slab, or basement
Materials List Available: Yes
Price Category: B

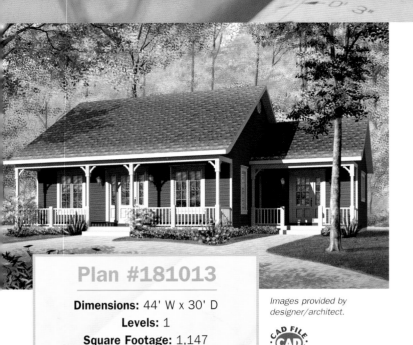

Plan #181013

Dimensions: 44' W x 30' D
Levels: 1
Square Footage: 1,147
Bedrooms: 3
Bathrooms: 1
Foundation: Full basement
Materials List Available: Yes
Price Category: B

Images provided by designer/architect.

CAD FILE AVAILABLE

9'-0" X 11'-0"
2,70 X 3,30

9'-0" X 10'-0"
2,70 X 3,00

16'-8" X 15'-4"
5,00 X 4,60

11'-0" X 12'-8"
3,30 X 3,70

14'-4" X 17'-4"
4,30 X 5,20

44'-0"
13,2 m

Copyright by designer/architect.

Plan #291006

Dimensions: 24' W x 25'4" D
Levels: 2
Square Footage: 965
Main Level Sq. Ft.: 547
Upper Level Sq. Ft.: 418
Bedrooms: 1
Bathrooms: 1½
Foundation: Crawl space
Materials List Available: No
Price Category: A

Images provided by designer/architect.

24'-0"

Main Level Floor Plan

25'-4"

1'-4"

D UTILITY HW
W F
PR
PANTRY
F.P.
KITCHEN
10'-0" x 8'-3"
LIVING ROOM
12'-0"x 13'-8"
OPEN TO ABOVE
DINING ROOM
10'-2" x 9'-0"
ENTRY PORCH

Upper Level Floor Plan

DN
LOFT
12'-0"x8'-0"
(8'-0" CLG)
OPEN TO ABOVE
RIDGE BEAM
TUB/SHWR
BATH
OPEN TO BELOW
MASTER BEDROOM
12'-0"x11'-0"
(12'-0" CEILING)
PLANT SHELF
WIC

Copyright by designer/architect.

Plan #271011

Dimensions: 36' W x 40'8" D
Levels: 2
Square Footage: 1,296
Main Level Sq. Ft.: 891
Upper Level Sq. Ft.: 405
Bedrooms: 3
Bathrooms: 2
Foundation: Basement
Materials List Available: Yes
Price Category: B

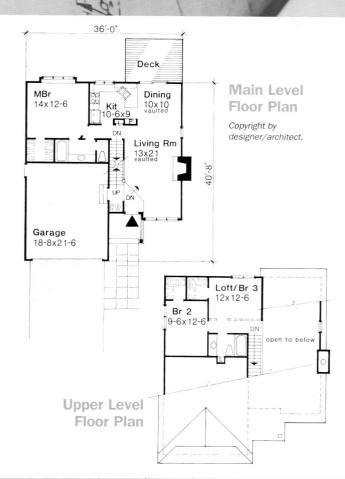

Images provided by designer/architect.

CAD FILE AVAILABLE

Main Level Floor Plan

Copyright by designer/architect.

36'-0"

Deck

MBr 14x12-6
Kit 10-6x9
Dining 10x10 vaulted
DN
Living Rm 13x21 vaulted
UP DN
Garage 18-8x21-6

40'-8"

Loft/ Br 3 12x12-6
Br 2 9-6x12-6
DN
open to below

Upper Level Floor Plan

Plan #361029

Dimensions: 40' W x 47'4" D
Levels: 1
Square Footage: 960
Bedrooms: 1
Bathrooms: 1
Foundation: Crawl space
Material List Available: No
Price Category: A

Images provided by designer/architect.

CAD FILE AVAILABLE

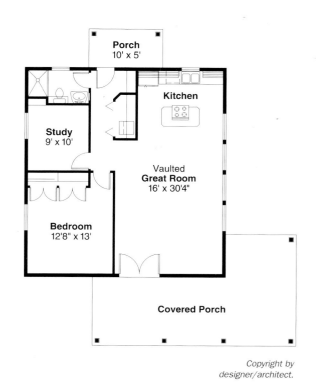

Porch 10' x 5'
Kitchen
Study 9' x 10'
Vaulted Great Room 16' x 30'4"
Bedroom 12'8" x 13'
Covered Porch

Copyright by designer/architect.

Plan #281023

Dimensions: 32' W x 46' D
Levels: 2
Square Footage: 1,011
Main Level Sq. Ft.: 768
Upper Level Sq. Ft.: 243
Bedrooms: 3
Bathrooms: 1
Foundation: Crawl space
Materials List Available: Yes
Price Category: B

Images provided by designer/architect.

Main Level Floor Plan

Upper Level Floor Plan

Copyright by designer/architect.

Plan #131053

Dimensions: 44' W x 39' D
Levels: 1 (2)
Square Footage: 1,056 (1,673)
Main Level Sq. Ft.: 1,056
Opt. Upper Level Sq. Ft.: 617
Bedrooms: 2 (4)
Bathrooms: 2 (3)
Foundation: Crawl space, slab, or basement
Materials List Available: Yes
Price Category: B (C)

Images provided by designer/architect.

Rear Elevation

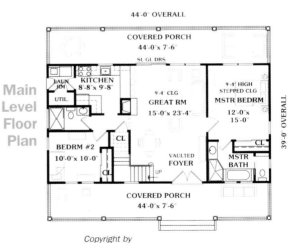

Main Level Floor Plan

Copyright by designer/architect.

Optional Upper Level Floor Plan

Plan #271013

Dimensions: 43' W x 45'8" D
Levels: 2
Square Footage: 1,498
Main Level Sq. Ft.: 1,044
Upper Level Sq. Ft.: 454
Bedrooms: 2
Bathrooms: 2½
Foundation: Basement
Materials List Available: Yes
Price Category: B

Images provided by designer/architect.

Main Level Floor Plan

Upper Level Floor Plan

Copyright by designer/architect.

Plan #181012

Dimensions: 34' W x 34' D
Levels: 1
Square Footage: 1,079
Bedrooms: 2
Bathrooms: 1
Foundation: Full basement
Materials List Available: Yes
Price Category: B

Images provided by designer/architect.

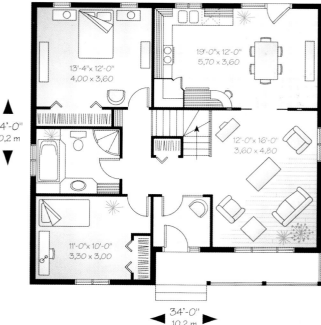

Copyright by designer/architect.

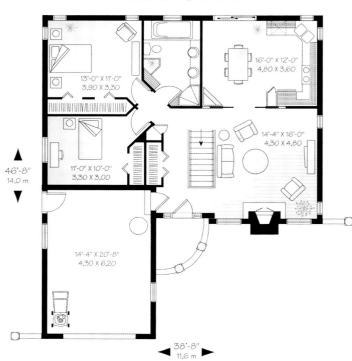

Images provided by designer/architect.

Plan #181016

Dimensions: 38'8" W x 46'8" D
Levels: 1
Square Footage: 1,080
Bedrooms: 2
Bathrooms: 1
Foundation: Full basement
Materials List Available: Yes
Price Category: B

CAD FILE AVAILABLE CAD

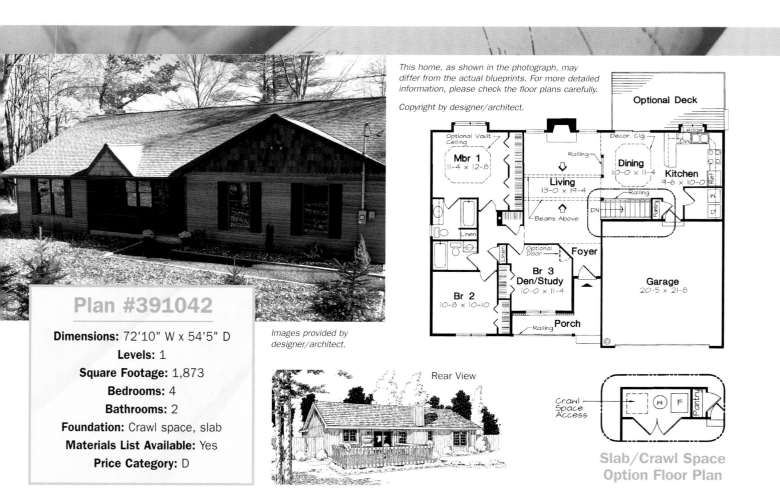

This home, as shown in the photograph, may differ from the actual blueprints. For more detailed information, please check the floor plans carefully.

Copyright by designer/architect.

Plan #391042

Dimensions: 72'10" W x 54'5" D
Levels: 1
Square Footage: 1,873
Bedrooms: 4
Bathrooms: 2
Foundation: Crawl space, slab
Materials List Available: Yes
Price Category: D

Images provided by designer/architect.

Rear View

Slab/Crawl Space Option Floor Plan

Plan #381021

Dimensions: 30' W x 30'8" D
Levels: 2
Square Footage: 1,425
Main Level Sq. Ft.: 1,025
Upper Level Sq. Ft.: 400
Bedrooms: 3
Bathrooms: 2
Foundation: Basement
Materials List Available: Yes
Price Category: B

Main Level Floor Plan

DECK

KIT. 13 x 10
w
d
P
DINING 11 x 10
BEDROOM 13 x 11
d
DEN 9 x 9
bench
LIVING 17 x 13
PORCH

Images provided by designer/architect.

BEDROOM 14 x 10
d
L
BEDROOM 9 x 10
OPEN

Upper Level Floor Plan

Copyright by designer/architect.

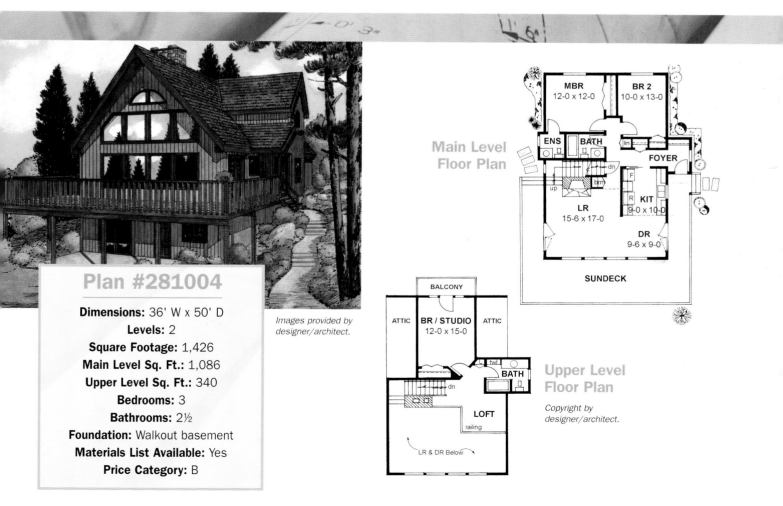

Plan #281004

Dimensions: 36' W x 50' D
Levels: 2
Square Footage: 1,426
Main Level Sq. Ft.: 1,086
Upper Level Sq. Ft.: 340
Bedrooms: 3
Bathrooms: 2½
Foundation: Walkout basement
Materials List Available: Yes
Price Category: B

Images provided by designer/architect.

Main Level Floor Plan

MBR 12-0 x 12-0
BR 2 10-0 x 13-0
ENS
BATH
lin
FOYER
dn
up
brm
F
R
KIT 9-0 x 10-0
LR 15-6 x 17-0
DR 9-6 x 9-0
SUNDECK

BALCONY
ATTIC
BR / STUDIO 12-0 x 15-0
ATTIC
twl
BATH
dn
LOFT
railing
LR & DR Below

Upper Level Floor Plan

Copyright by designer/architect.

Plan #341010

Dimensions: 42'6" W x 35'4" D

Levels: 1

Square Footage: 1,261

Bedrooms: 3

Bathrooms: 2

Foundation: Crawl space, slab, or basement

Materials List Available: Yes

Price Category: B

Images provided by designer/architect.

CAD FILE AVAILABLE

Copyright by designer/architect.

Floor plan labels: PORCH, GARDEN TUB, WH, KITCHEN/DINING 14'-7" X 14'-9", PANTRY, COATS, CLOSET, BEDROOM 3 10'-0" X 10'-0", BATH 1, UTILITIES, SHWR, DRY, WASH, SINK, DW, RANGE, REF, LINENS, CLOSET, BATH 2, VAULTED CEILING, BEDROOM 1 12'-8" X 15'-5", FAMILY ROOM 14'-7" X 14'-5", CLOSET, BEDROOM 2 11'-2" X 10'-5", TRAY CEILING, PORCH, 35'-4", 42'-6"

Plan #131013

Dimensions: 50' W x 41'8" D

Levels: 1

Square Footage: 1,489

Bedrooms: 3

Bathrooms: 2

Foundation: Crawl space, slab or basement

Materials List Available: Yes

Price Category: C

Images provided by designer/architect.

Copyright by designer/architect.

Floor plan labels: BKFST RM 8'-2" / 10'-4" x 15'-8", WICL, TRAY CEIL, MSTR BEDRM 12'-4" x 15'-2", 10'-0" CLG STEPPED CLG, GREAT RM 15'-4" x 20'-6", KIT, LAUN RM, OPTIONAL TWO CAR GARAGE 20'-4" x 19'-6", MSTR BATH, STEPPED CLG DINING RM 10'-0" x 11'-0", BATH, VAULTED BEDRM #2 11'-2" x 10'-0", VAULTED BEDRM #3 10'-4" x 12'-0", COV. PORCH, SEAT

Rear View

Plan #181109

Dimensions: 26' W x 30' D
Levels: 2
Square Footage: 1,295
Main Level Sq. Ft.: 772
Second Level Sq. Ft.: 523
Bedrooms: 2 or 3
Bathrooms: 2
Foundation: Basement
Materials List Available: Yes
Price Category: B

This charming home with beautiful windows is the perfect starter or retirement home.

Features:

• Ceiling Height: 8 ft. unless otherwise noted.

• Living Room: This front living room is the centerpiece of a well-designed floor plan that makes excellent use of space. The living room itself has plenty of room for family and friends to gather and relax.

• Kitchen: This bright and efficient kitchen includes an eat-in area that is perfect for informal dining. The eating area flows easily into the living room.

• Guest Bedroom: Guests will stay in comfort thanks to this pleasant downstairs guest room with its own closet and full bath.

• Master Suite: Retire at the end of the day in comfort and privacy in this upstairs master suite, which features a nicely appointed full bathroom and a walk-in closet.

• Mezzanine: This lovely balcony is open to the family room below. It provides space for a reading area or a home office.

Main Level Floor Plan

12'-0" X 11'-4"
3,60 X 3,40

30'-0"
9,0 m

14'-8" X 13'-4"
4,40 X 4,00

10'-0" X 26'-8"
3,00 X 8,00

10'-0" X 16'-8"
3,00 X 5,00

Copyright by designer/architect.

26'-0"
7,8 m

15'-0" X 11'-4"
4,50 X 3,40

12'-4" 13'-4"
3,70 X 4,00

Upper Level Floor Plan

Images provided by designer/architect.

Plan #131008

Dimensions: 45'4" W x 36'4" D
Levels: 1
Square Footage: 1,299
Bedrooms: 3
Bathrooms: 2
Foundation: Crawl space, basement
Materials List Available: Yes
Price Category: C

Build this home in a vacation spot or any other location where you'll treasure the convenience of having three different outdoor entrances.

Features:

• Ceiling Height: 8 ft.

• Living Room: Sliding glass doors open onto the large deck area and serve to let bright, natural light stream into the home during the day. Add drapes to keep the house cozy at night and on cloudy winter days.

• Kitchen: Shaped like a galley, this kitchen is so well designed that you'll love working in it. Counter space and cabinets add to its practicality, and a windowed nook makes it charming.

• Master Suite: Enjoy the private bath attached to the bedroom in this quiet area.

• Additional Bedrooms: These nicely sized rooms share another full bathroom.

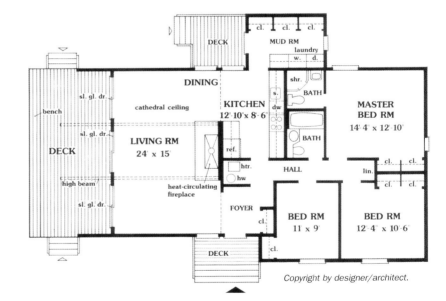

Copyright by designer/architect.

Rear View

Plan #181111

Dimensions: 24'8" W x 38'4" D
Levels: 2
Square Footage: 1,304
Main Level Sq. Ft.: 945
Upper Level Sq. Ft.: 359
Bedrooms: 2
Bathrooms: 1
Foundation: Crawl space
Materials List Available: Yes
Price Category: B

Images provided by designer/architect.

CAD FILE AVAILABLE

Main Level Floor Plan

Upper Level Floor Plan

Copyright by designer/architect.

Plan #271050

Dimensions: 40' W x 40' D
Levels: 2
Square Footage: 1,188
Main Level Sq. Ft.: 936
Upper Level Sq. Ft.: 252
Bedrooms: 3
Bathrooms: 2
Foundation: Daylight basement
Materials List Available: Yes
Price Category: B

Images provided by designer/architect.

CAD FILE AVAILABLE

Main Level Floor Plan

Copyright by designer/architect.

Upper Level Floor Plan

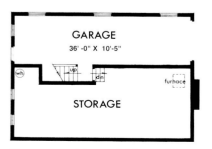

Basement Level Floor Plan

Plan #101010

Dimensions: 70' W x 47' D

Levels: 1

Square Footage: 2,187

Bedrooms: 4

Bathrooms: 2½

Foundation: Crawl space, slab, or basement

Materials List Available: Yes

Price Category: D

This stately ranch features a brick-and-stucco exterior, layered trim, and copper roofing returns.

Features:

• Ceiling Height: 11 ft. unless otherwise noted.

• Special Ceilings: Vaulted and raised ceilings adorn the living room, family room, dining room, foyer, kitchen, breakfast room, and master suite.

• Kitchen: This roomy kitchen is brightened by an abundance of windows.

• Breakfast Room: Located off the kitchen, this breakfast room is the perfect spot for informal family meals.

• Master Suite: This truly exceptional master suite features a bath, and a spacious walk in closet.

• Morning Porch: Step out of the master bedroom, and greet the day on this lovely porch.

• Additional Bedrooms: The three additional bedrooms each measure approximately 11 ft. x 12 ft. Two of them have walk-in closets.

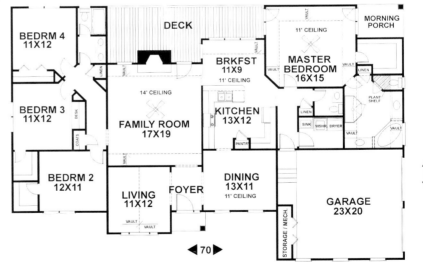

SMARTtip
Using Slipcovers in Your Dining Area

Change the look of your dining room by slipcovering chairs. Short-skirted slipcovers give a more informal appearance; fabrics in graphic patterns, such as checks or floral prints, complement this style of slipcover best. Long-skirted covers are elegant additions to a formal dining room, particularly in solid color or tone-on-tone fabrics. Ties, buttons, or trim can add personality.

Plan #291005

Dimensions: 16' W x 28' D
Levels: 2
Square Footage: 896
Main Level Sq. Ft.: 448
Upper Level Sq. Ft.: 448
Bedrooms: 2
Bathrooms: 1½
Foundation: Crawl space
Materials List Available: No
Price Category: A

You'll be as charmed by the interior of this small home as you are by the wood-shingled roof, scroll-saw rake detailing, and board-and-batten siding on the exterior.

Features:

- Porch: Relax on this porch, which is the ideal spot for a couple of rockers or a swing.

- Entryway: Double doors reveal an open floor plan that makes everyone feel welcome.

- Living Room: Create a cozy nook by the windows here.

- Kitchen: Designed for convenience, this kitchen has ample counter space as well as enough storage to suit your needs. The stairway to the upper floor and the half-bath divide the kitchen from the living and dining areas.

- Upper Level: 9-ft. ceilings give a spacious feeling to the two bedrooms and full bathroom that you'll find on this floor.

Images provided by designer/architect.

Main Level Floor Plan

Upper Level Floor Plan

Copyright by designer/architect.

Images provided by designer/architect.

Plan #121013

Dimensions: 40' W x 55'8" D
Levels: 1
Square Footage: 1,375
Bedrooms: 1
Bathrooms: 2
Foundation: Basement
Materials List Available: Yes
Price Category: B

This convenient open plan is well-suited to retirement or as a starter home.

Features:

- Ceiling Height: 8 ft., unless otherwise noted.
- Den: To the left of the entry, French doors lead to a den that can convert to a second bedroom.
- Kitchen: A center island doubles as a snack bar while the breakfast area includes a pantry and a desk for compiling shopping lists and menus.

- Open Plan: The sense of spaciousness is enhanced by the large open area that includes the family room, kitchen, and breakfast area.
- Family Room: A handsome fireplace invites family and friends to gather in this area.
- Porch: Step through the breakfast area to enjoy the fresh air on this secluded porch.
- Master Bedroom: This distinctive bedroom features a boxed ceiling. It's served by a private bath with a walk-in closet.

SMARTtip
Paint Color Choices for Your Home

Earth tones are easy to decorate with because they are neutral colors. Use neutral or muted tones, such as light grays, browns, or greens with either lighter or darker shades for accenting.

Use bright colors sparingly, to catch the eye. Painting the front door a bright color creates a cheerful entryway.

Investigate home shows, magazines, and houses in your area for color ideas. Paint suppliers can also give you valuable tips on appropriate color schemes.

Colors that look just right on a color card may need to be toned down for painting large areas. If in doubt, buy a quart of paint and test it.

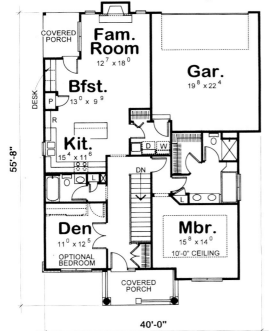

Copyright by designer/architect.

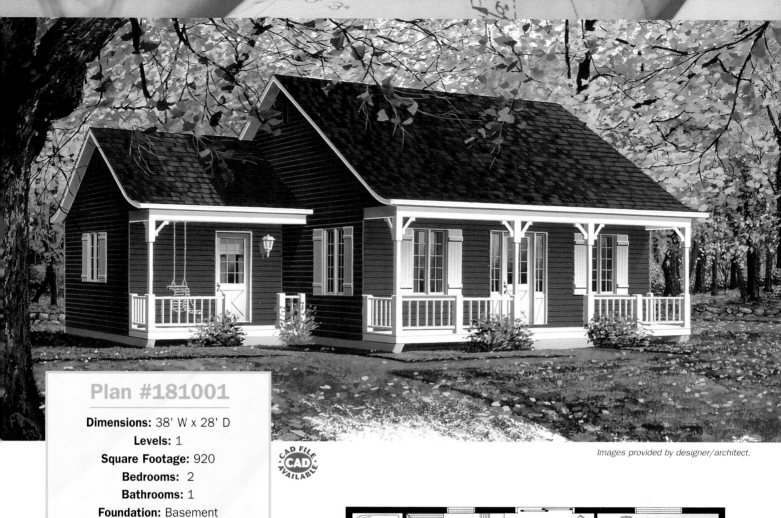

Plan #181001

Dimensions: 38' W x 28' D
Levels: 1
Square Footage: 920
Bedrooms: 2
Bathrooms: 1
Foundation: Basement
Materials List Available: Yes
Price Category: A

Images provided by designer/architect.

This cozy and charming one-story cottage offers many amenities in its well-designed layout.

Features:

- Ceiling Height: 8 ft.

- Porch: Enjoy summer evenings relaxing on the front porch.

- Kitchen: This kitchen has ample work and storage space as well as a breakfast bar and enough room for the family to dine together.

- Family Room: Natural light streaming through the windows makes this an appealing place for family activities.

- Bedrooms: There's a generous master bedroom and one secondary bedroom. Each has its own closet.

- Laundry Room: A fully equipped laundry room is conveniently located adjacent to the kitchen.

- Full Basement: Here is plenty of storage room as well as the opportunity for expanded living space.

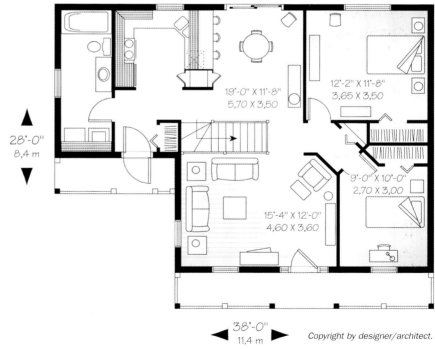

19'-0" X 11'-8"
5,70 X 3,50

12'-2" X 11'-8"
3,65 X 3,50

9'-0" X 10'-0"
2,70 X 3,00

15'-4" X 12'-0"
4,60 X 3,60

28'-0"
8,4 m

38'-0"
11,4 m

Copyright by designer/architect.

Plan #401047

Dimensions: 38' W x 34' D
Levels: 1
Square Footage: 1,064
Bedrooms: 2
Bathrooms: 1
Foundation: Basement
Materials List Available: Yes
Price Category: B

Images provided by designer/architect.

This farmhouse squeezes space-efficient features into its compact plan. Twin dormer windows flood the vaulted interior with natural light and accentuate the high ceilings.

CAD FILE AVAILABLE

Features:

- **Porch:** This cozy front porch opens into a vaulted great room and its adjoining dining room.
- **Great Room:** A warm hearth in this gathering place for the family adds to its coziness.
- **Kitchen:** This U-shaped kitchen has a breakfast bar open to the dining room and a sink overlooking a flower box. Nearby side-door access is found in the handy laundry room.
- **Bedrooms:** Vaulted bedrooms are positioned along the back of the plan. They contain wall closets and share a full bathroom with a soaking tub.
- **Future Expansion:** An open-rail staircase leads to the basement, which can be developed into living or sleeping space at a later time, if needed.

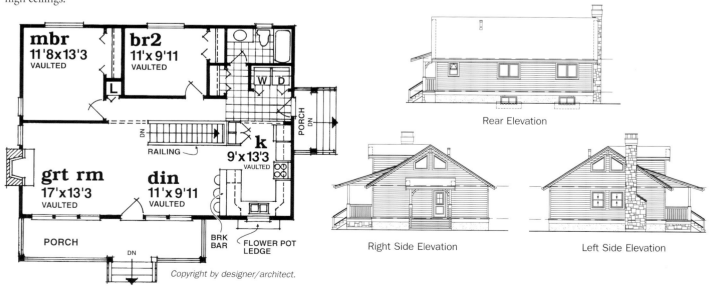

Copyright by designer/architect.

Plan #391069

Dimensions: 56' W x 48' D
Levels: 1
Square Footage: 1,492
Bedrooms: 3
Bathrooms: 2
Foundation: Crawl space, slab, or basement
Materials List Available: Yes
Price Category: B

Images provided by designer/architect.

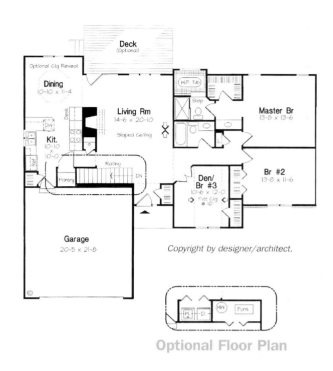

Copyright by designer/architect.

Optional Floor Plan

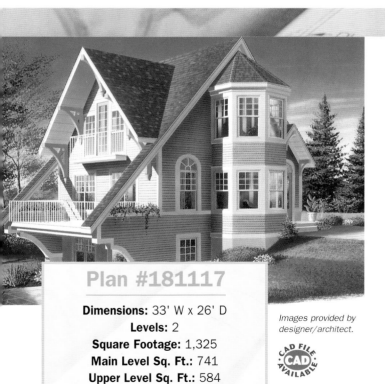

Plan #181117

Dimensions: 33' W x 26' D
Levels: 2
Square Footage: 1,325
Main Level Sq. Ft.: 741
Upper Level Sq. Ft.: 584
Bedrooms: 2
Bathrooms: 1½
Foundation: Walkout basement
Materials List Available: Yes
Price Category: B

Images provided by designer/architect.

CAD FILE AVAILABLE

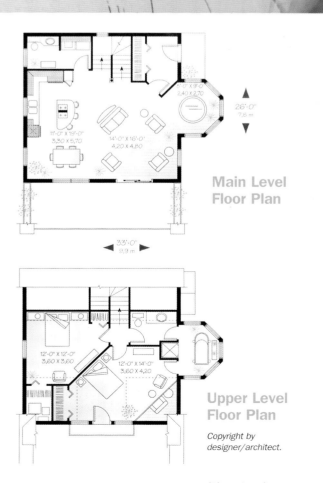

Main Level Floor Plan

Upper Level Floor Plan

Copyright by designer/architect.

Plan #181011

Dimensions: 41'4" W x 42' D

Levels: 1

Square Footage: 1,347

Bedrooms: 3

Bathrooms: 1

Foundation: Full basement

Materials List Available: Yes

Price Category: B

Images provided by designer/architect.

CAD FILE AVAILABLE

Copyright by designer/architect.

8'-8" X 12'-0"
2,60 X 3,60

10'-8" X 14'-0"
3,20 X 4,20

10'-0" X 9'-0"
3,00 X 2,70

10'-8" X 9'-0"
3,20 X 2,70

17'-4" X 12'-0"
5,20 X 3,60

14'-0" X 11'-0"
4,20 X 3,30

42'-0"
12,6 m

41'-4"
12,4 m

Plan #281005

Dimensions: 35' W x 40' D

Levels: 2

Square Footage: 1,362

Main Level Sq. Ft.: 864

Upper Level Sq. Ft.: 498

Bedrooms: 3

Bathrooms: 2

Foundation: Crawl space

Materials List Available: Yes

Price Category: B

Images provided by designer/architect.

Upper Level Floor Plan

attic

Ensuite

attic

attic

MBR
16-0 x 19-6

attic

DECK

Main Level Floor Plan

BR 2
11-0 x 11-0

Bath

Utility

Hall

KITCHEN
11-0 x 9-0

LR
14-6 x 16-0

DR
11-6 x 10-0

SUNDECK

Copyright by designer/architect.

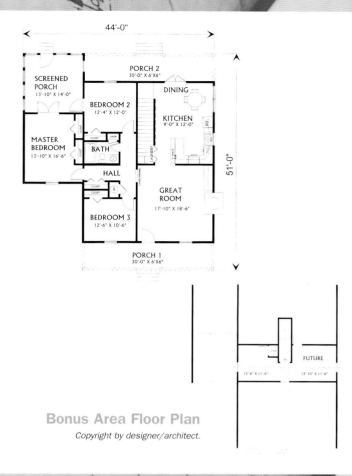

Images provided by designer/architect.

Plan #191022

Dimensions: 44' W x 51' D
Levels: 1
Square Footage: 1,377
Bedrooms: 3
Bathrooms: 1
Foundation: Crawl space or slab
Material List Available: No
Price Category: B

Bonus Area Floor Plan

Copyright by designer/architect.

PORCH 2
30'-0" X 6'X6"
SCREENED PORCH
13'-10" X 14'-0"
DINING
BEDROOM 2
12'-4" X 12'-0"
KITCHEN
9'-0" X 12'-0"
MASTER BEDROOM
13'-10" X 16'-6"
BATH
LAUNDRY
HALL
GREAT ROOM
17'-10" X 18'-6"
BEDROOM 3
12'-6" X 10'-6"
PORCH 1
30'-0" X 6'X6"
FUTURE
12'-6" X 11'-6"
13'-10" X 11'-6"

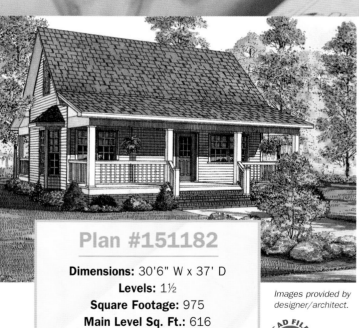

Plan #151182

Dimensions: 30'6" W x 37' D
Levels: 1½
Square Footage: 975
Main Level Sq. Ft.: 616
Upper Level Sq. Ft.: 359
Bedrooms: 2
Bathrooms: 1
Foundation: Crawl space, slab; basement or walkout basement available for fee
CompleteCost List Available: Yes
Price Category: A

Images provided by designer/architect.

Main Level Floor Plan

GRILLING PORCH
29'-0" X 8'-0"
BATH
DINING
KITCHEN
15'-8" X 9'-0"
MASTER BEDROOM
8'-6" X 14'-0"
GREAT ROOM
15'-8" X 16'-4"
COVERED PORCH
29'-0" X 8'-0"

Upper Level Floor Plan

LOFT
16'-0" X 10'-0"
BEDROOM 2
8'-6" X 12'-0"

Copyright by designer/architect.

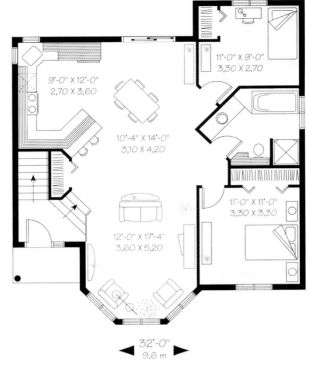

Images provided by designer/architect.

Plan #181025

Dimensions: 32' W x 36'8" D
Levels: 1
Square Footage: 975
Bedrooms: 2
Bathrooms: 1
Foundation: Full basement
Materials List Available: Yes
Price Category: A

36'-8"
11,0 m

32'-0"
9,6 m

9'-0" X 12'-0"
2,70 X 3,60

10'-4" X 14'-0"
3,10 X 4,20

12'-0" X 17'-4"
3,60 X 5,20

11'-0" X 9'-0"
3,30 X 2,70

11'-0" X 11'-0"
3,30 X 3,30

Copyright by designer/architect.

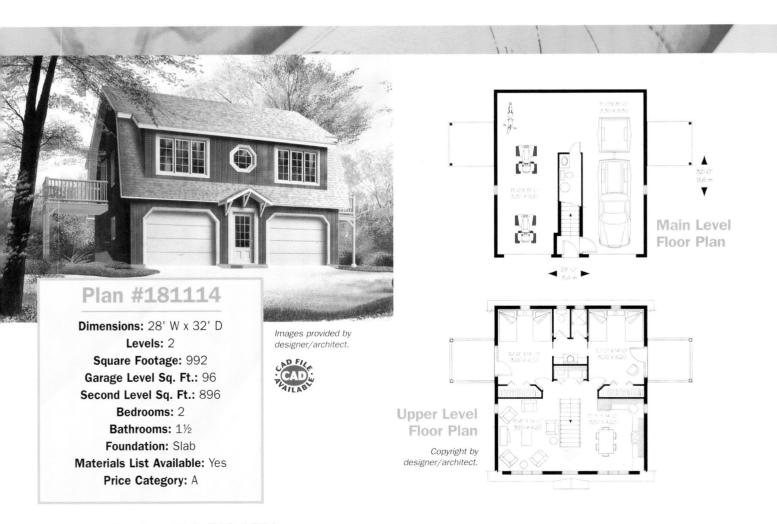

Plan #181114

Dimensions: 28' W x 32' D
Levels: 2
Square Footage: 992
Garage Level Sq. Ft.: 96
Second Level Sq. Ft.: 896
Bedrooms: 2
Bathrooms: 1½
Foundation: Slab
Materials List Available: Yes
Price Category: A

Images provided by designer/architect.

Main Level Floor Plan

Upper Level Floor Plan

Copyright by designer/architect.

Plan #321038

Dimensions: 30' W x 51' D
Levels: 1
Square Footage: 1,452
Bedrooms: 4
Bathrooms: 2
Foundation: Basement
Materials List Available: Yes
Price Category: B

Images provided by designer/architect.

Copyright by designer/architect.

Plan #121056

Dimensions: 48' W x 50' D
Levels: 1
Square Footage: 1,479
Bedrooms: 2
Bathrooms: 2
Foundation: Basement
Materials List Available: Yes
Price Category: B

Images provided by designer/architect.

Copyright by designer/architect.

Optional Third Bedroom Floor Plan

Kitchens for Entertaining

From every standpoint, the importance of the kitchen and its design cannot be underestimated. The heart of the home beats in the kitchen. There's the hum of the refrigerator, the whir of the food processor, the crunch of the waste-disposal unit, and the bubbling of dinner simmering on the stove. These are the reassuring sounds of a home in action. The kitchen is also a warehouse, a communications center, a place to socialize, and the hub of family life. According to industry studies, 90 percent of American families eat some or all of their meals in the kitchen. It is also the command center where household bills are paid and vacations are planned. The kitchen is even a playroom at times. Emotions, as well as tasks, reside here. When you were little, this is where you could find mom whenever you needed her. It's where the cookies were kept. When other rooms were cold and empty, the kitchen was a place of warmth and companionship. It is from the kitchen that the family sets off into the day. And it is to the kitchen that they return at nightfall.

The Great Room Concept

Today, the family life that was once contained by the kitchen is spilling into an adjoining great room. Usually a large, open room, great rooms and kitchens are often considered part of the same space. It is here where the family gathers to watch TV, share meals, and do homework. In short, great rooms/kitchens are the new heart of the home and the places where families do most of their living. In most designs, a kitchen and great room are separated by a snack counter, an island, or a large pass-through.

Kitchen Layouts That Work

The basic layout of your kitchen will depend on the home design you choose. Look for aisles that have at least 39 inches between the front of the cabinets and appliances or an opposite-facing island. If it's possible, a clearance of 42 inches is better. And given more available space, a clear-

Large kitchen/great rooms, below, are now considered the true heart of the family home.

In large kitchens, opposite, look for plenty of counter and storage space, but insist on compact, efficient work areas.

ance of 48 to 49 inches is ideal. It means that you can open the dishwasher to load or unload it, and someone will still be able to walk behind you without doing a side-to-side shuffle or a crab walk. It also means that two people can work together in the same area. Any more than 49 inches, and the space is too much and involves a lot of walking back and forth. Fifty-four inches, for example, is too big a stretch. In large kitchens, look for balance; the work areas should have generous proportions, but to be truly efficient they should be compact and well designed.

Food Prep Areas and Surfaces. In many families, much of the food preparation takes place between the sink and the refrigerator. When you think of the work triangle, think of how much and how often you use an appliance. For example, sinks are generally used the most, followed by the refrigerator. The use of the cooktop is a matter of personal habit. Some families use it everyday, others use it sporadically. How close does it really need to be in relation to

the sink and refrigerator? Make your primary work zone the link between the sink and the refrigerator; then make the cooktop a secondary zone that's linked to them.

Cabinets Set the Style

Cabinets are the real furniture of a kitchen, making their selection both an aesthetic and functional choice. They are also likely to account for the largest portion of the budget.

Laminate. There are different brands and grades of plastic laminate, but cabinets made from this material generally are the least expensive you can buy. For the most part, they are devoid of detail and frameless, so don't look for raised panels, moldings, or inlaid beads on plastic laminate cabinets.

Although the surface is somewhat vulnerable (depending on the quality) to scratches and chips, plastic laminate cabinets can be refaced relatively inexpensively. Laminates come in a formidable range of

colors and patterns. Some of the newer speckled and patterned designs, which now even include denim and canvas, not only look great but won't show minor scratches and scars.

Wood. Wood cabinets offer the greatest variety of type, style, and finish. Framed cabinets (the full frame across the face of the cabinets may show between the doors) are popular for achieving a traditional look, but they are slightly less roomy inside. That's because you lose the width of the frame, which can be as much as an inch on each side. Frameless cabinets have full overlay doors and drawer fronts. With frameless cabinets, you gain about 2 inches of interior space per cabinet unit. Multiply that by the number of cabinet doors or drawer units you have, and add it up. It's easy to see that if space is at a premium, choose the frameless or full-overlay type. Besides, most cabinet companies now offer enough frameless styles to give you a traditional look in cabinetry, if that's your style.

The Decorative Aspect of Cabinets

While the trend in overall kitchen style is toward more decorative moldings and carvings, the trend in cabinet doors is toward simpler designs. Plain panels, for instance, are now more popular than raised panels. They allow you to have more decoration elsewhere. Ornamentation is effective when it is used to provide a focal point over a hood, fridge, or sink. Instead of installing a single crown profile, you might create a three- or four-piece crown treatment, or add a carving of grapevines, acanthus leaves, or another decorative motif. In the traditional kitchen, add them, but sparingly.

Finishes. Of all of the choices you will need to make regarding wood cabinets, the selection of the finish may be the hardest. Wood can be stained, pickled, painted, or oiled. Your selection will be determined in part by whether you order stock or custom cabinets. Finishing options on stock cabinets are usually limited, and variations are offered as an upgrade. Translation: more money. Try working with the manufacturer's stock cabinets. It not only costs less but also speeds up the process. There is usually

a reason why manufacturers offer certain woods in certain choices: it's because those choices work best with other elements in the room.

Wood Stains. Today, stains that are close to natural wood tones are popular, particularly natural wood finishes. Cherry is quickly becoming the number-one wood in the country. Pickled finishes, very popular in the early 1990s, are now looking dated. Some woods, particularly oak, have more grain than others. Some, such as maple, are smoother. And others, such as birch, dent more easily. The quality and inherent characteristics of the wood you choose will help determine whether it is better to stain, pickle, or paint. For staining, you need a good-quality clear wood. Pickling, because it has pigment in the stain, masks more of the grain but is still translucent. Because paint completely covers the grain, painted wood cabinets are usually made of lesser-quality paint-grade wood.

Painted Wood. Paint gives wood a smooth, clean finish. You can paint when you want a change or if the finish starts to show wear. This comes at no small expense, though, because the painter will have to sand the surfaces well before applying several coats of paint. If you choose painted cabinets, be sure to obtain a small can of the exact same paint from your kitchen vendor. There is usually a charge for this, but it allows you to do small touch-ups yourself, ridding your cabinets of particularly hideous scars without a complete repainting. While in theory the color choice for painted cabinets is infinite, manufacturers generally offer four shades of white and a few other standard color options from which to choose.

Pickled Wood. Pickled cabinets fall midway between full-grain natural cabinets and painted ones. Pickling is a combination of stain and paint, allowing some of the grain to show. It subdues the strongest patterns, while it covers over the lesser ones. The degree depends on your choice and on the options available from the manufacturer.

Be creative with storage. A tall cabinet, above, tops a drawer unit that holds dish towels and tablecloths.

A great room, below, works best when a well-defined kitchen area flows effortlessly into the living area.

Hardware. Handles are easier to maneuver than knobs. Advocates of universal design, which takes into consideration the capabilities of all people—young and old, with and without physical limitations—recommend them. Knobs do not work easily for children or elderly people with arthritis. A handle with a backplate will keep fingerprints off the cabinet door.

Fitting Cabinets into Your Layout

This calls for attention to the kitchen layout. In specifying cabinets, first let common sense and budget be your guide. Kitchen geography can help you determine how much storage you need and where it should be. Mentally divide your kitchen into zones: food preparation, food consumption, and so on. And don't forget about the nonfood areas. Do you see yourself repotting plants or working on a hobby in the kitchen? You'll need work space and cabinet space for those extra activities.

A kitchen workhorse, the island, is not new to kitchen design. It's as old as the solid, slightly elevated, central table of medieval kitchens in England. But where that table was a work surface, today's island can hold cabinets, a sink, a cooktop, a beverage refrigerator, and it can serve to divide areas of the kitchen.

How Tall Is Too Tall?

Upper cabinets are typically 12 inches deep; base, or lower, cabinets are 24 inches deep. With the exception of a desk unit, standard base cabinets are always the same height, 36 inches. Although most people prefer clean lines and planes as much as possible, some circumstances call for variations in the height of lower cabinets. There may be an often-used area where you want a countertop at which you can work while seated, for example.

Upper cabinets come in two or three standard heights: 30, 36, and 42 inches. The 30-inch ones look short; 36-inch cabinets look standard, and 42-inch ones can look too tall if your ceiling is not unusually high. In general, there is a slight up-charge for 30-inch cabinets and a big jump in price for 42-inch units. Order another size and you will pay double-custom prices. But you don't need to. For greater variation, install upper cabinets at varying heights. The old standard was to install 30-inch upper cabinets under a soffit—the often,

but not always, boxed-in area just under the ceiling and above the wall cabinets. Now, unless you have very tall ceilings, soffits are practically obsolete. Provided you have standard-height, 8-foot ceilings, the way to go now seems to be 36-inch cabinets with the remaining space of 6 inches or so filled with decorative trim up to the ceiling. It is a nicer, more refined look than cabinets that extend all the way to the ceiling, unless you prefer something contemporary and totally sleek and without ornament.

Size and Space. You don't want a massive bank of cabinets, either. Add up the dimensions wherever you're considering wall units. The counter is 36 inches high; backsplashes typically range from 15 to 17 inches. So with 36-inch-high upper cabinets, we're talking 7½ feet in all, 8 feet if you chose 42-inch-high wall units. Your own size can help determine which ones to choose. Determine what's comfortable by measuring your reach. A petite person will lose access to the top third of a cabinet. An inch or two can make a very big difference.

Also, be sure that the small appliances you keep on the countertop fit under the wall cabinets. Having them sit at the front edge of a countertop is an accident waiting to happen. A lot of people who have "appliance garages" discovered this. Whenever they pulled out the appliance, which places it nearer the counter's edge, they watched their mixer or coffeemaker tumble to the floor.

Often people need extra storage, so they extend the cabinets up to the ceiling. This provides the added extra storage space, but it can only be reached by a step stool. An open soffit above the upper cabinets provides just as much space for oversize, infrequently used objects, and it is equally accessible by stepladder. Plus it can be both a display area and perfect home for hard-to-store items: pitchers, trays, salad bowls, vases, collectibles, platters, covered servers, and so forth.

Light, natural wood finishes, left, are a popular cabinet choice.

Just remember to allow plenty of room for air to circulate around the TV.

Kitchen Storage Solutions

There are many storage options that are extremely useful. At the top of the list is a spice drawer or rack attached to an upper cabinet or door. Both drawer and door spice racks are offered as factory options when you order cabinets, or you can retro-fit them into existing cabinets. They provide visible access to all spices, so you don't end up with three tins of cinnamon, nine jars of garlic salt, four tiny bottles of vanilla, and no red pepper.

Lazy Susans. These rotating trays make items in the back of corner cabinets accessible. Consider adding inexpensive, plastic lazy Susans in a small upper cabinet. They will make the seasonings and cooking items you use everyday easily accessible.

Pie-cut door attachments can provide the same accessibility as a lazy Susan. Your choice depends on how much and what kind of storage you need. If a corner cabinet is home to sodas, chips, and cooking materials, install a pie-cut. A lazy Susan is more stable, best for pots, bowls, and larger, heavier objects.

The Kitchen Desk

Consider whether you will actually sit at a kitchen desk. Many people don't. Instead, they use it as the family message center and generally stand or perch on a stool. An additional, taller counter simply introduces more clutter to a room that is already overburdened with paraphernalia. And forget a desk-high cabinet, too. Instead use a standard counter-height cabinet to streamline whenever and wherever you can in the room.

Think about outfitting the desk area with a phone and answering machine and a corkboard for notes, your family's social schedule, invitations, and reminders. If you have room, a file drawer makes sense for storing school and business papers that need to be easy to retrieve. Also, if you don't have a separate study, and there's room, the kitchen may be a place to keep the family computer. Not only will you likely be using it more in the future for household record-keeping, but you can also help the kids with their homework and monitor their Internet use. In those cases, it makes sense to add a desk for comfort.

A Niche for the TV. Many people also want a TV in the kitchen. Plan for it. Who wants to see the back of the set or look at cords stretching across work areas, atop the refrigerator or the stove? Space and an outlet can be built into the lower portion of a well-placed wall cabinet or an open unit.

Pullouts, Rollouts, and Dividers.

Pullout fittings maximize the use of very narrow spaces. There are just two options for these areas: vertical tray-storage units or pullout pantries. You can find a 12-inch-wide base cabinet that is a pullout pantry with storage for canned goods and boxed items.

Pullout racks for cabinets and lid-rack dividers for drawers are also available from some cabinet suppliers. They are handy, but if you have enough cabinet storage space, the best thing is to store pots and pans with the lids on them in a couple of large cabinets.

Rollout cabinets are great and offer a lot of flexibility. They are adjustable to accommodate bulky countertop appliances and

Pullout cutting boards, above left, increase usable counter space.

Accessories for tall, narrow cabinets, left, home in handy for storing cookie sheets and trays.

Decorative molding, above, can enhance any cabinet. Most manufacturers offer a variety of molding options.

Knife, Towel, and Bread Storage. If you want a place to store knives, use slotted storage on a countertop. Frequently islands have false backs because they are deeper than base cabinets. Slots for knives can be cut into the area of the countertop that covers the void behind the base cabinet.

You can obtain all these storage options at the time you buy your cabinets. But you don't have to and may not even want to until you see how you really end up using your kitchen. A carpenter or handyman can often make them or install off-the-shelf units. Think outside of the box. We get in a rut; it is hard to be objective. Ask friends where they keep their kitchen stuff, and analyze every aspect of how you use your kitchen. Store things at point of use, such as leftover containers and sandwich bags near the refrigerator; mixing bowls and carving knives near the sink.

stock pots, and they can save a lot of steps and banging around.

You can also divide a base cabinet vertically into separate parts. Some of the vertical spaces are further subdivided horizontally—good places for storing cutting boards, cookie trays, baking tins, and big glass baking dishes.

Other Organizers

Buy cutlery drawers carefully. They are often too big and too clumsy, and they fail to take advantage of the full interior of the drawer. They are as bad as bookshelves spread too far apart. Consider cutlery dividers that are almost no wider than a spoon, with separate sections for teaspoons, cereal spoons, breakfast and dinner knives, lunch forks, dinner forks, and serving pieces. Add to this a section for miscellaneous utensils such as spoons for iced tea, chopsticks, and so on. Drawer dividers should be adjustable in case your needs, or your cutlery, change.

Plan #131034

Dimensions: 40' W x 32' D
Levels: 2 (upper unfinished)
Square Footage: 1,040
Bedrooms: 5
Bathrooms: 2½
Foundation: Crawl space, slab, or basement
Materials List Available: Yes
Price Category: C

Images provided by designer/architect.

You'll love the versatility this expandable ranch-style home gives, with its unfinished, second story that you can transform into two bedrooms and a bath if you need the space.

Features:

- Porch: Decorate this country-style porch to accentuate the charm of this warm home.

- Living Room: This formal room features a wide, dramatic archway that opens to the kitchen and the dining room.

- Kitchen: The angled shape of this kitchen gives it character, while the convenient island and well-designed floor plan make cooking and cleaning tasks unusually efficient.

- Bedrooms: Use the design option in the blueprints of this home to substitute one of the bedrooms into an expansion of the master bedroom, which features an amenity-laden, private bathroom for total luxury.

Optional Main Level Floor Plan

Main Level Floor Plan

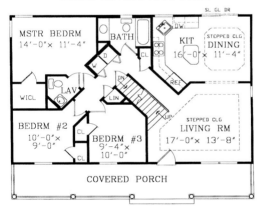

Kitchen

Upper Level Floor Plan

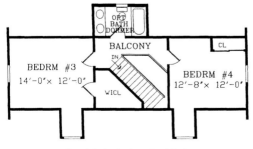

Copyright by designer/architect.

Plan #181003

Dimensions: 30' W x 35'4" D
Levels: 1
Square Footage: 958
Bedrooms: 2
Bathrooms: 1
Foundation: Basement
Materials List Available: Yes
Price Category: A

CAD FILE AVAILABLE

Images provided by designer/architect.

A front bay and an arched window prove that a house needn't be big to be beautiful.

Features:

- Ceiling Height: 8 ft.

- Porch: This charming covered entry porch invites you to enjoy summer breezes in an old-fashioned rocker or porch swing.

- Family Room: This large family gathering area enjoys plenty of sunlight from the multi-pane corner windows.

- Dining Room: Located adjacent to the family room for convenient entertaining, this dining room has a sliding glass door for access to the backyard.

- Kitchen: This convenient and pleasant kitchen features a single large sink overlooked by double windows.

- Bedroom: Each of the two bedrooms has its own closet. They share a luxurious full bathroom equipped with both a shower and a tub.

- Basement: The full basement provides plenty of storage and room for future expansion.

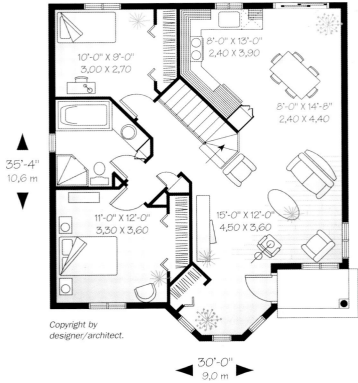

35'-4"
10,6 m

10'-0" X 9'-0"
3,00 X 2,70

8'-0" X 13'-0"
2,40 X 3,90

8'-0" X 14'-8"
2,40 X 4,40

11'-0" X 12'-0"
3,30 X 3,60

15'-0" X 12'-0"
4,50 X 3,60

30'-0"
9,0 m

Copyright by designer/architect.

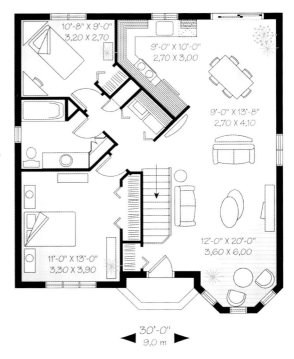

Plan #181006

Dimensions: 30' W x 35' D
Levels: 1
Square Footage: 972
Bedrooms: 2
Bathrooms: 1
Foundation: Full basement
Materials List Available: Yes
Price Category: A

Images provided by designer/architect.

CAD FILE AVAILABLE

35'-0"
10,5 m

10'-8" X 9'-0"
3,20 X 2,70

9'-0" X 10'-0"
2,70 X 3,00

9'-0" X 13'-8"
2,70 X 4,10

11'-0" X 13'-0"
3,30 X 3,90

12'-0" X 20'-0"
3,60 X 6,00

30'-0"
9,0 m

Copyright by designer/architect.

Plan #181022

Dimensions: 46' W x 40'4" D
Levels: 1
Square Footage: 1,098
Bedrooms: 2
Bathrooms: 1
Foundation: Full basement
Materials List Available: Yes
Price Category: B

Images provided by designer/architect.

CAD FILE AVAILABLE

40'-4"
12,1 m

9'-6" X 9'-5"
2,85 X 2,83

12'-0" X 18'-0"
3,60 X 5,40

12'-0" X 13'-0"
3,60 X 3,90

11'-4" X 20'-8"
3,40 X 6,20

14'-8" X 12'-0"
4,40 X 3,60

46'-0"
13,8 m

Copyright by designer/architect.

Plan #121012

Dimensions: 40' W x 48'8" D
Levels: 1
Square Footage: 1,195
Bedrooms: 3
Bathrooms: 2
Foundation: Basement
Materials List Available: Yes
Price Category: B

This home, as shown in the photograph, may differ from the actual blueprints. For more detailed information, please check the floor plans carefully.

Images provided by designer/architect.

This compact one-level home uses an open plan to make the most of its square footage.

Features:

- Ceiling Height: 8 ft.
- Covered Porch: This delightful area, located off the kitchen, provides a private spot to enjoy some fresh air.
- Open Plan: The family room, dining area and kitchen share a big open space to provide a sense of spaciousness. Moving so easily between these interrelated areas provides the convenience demanded by a busy lifestyle.
- Master Suite: An open plan is convenient, but it is still important for everyone to have their private space. The master suite enjoys its own bath and walk-in closet. The secondary bedrooms share a nearby bath.
- Garage: Here you will find parking for two cars and plenty of extra storage space as well.

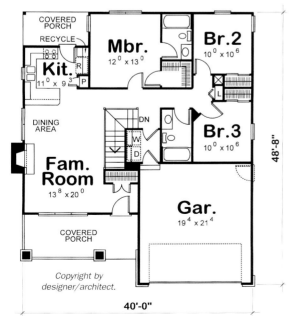

Copyright by designer/architect.

Rendering reflects floor plan

Plan #321025

Dimensions: 28' W x 28' D

Levels: 1

Square Footage: 914

Bedrooms: 2

Bathrooms: 1

Foundation: Basement, walkout

Materials List Available: Yes

Price Category: A

This cute little home's great layout packs in an abundance of features.

Features:

- Living Room: The cozy fireplace in this open, welcoming room invites you to relax awhile.

- Dining Room: This area has a bay window and is open to the kitchen and the living room.

- Kitchen: This compact kitchen has everything you'll need, including a built-in pantry.

- Master Bedroom: Generously sized, with a large closet, this room has a private door into the common bathroom.

- Bedroom: This secondary bedroom can also be used as a home office.

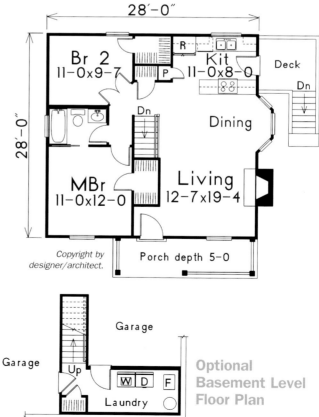

Plan #151561

Dimensions: 36' W x 65' D
Levels: 1
Square Footage: 1,374
Bedrooms: 3
Bathrooms: 2
Foundation: Crawl space or slab
CompleteCost List Available: Yes
Price Category: B

CAD FILE AVAILABLE

A covered porch with brick columns and railing adds great street appeal to this Arts and Crafts style ranch home.

Features:

- **Great Room:** Enjoy conversation with friends and loved ones in this room, which has a cozy fireplace. The area is open to the foyer, giving a large open feeling.

- **Kitchen:** Easy access from this kitchen to the dining room across the angled bar counter makes serving your meals a delight. Close by is the laundry area, which can conveniently serve the whole house.

- **Master Suite:** For privacy and convenience, this suite, with its private bath and large walk-in closet, is located at the rear of the house. Large windows allow the area to be flooded with natural light.

- **Bedrooms:** The house design offers this double bedroom area with full bathroom, which is ideal for the kids or overnight guests while separate from the master suite entry.

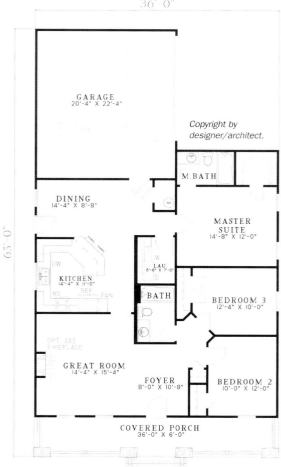

Plan #211081

Dimensions: 32' W x 34' D
Levels: 2
Square Footage: 1,110
Main Level Sq. Ft.: 832
Upper Level Sq. Ft.: 278
Bedrooms: 2
Bathrooms: 2
Foundation: Crawl space
Materials List Available: No
Price Category: B

Images provided by designer/architect.

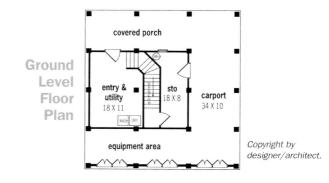

Ground Level Floor Plan

Copyright by designer/architect.

Main Level Floor Plan　　**Upper Level Floor Plan**

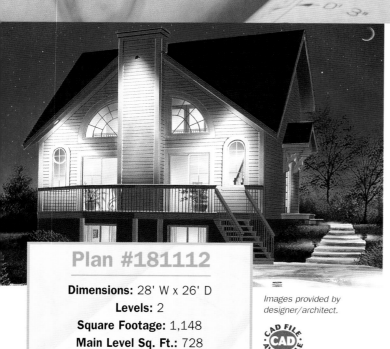

Plan #181112

Dimensions: 28' W x 26' D
Levels: 2
Square Footage: 1,148
Main Level Sq. Ft.: 728
Upper Level Sq. Ft.: 420
Bedrooms: 1
Bathrooms: 1½
Foundation: Full basement
Materials List Available: Yes
Price Category: B

Images provided by designer/architect.

CAD FILE AVAILABLE

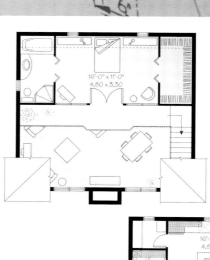

Upper Level Floor Plan

Copyright by designer/architect.

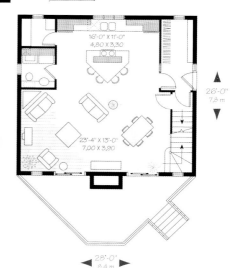

Main Level Floor Plan

Main Level Floor Plan

Deck

Brkfst

Fam/Kit
25-4x12

Dining
12-6x9-4

Great Room
16-4x12-8

Gar
19-4x19-4

Dn

Up

Dn Entry

W D

P

40'-0"

41'-4"

Images provided by designer/architect.

CAD FILE AVAILABLE

Mbr
12-4x14

Loft
12-8x11-2

Br 3
9x11-2

Br 2
12-4x10-2

Open to below

Dn

Upper Level Floor Plan

Copyright by designer/architect.

Plan #271033

Dimensions: 40' W x 41'4" D
Levels: 2
Square Footage: 1,516
Main Level Sq. Ft.: 817
Upper Level Sq. Ft.: 699
Bedrooms: 3
Bathrooms: 2½
Foundation: Basement
Materials List Available: Yes
Price Category: C

Main Level Floor Plan

38'-0"

39'-4"

Patio

Living
17-8x12-0

MBr
12-4x15-4

Kit
10-6x10-6

Dining
10-6x9-10

Garage
19-4x20-4

Up

Dn

P

R

Porch

Images provided by designer/architect.

Upper Level Floor Plan

Br 2
17-8x12-0

Br 3
10-6x13-0

Dn

open to below

Copyright by designer/architect.

Plan #321057

Dimensions: 38' W x 39'4" D
Levels: 2
Square Footage: 1,524
Main Level Sq. Ft.: 951
Upper Level Sq. Ft.: 573
Bedrooms: 3
Bathrooms: 2½
Foundation: Basement
Materials List Available: Yes
Price Category: C

Plan #151413

Dimensions: 32' W x 42' D
Levels: 1.5
Square Footage: 1,400
Main Level Sq. Ft.: 948
Upper Level Sq. Ft.: 452
Bedrooms: 2
Bathrooms: 2
Foundation: Crawl space or slab
CompleteCost List Available: Yes
Price Category: B

Images provided by designer/architect.

Relax on the front porch of this lovely little cottage. It's a great starter home or a weekend getaway.

Features:

• Great Room: Enter from the front porch into this large room, with its vaulted ceiling and stone fireplace.

• Kitchen: This large kitchen has plenty of cabinets and counter space; there is even a raised bar.

• Grilling Porch: Just off the kitchen is this porch. Bedroom 1 has access to this area as well.

• Upper Level: Located on this level are a loft area, a full bathroom, and a bedroom.

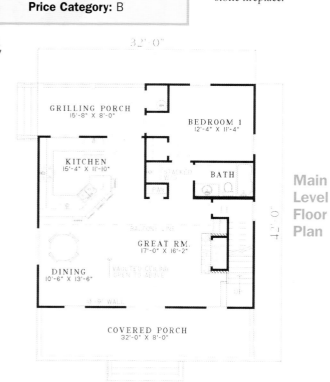

Main Level Floor Plan

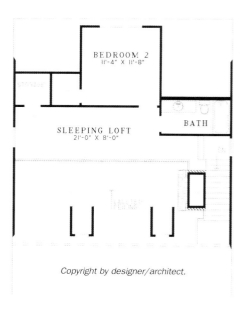

Upper Level Floor Plan

Copyright by designer/architect.

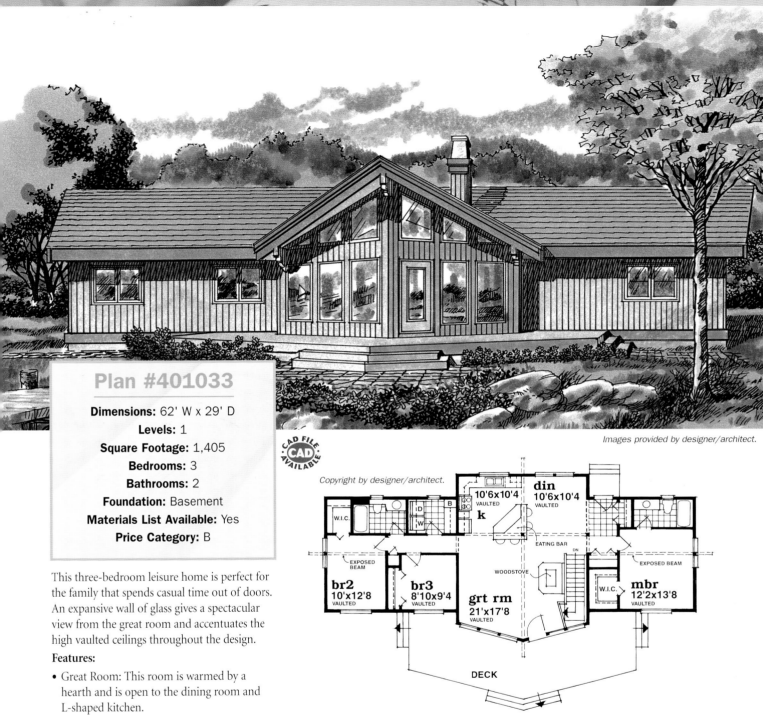

Images provided by designer/architect.

Plan #401033

Dimensions: 62' W x 29' D
Levels: 1
Square Footage: 1,405
Bedrooms: 3
Bathrooms: 2
Foundation: Basement
Materials List Available: Yes
Price Category: B

This three-bedroom leisure home is perfect for the family that spends casual time out of doors. An expansive wall of glass gives a spectacular view from the great room and accentuates the high vaulted ceilings throughout the design.

Features:

- Great Room: This room is warmed by a hearth and is open to the dining room and L-shaped kitchen.

- Kitchen: A triangular snack bar graces this kitchen and provides space for casual meals.

- Bedrooms: The bedrooms are split, with the master bedroom on the right side of the plan and family bedrooms on the left.

Copyright by designer/architect.

br2 10'x12'8 VAULTED

br3 8'10x9'4 VAULTED

grt rm 21'x17'8 VAULTED

W.I.C.

EXPOSED BEAM

WOODSTOVE

k 10'6x10'4 VAULTED

din 10'6x10'4 VAULTED

EATING BAR

DN

EXPOSED BEAM

W.I.C.

mbr 12'2x13'8 VAULTED

DECK

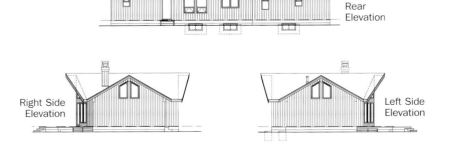

Rear Elevation

Right Side Elevation

Left Side Elevation

Plan #321040

Dimensions: 35' W x 40'8" D

Levels: 1

Square Footage: 1,084

Bedrooms: 2

Bathrooms: 2

Foundation: Basement

Materials List Available: Yes

Price Category: B

Images provided by designer/architect.

This cute cottage, with its front porch, would make a great starter home or a weekend getaway home.

Features:

- Living Room: This room features an entry closet and a cozy fireplace.

- Kitchen: This well-designed kitchen opens into the breakfast area.

- Master Suite: This retreat has a walk-in closet and a private bath.

- Bedroom: This second bedroom features a walk-in closet and has access to the hall bathroom.

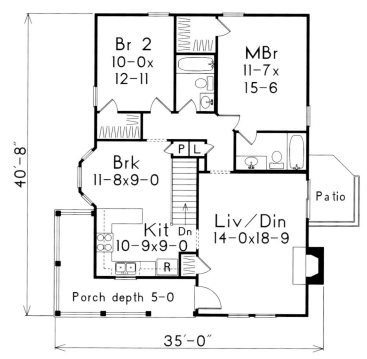

Copyright by designer/architect.

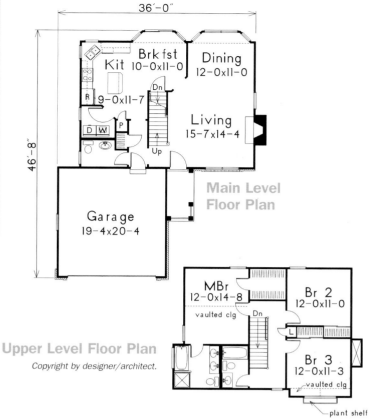

36'-0"

46'-8"

Brk fst
Kit 10-0x11-0
9-0x11-7

Dining
12-0x11-0

Dn

Living
15-7x14-4

D W

P

Up

Garage
19-4x20-4

Main Level Floor Plan

Images provided by designer/architect.

Plan #321060

Dimensions: 36' W x 46'8" D

Levels: 2

Square Footage: 1,575

Main Level Sq. Ft.: 802

Upper Level Sq. Ft.: 773

Bedrooms: 3

Bathrooms: 2½

Foundation: Basement

Materials List Available: Yes

Price Category: C

MBr
12-0x14-8
vaulted clg

Br 2
12-0x11-0

Dn

Br 3
12-0x11-3
vaulted clg

plant shelf

Upper Level Floor Plan

Copyright by designer/architect.

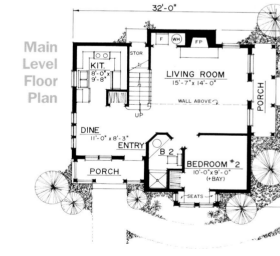

32'-0"

F WH FP

Main Level Floor Plan

KIT.
8'-0" x 9'-8"

STOR

LIVING ROOM
15'-7" x 14'-0"

PORCH

WALL ABOVE

UP

28'-7"

DINE
11'-0" x 8'-3"

ENTRY

B 2

BEDROOM #2
10'-0" x 9'-0"
(+ BAY)

PORCH

SEATS

Plan #291008

Dimensions: 32' W x 28'7" D

Levels: 2

Square Footage: 1,183

Main Level Sq. Ft.: 772

Upper Level Sq. Ft.: 411

Bedrooms: 2

Bathrooms: 2

Foundation: Crawl space

Materials List Available: No

Price Category: B

Images provided by designer/architect.

DOWN

OPEN TO LIVING ROOM

D

W

Upper Level Floor Plan

WOOD BEAMS

BATH #1

WIC

MASTER BEDROOM
10'-5" x 13'-8"
(11'-8" CEILING)

BUILT-IN CABINETS

Copyright by designer/architect.

Plan #401020

Dimensions: 55'6" W x 30' D

Levels: 1

Square Footage: 1,230

Bedrooms: 3

Bathrooms: 2

Foundation: Basement

Materials List Available: Yes

Price Category: B

This is a grand vacation or retirement home, designed for views and the outdoor lifestyle. The full-width deck complements the abundant windows in the rooms that face it.

Features:

- Living Room: This area, with a vaulted ceiling, a fireplace, and full-height windows overlooking the deck, is made for gathering.

- Dining Room: This room is open to the living room; it has sliding glass doors that lead to the outdoors.

- Kitchen: This room has a pass-through counter to the dining room and is U-shaped in design.

- Bedrooms: Two family bedrooms in the middle of the plan share a full bath.

- Master Suite: This area has a private bath and deck views.

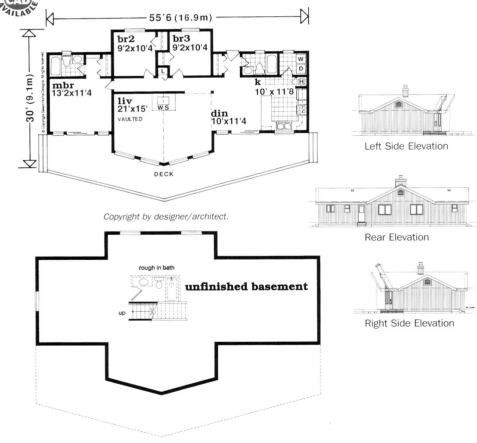

Copyright by designer/architect.

Optional Basement Level Floor Plan

Left Side Elevation

Rear Elevation

Right Side Elevation

Images provided by designer/architect.

Plan #151751

Dimensions: 39'10" W x 39'5" D
Levels: 1.5
Square Footage: 1,449
Main Level Sq. Ft.: 1,059
Upper Level Sq. Ft.: 390
Bedrooms: 2
Bathrooms: 2½
Foundation: Crawl space
CompleteCost List Available: Yes
Price Category: B

Comfort is the key with this magnificent log home.

Features:

• **Entry:** Step up to the covered porch, which has two sets of French doors that open into the great room: inside, you are greeted with a fireplace.

• **Kitchen:** Open to the great room, this cooking space has bar seating and view of a bay-shaped dining area.

• **Master Suite:** This main-level suite includes a large walk-in closet and a bath with an extra-large shower, double vanities, and a closet for a stacked washer-dryer.

• **Upper Level:** This space has a bedroom and bathroom with creative ceiling heights and a balcony view to the great room below.

Upper Level Floor Plan

Copyright by designer/architect.

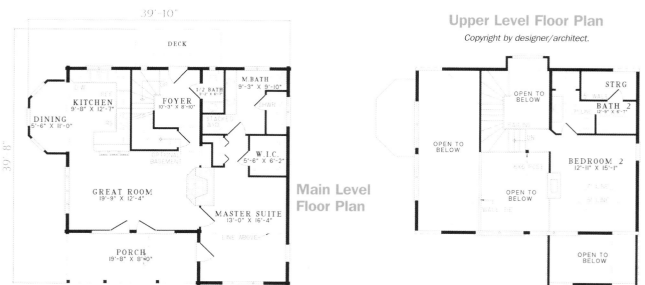

Main Level Floor Plan

Plan #151411

Dimensions: 44'2" W x 39' D
Levels: 1.5
Square Footage: 1,472
Main Level Sq. Ft.: 1,140
Upper Level Sq. Ft.: 332
Bedrooms: 4
Bathrooms: 2
Foundation: Crawl space or slab
CompleteCost List Available: Yes
Price Category: B

Images provided by designer/architect.

The front porch and roof dormers add a genuine country look to this home.

Features:

- Great Room: This large gathering area features a fireplace and windows looking onto the front yard.

- Kitchen: This large U-shaped kitchen has a raised bar and is open to the dining room.

- Bedrooms: Two bedrooms are located on the main level and share a common bathroom. The remaining two bedrooms are located on the upper level and share a full bathroom.

- Loft: This large area overlooks the great room and is ideal for extra sleeping areas for overnight guests.

Main Level Floor Plan

44' 2"

BEDROOM 1
11'-0" X 13'-0"

BEDROOM 2
10'-8" X 9'-2"

BATH

GRILLING PORCH
13'-4" X 9'-6"

CLEANING TABLE

STACKED W/D

SUPPLY ROOM

PAN

GREAT RM.
17'-0" X 16'-0"

KITCHEN
13'-4" X 12'-6"

39' 0"

8' COVERED PORCH

DINING
13'-4" X 12'-6"

Upper Level Floor Plan

Copyright by designer/architect.

BEDROOM 3
10'-8" X 9'-2"

BATH

OPTIONAL BEDROOM 4
13'-4" X 13'-7"

LOFT
17'-0" X 6'-0"

OPEN TO BELOW

Plan #151797

Dimensions: 53' W x 41'10" D
Levels: 1
Square Footage: 1,480
Bedrooms: 3
Bathrooms: 2
Foundation: Crawl space
CompleteCost List Available: Yes
Price Category: B

Southern traditional styling is blended into this fantastic log home plan.

Features:

- Living Room: Two gable windows let natural light pour into the vaulted ceiling in this room.

- Dining Room: This area shares the cozy stone fireplace with the living room. Step through the French doors, and you'll find yourself on the rear screened porch, which stretches the entire length of the home.

- Master Suite: This massive suite has French-door access to the rear screened porch and a private master bath.

- Bedrooms: The two bedrooms, in addition to the master suite, are placed near the central laundry closet and bathroom with corner shower, which separate the bedrooms from the main family areas.

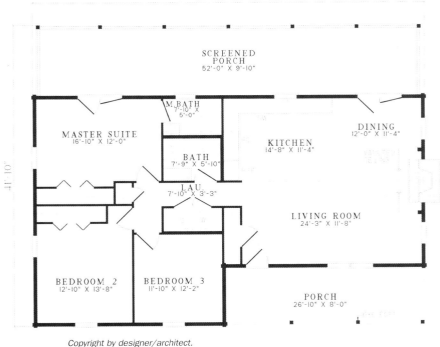

Plan #121045

Dimensions: 40' W x 48' D
Levels: 2
Square Footage: 1,575
Main Level Sq. Ft.: 787
Upper Level Sq. Ft.: 788
Bedrooms: 3
Bathrooms: 2½
Foundation: Basement
Materials List Available: Yes
Price Category: C

Images provided by designer/architect.

This home, as shown in the photograph, may differ from the actual blueprints. For more detailed information, please check the floor plans carefully.

Upper Level Floor Plan

Main Level Floor Plan

Copyright by designer/architect.

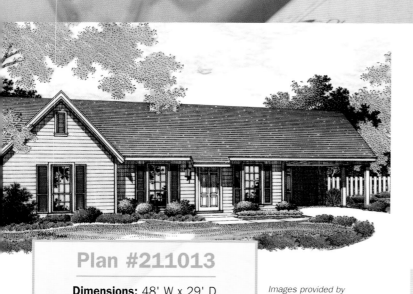

Plan #211013

Dimensions: 48' W x 29' D
Levels: 1
Square Footage: 998
Bedrooms: 3
Bathrooms: 1
Foundation: Slab; crawl space for fee
Materials List Available: Yes
Price Category: A

Images provided by designer/architect.

Copyright by designer/architect.

SMARTtip
Mixing Patterns

A trick for mixing patterns is to provide links of scale, motif, and color. The regularity of checks, stripes, textural looks, and geometrics, particularly if small-scale and low-contrast, tends to make them easy-to-mix "neutral" patterns. A small floral can play off a thin ticking stripe, while a cabbage-rose chintz may require a bolder stripe as a same-scale foil. Use the same or similar patterns in varying sizes, or develop a them by focusing on florals, geometric, or ethnic prints.

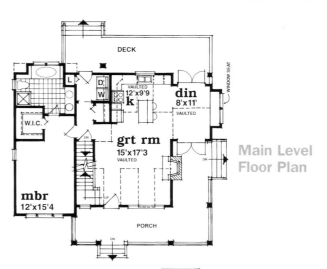

**Main Level
Floor Plan**

Images provided by designer/architect.

CAD FILE AVAILABLE

Plan #401036

Dimensions: 42' W x 38' D
Levels: 2
Square Footage: 1,583
Main Level Sq. Ft.: 1,050
Upper Level Sq. Ft.: 533
Bedrooms: 3
Bathrooms: 2
Foundation: Basement
Materials List Available: Yes
Price Category: C

**Upper Level
Floor Plan**

Copyright by designer/architect.

Plan #431003

Dimensions: 34' W x 36' D
Levels: 2
Square Footage: 1,330
Main Level Sq. Ft.: 1,030
Upper Level Sq. Ft.: 300
Bedrooms: 2
Bathrooms: 1
Foundation: Crawl space or basement
Material List Available: Yes
Price Category: B

Images provided by designer/architect.

**Main Level
Floor Plan**

Copyright by designer/architect.

Great Room

Upper Level Floor Plan

Plan #431004

Dimensions: 41' W x 30' D
Levels: 2
Square Footage: 1,156
Main Level Sq. Ft.: 810
Upper Level Sq. Ft.: 346
Bedrooms: 2
Bathrooms: 2
Foundation: Crawl space
Material List Available: Yes
Price Category: B

Images provided by designer/architect.

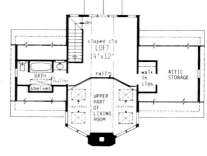

Upper Level Floor Plan

Copyright by designer/architect.

Main Level Floor Plan

Plan #271034

Dimensions: 45' W x 43' D
Levels: 2
Square Footage: 1,531
Main Level Sq. Ft.: 1,062
Upper Level Sq. Ft.: 469
Bedrooms: 4
Bathrooms: 2
Foundation: Basement
Materials List Available: Yes
Price Category: C

Images provided by designer/architect.

CAD FILE AVAILABLE

Upper Level Floor Plan

Copyright by designer/architect.

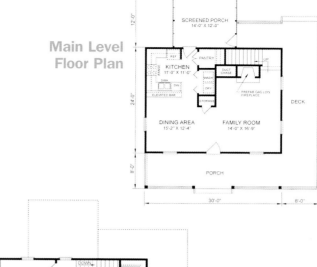

Main Level Floor Plan

SCREENED PORCH
14'-0" X 12'-0"

KITCHEN
11'-0" X 11'-0"

PANTRY

DUCT CHASE

PREFAB GAS LOGS FIREPLACE

DECK

DINING AREA
15'-2" X 12'-4"

FAMILY ROOM
14'-0" X 16'-9"

PORCH

Plan #341045

Dimensions: 38' W x 44' D
Levels: 2
Square Footage: 1,440
Main Level Sq. Ft.: 720
Upper Level Sq. Ft.: 720
Bedrooms: 3
Bathrooms: 2
Foundation: Crawl space, slab; basement option for fee
Materials List Available: Yes
Price Category: B

Upper Level Floor Plan

BEDROOM 2
11'-0" X 10'-3"

CLOSET

DUCT CHASE

CLOSET

BEDROOM 1
14'-0" X 11'-5"

BEDROOM 3
11'-0" X 10'-1"

BATH 2

BATH 1

LINE OF 8 FT CEILING

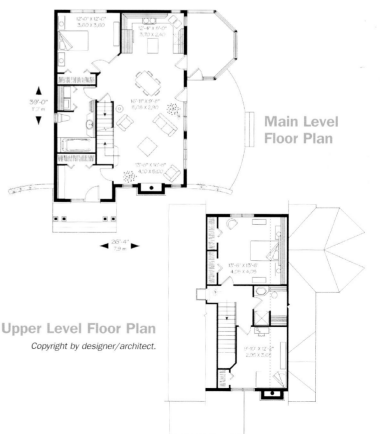

Main Level Floor Plan

39'-0"
11.7 m

26'-4"
7.9 m

Upper Level Floor Plan

Plan #181131

Dimensions: 26'4" W x 39' D
Levels: 2
Square Footage: 1,590
Main Level Sq. Ft.: 996
Upper Level Sq. Ft.: 594
Bedrooms: 3
Bathrooms: 2
Foundation: Full basement
Materials List Available: Yes
Price Category: B

Plan #131017

Dimensions: 69'8" W x 39'4" D
Levels: 1
Square Footage: 1,480
Bedrooms: 3
Bathrooms: 2
Foundation: Crawl space, slab, or basement
Materials List Available: Yes
Price Category: C

Images provided by designer/architect.

Alternate Floor Plan

Part Plan with Optional Basement

Rear Elevation

Copyright by designer/architect.

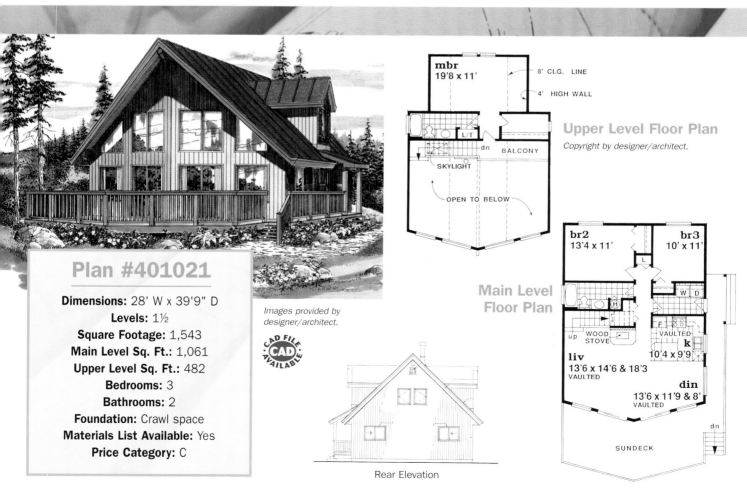

Plan #401021

Dimensions: 28' W x 39'9" D
Levels: 1½
Square Footage: 1,543
Main Level Sq. Ft.: 1,061
Upper Level Sq. Ft.: 482
Bedrooms: 3
Bathrooms: 2
Foundation: Crawl space
Materials List Available: Yes
Price Category: C

Images provided by designer/architect.

CAD FILE AVAILABLE

Upper Level Floor Plan

Copyright by designer/architect.

Main Level Floor Plan

Rear Elevation

Plan #151761

Dimensions: 39' W x 41'8" D
Levels: 1
Square Footage: 1,092
Bedrooms: 2
Bathrooms: 1
Foundation: Crawl space
CompleteCost List Available: Yes
Price Category: B

This log home has a simple straight-lined design featuring a front covered porch, perfect for stargazing and a cup of hot chocolate.

Features:

- Front Porch: This covered porch, with plenty of room for relaxing, runs the full width of the home.

- Entry: This cozy entry leads to the open floor plan, with its spacious great room, kitchen, and large dining room.

- Kitchen: This kitchen has ample counter and cabinet space and is open to the dining room. Nearby is the grilling porch with columns for lazy summer afternoons.

- Bedrooms: The two bedrooms are surprisingly large for a home of this size. They share the common bathroom, which has dual vanities.

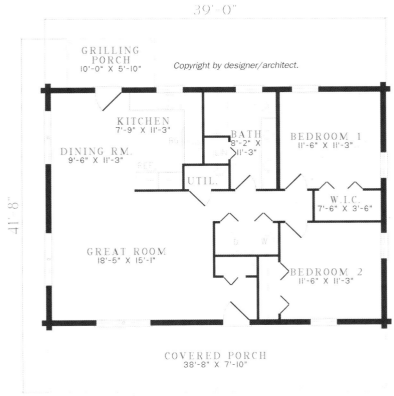

GRILLING PORCH 10'-0" X 5'-10"

KITCHEN 7'-9" X 11'-3"

BATH 8'-2" X 11'-3"

BEDROOM 1 11'-6" X 11'-3"

DINING RM. 9'-6" X 11'-3"

UTIL.

W.I.C. 7'-6" X 3'-6"

GREAT ROOM 18'-5" X 15'-1"

BEDROOM 2 11'-6" X 11'-3"

COVERED PORCH 38'-8" X 7'-10"

39'-0"

41'8"

Plan #131007

Dimensions: 59'10" W x 47'8" D
Levels: 1
Square Footage: 1,595
Bedrooms: 3
Bathrooms: 2
Foundation: Crawl space, slab, basement, or walkout
Materials List Available: Yes
Price Category: D

Imagine living in this home, with its traditional country comfort and individual brand of charm.

Features:

- Exterior elements: The mixture of a front porch with a cameo front door, decorative posts, bay windows, and dormers will delight you.

- Great Room: A tray ceiling gives distinction to this large room, and a wet bar eases entertaining.

- Screened Porch: At dusk and dawn, this porch is sure to be your favorite outdoor spot.

- Kitchen: Eat any meal in this large kitchen for a touch of homey charm.

- Dining Room: Perfect for hosting a formal dinner, this bayed dining room can increase your enjoyment of simple family meals.

- Master Bedroom: For the sake of privacy, this room is somewhat secluded. Decorate to emphasize the elegant tray ceiling.

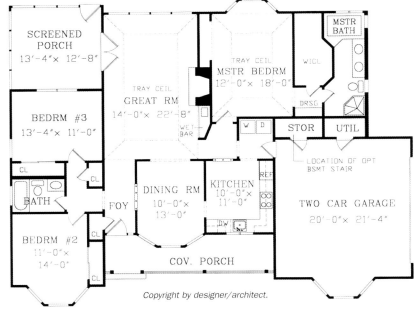

Copyright by designer/architect.

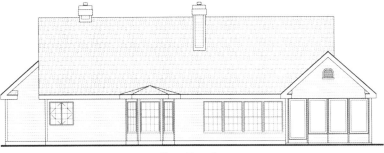

Rear Elevation

Alternate Front View

Foyer / Dining Room

Great Room

Add the Extras

Simple or plain, it's the little conveniences and miscellaneous touches that push the dining experience to perfection. Here are some extra things to think about.

- You can never have too many serving trays when you entertain outside. For carrying food or drinks from the kitchen or the grill, trays are indispensable.

- A serving cart on wheels makes a perfect movable outdoor bar and provides an additional serving surface. Look for one at yard sales or buy one new.

- Chances are you won't have a sideboard, but a few small tables to hold excess items are great substitutes for one. They're also easier to position in the different places where you need them.

- For cooler weather or even a summer's evening with a bit of nip in the air, nothing beats an outdoor fireplace for comfort. You could build one into the house, but various types of stand-alone units are sold in home centers. To add a Southwest ambiance, consider a chiminea, a clay fireplace. Try burning some piñon pine, and you'll feel as if you're in Santa Fe. Be sure to follow manufacturers' instructions when using these fireplaces. You might also have to store them during the winter.

- Pots of fragrant plants—lavender, scented geraniums, flowering tobacco, or jasmine—provide a sensual aroma. Flowers such as roses climbing up an arbor or trellis are beautiful, evoke a romantic feeling, and lend a delicate scent to the atmosphere as well.

Nothing adds romance and intrigue to an evening soiree as candlelight does. Include just a few candles for an intimate dinner. Use more for a larger gathering, placing one or more on each table. Scatter luminaries around the yard. As the beautiful evening dusk begins, light candles, a few at a time, so your eyes can adjust to the dimming light. Not only do the candles illuminate the night in a magical way but they can also keep bugs at bay.

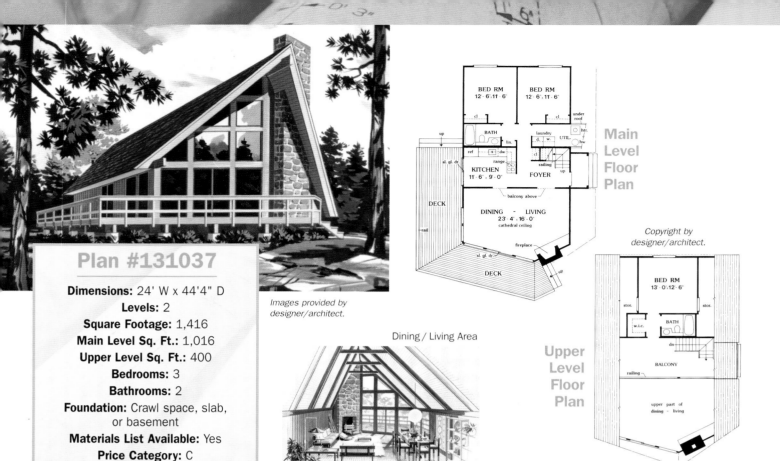

Plan #131037

Dimensions: 24' W x 44'4" D
Levels: 2
Square Footage: 1,416
Main Level Sq. Ft.: 1,016
Upper Level Sq. Ft.: 400
Bedrooms: 3
Bathrooms: 2
Foundation: Crawl space, slab, or basement
Materials List Available: Yes
Price Category: C

Images provided by designer/architect.

Dining / Living Area

Main Level Floor Plan

Upper Level Floor Plan

Copyright by designer/architect.

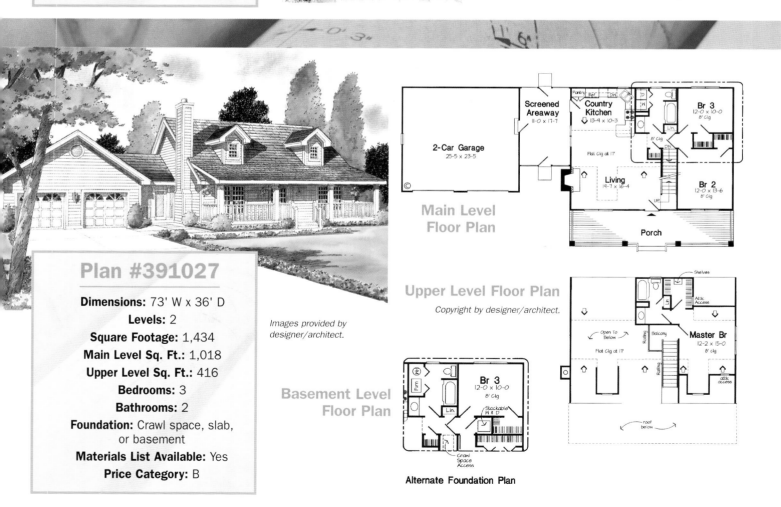

Plan #391027

Dimensions: 73' W x 36' D
Levels: 2
Square Footage: 1,434
Main Level Sq. Ft.: 1,018
Upper Level Sq. Ft.: 416
Bedrooms: 3
Bathrooms: 2
Foundation: Crawl space, slab, or basement
Materials List Available: Yes
Price Category: B

Images provided by designer/architect.

Main Level Floor Plan

Upper Level Floor Plan

Copyright by designer/architect.

Basement Level Floor Plan

Alternate Foundation Plan

Plan #181132

Dimensions: 44' W x 26' D
Levels: 2
Square Footage: 1,437
Main Level Sq. Ft.: 856
Upper Level Sq. Ft.: 581
Bedrooms: 3
Bathrooms: 1½
Foundation: Walkout basement
Materials List Available: Yes
Price Category: B

Images provided by designer/architect.

CAD FILE AVAILABLE

Main Level Floor Plan

Upper Level Floor Plan

Copyright by designer/architect.

Plan #191036

Dimensions: 45'6" W x 51' D
Levels: 1
Square Footage: 1,438
Bedrooms: 3
Bathrooms: 1
Foundation: Crawl space, slab
Materials List Available: No
Price Category: B

Images provided by designer/architect.

Copyright by designer/architect.

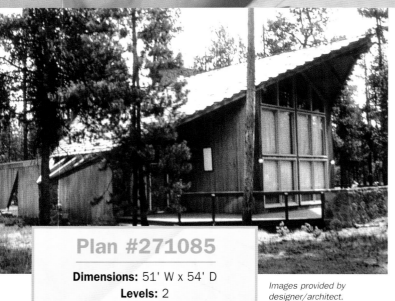

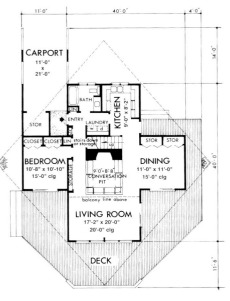

Main Level Floor Plan

CARPORT
11'-0"
x
21'-0"

BATH

KITCHEN
9'-0" x 8'-2"

STOR

ENTRY
LAUNDRY
w d

BEDROOM
10'-8" x 10'-10"
15'-0" clg

STORAGE

stairs down
or storage

up

DINING
11'-0" x 11'-0"
15'-0" clg

STOR STOR

CLOSET CLOSET LIN

CONVERSATION
PIT
9'-0" x 8'-2"

balcony line above

LIVING ROOM
17'-2" x 20'-0"
20'-0" clg

DECK

Plan #271085

Dimensions: 51' W x 54' D
Levels: 2
Square Footage: 1,541
Main Level Sq. Ft.: 1,028
Upper Level Sq. Ft.: 513
Bedrooms: 3
Bathrooms: 2
Foundation: Basement
Materials List Available: No
Price Category: C

Images provided by designer/architect.

BATH
Sh'wr
LIN

BEDROOM
9'-0" x 12'-7"

down

CLOS
CLOS

BALCONY BEDR'M
17'-2" x 9'-8"
11'-0" clg

railing

upper part of
living room

Upper Level Floor Plan

Copyright by designer/architect.

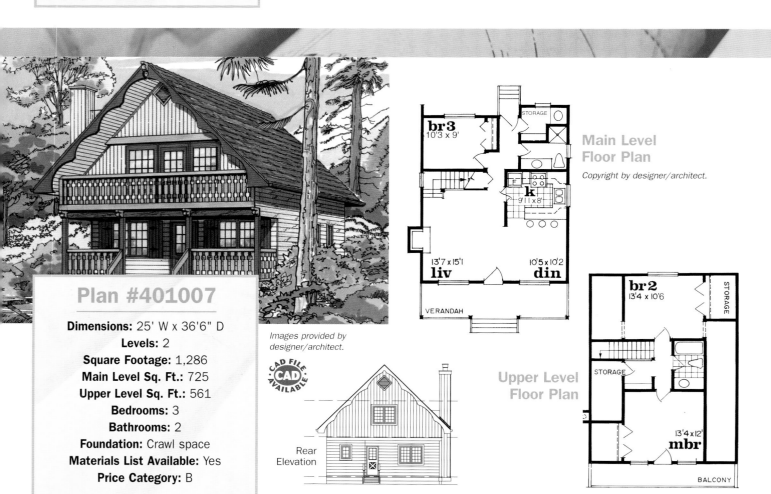

Plan #401007

Dimensions: 25' W x 36'6" D
Levels: 2
Square Footage: 1,286
Main Level Sq. Ft.: 725
Upper Level Sq. Ft.: 561
Bedrooms: 3
Bathrooms: 2
Foundation: Crawl space
Materials List Available: Yes
Price Category: B

Images provided by designer/architect.

Main Level Floor Plan

Copyright by designer/architect.

br3
10'3 x 9'

STORAGE

liv
13'7 x 15'1

k
9'11 x 8'

din
10'5 x 10'2

VERANDAH

Rear Elevation

Upper Level Floor Plan

br2
13'4 x 10'6

STORAGE

STORAGE

mbr
13'4 x 12'

BALCONY

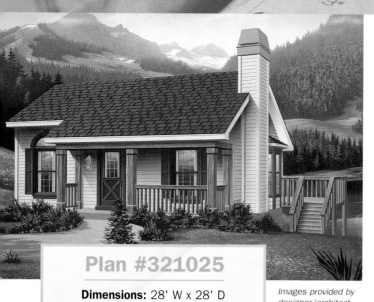

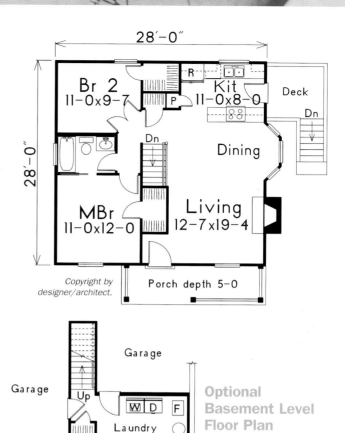

Plan #321025

Dimensions: 28' W x 28' D

Levels: 1

Square Footage: 914

Bedrooms: 2

Bathrooms: 1

Foundation: Basement, walkout

Materials List Available: Yes

Price Category: A

Images provided by designer/architect.

Copyright by designer/architect.

Optional Basement Level Floor Plan

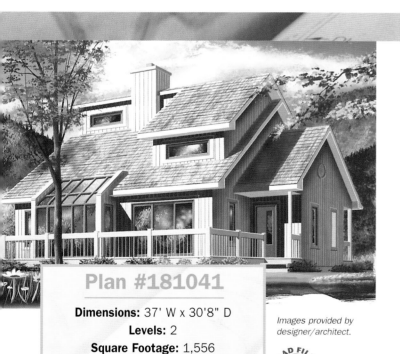

Plan #181041

Dimensions: 37' W x 30'8" D

Levels: 2

Square Footage: 1,556

Main Level Sq. Ft.: 952

Upper Level Sq. Ft.: 604

Bedrooms: 3

Bathrooms: 2

Foundation: Full basement

Materials List Available: Yes

Price Category: C

Images provided by designer/architect.

CAD FILE AVAILABLE

Upper Level Floor Plan

Copyright by designer/architect.

Main Level Floor Plan

Main Level Floor Plan

Images provided by designer/architect.

CAD FILE AVAILABLE

Plan #341038

Dimensions: 26' W x 39' D
Levels: 2
Square Footage: 1,560
Main Level Sq. Ft.: 1,014
Upper Level Sq. Ft.: 546
Bedrooms: 3
Bathrooms: 2½
Foundation: Crawl space, slab; basement option available for fee
Materials List Available: Yes
Price Category: C

Upper Level Floor Plan

Copyright by designer/architect.

Images provided by designer/architect.

Plan #191037

Dimensions: 57'4" W x 65' D
Levels: 1
Square Footage: 1,575
Bedrooms: 3
Bathrooms: 2
Foundation: Crawl space, slab
Materials List Available: No
Price Category: C

Copyright by designer/architect.

Images provided by designer/architect.

Plan #211069

Dimensions: 58' W x 42' D
Levels: 1.5
Square Footage: 1,600
Main Level Sq. Ft.: 1,136
Upper Level Sq. Ft.: 464
Bedrooms: 3
Bathrooms: 2
Foundation: Crawl space
Materials List Available: Yes
Price Category: C

Enjoy the large front porch on this traditionally styled home when it's too sunny for the bugs, and use the screened back porch at dusk and dawn.

Features:

• Living Room: Call this the family room if you wish, but no matter what you call it, expect friends and family to gather here, especially when the fireplace gives welcome warmth.

• Kitchen: You'll love the practical layout that pleases everyone from gourmet chefs to beginning cooks.

• Master Suite: Positioned on the main floor to give it privacy, this suite has two entrances for convenience. You'll find a large walk-in closet here as well as a dressing room that includes a separate vanity and mirror makeup counter.

• Storage Space: The 462-sq.-ft. garage is roomy enough to hold two cars and still have space to store tools, out-of-season clothing, or whatever else that needs a dry, protected spot.

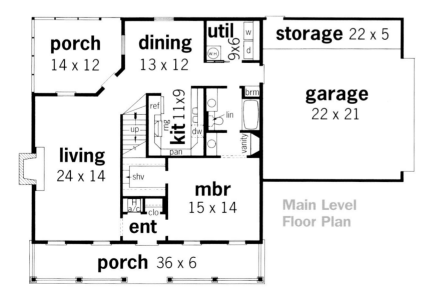

Main Level Floor Plan

Upper Level Floor Plan

Copyright by designer/architect.

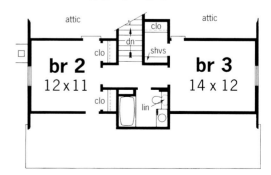

Plan #161081

Dimensions: 50' W x 55'8" D
Levels: 1
Square Footage: 1,390
Bedrooms: 3
Bathrooms: 2
Foundation: Walkout basement
Materials List Available: Yes
Price Category: B

Images provided by designer/architect.

The stone-and-siding facade, front porch, and multiple gables decorate the exterior of this charming one-floor plan.

Features:

- **Great Room:** The standard 8–ft. ceiling height vaults to an 11-ft. height through this room.

- **Kitchen:** This kitchen can accommodate a small dining area or can be designed to offer more cabinets and allow for a larger great room.

- **Master Suite:** This suite enjoys a raised center ceiling and a private bath.

- **Basement:** The home is designed with this unfinished walk-out basement, which can be finished to provide additional living space.

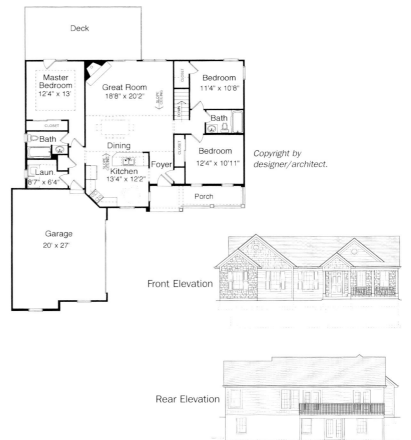

Deck

Master Bedroom
12'4" x 13'

Great Room
18'8" x 20'2"

Bedroom
11'4" x 10'8"

CLOSET

Bath

Bath

Dining

Bedroom
12'4" x 10'11"

Laun.
8'7" x 6'4"

Kitchen
13'4" x 12'2"

Foyer

Porch

Copyright by designer/architect.

Garage
20' x 27'

Front Elevation

Rear Elevation

Plan #181120

Dimensions: 32' W x 40' D
Levels: 2
Square Footage: 1,480
Main Level Sq. Ft.: 1,024
Second Level Sq. Ft.: 456
Bedrooms: 2
Bathrooms: 2
Foundation: Basement
Materials List Available: Yes
Price Category: B

Escape to this charming all-season vacation home with lots of view-capturing windows.

Images provided by designer/architect.

Features:

- Ceiling Height: 8 ft. unless otherwise noted.

- Living/Dining Area: The covered back porch opens into this large, inviting combined area. Its high ceiling adds to the sense of spaciousness.

- Family Room: After relaxing in front of the fireplace that warms this family room, family and guests can move outside onto the porch to watch the sun set.

- Kitchen: Light streams through a triple window in this well-designed kitchen. It's conveniently located next to the dining area and features a center island with a breakfast bar and double sinks.

- Master Suite: This first floor suite is located in the front of the house and is enhanced by its large walk-through closet and the adjoining private bath.

CAD FILE AVAILABLE

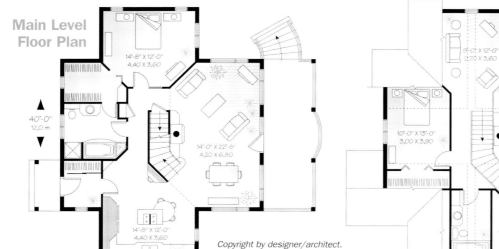

Main Level Floor Plan

40'-0"
12,0 m

14'-8" X 12'-0"
4,40 X 3,60

14'-0" X 22'-8"
4,20 X 6,80

14'-8" X 12'-0"
4,40 X 3,60

Copyright by designer/architect.

32'-0"
9,6 m

Upper Level Floor Plan

9'-0" X 12'-0"
2,70 X 3,60

10'-0" X 13'-0"
3,00 X 3,90

Plan #181019

Dimensions: 59'8" W x 44'4" D
Levels: 1
Square Footage: 1,494
Bedrooms: 3
Bathrooms: 1
Foundation: Basement
Materials List Available: Yes
Price Category: B

Images provided by designer/architect.

This elegantly styled home with an open floor plan has something for everyone.

Features:

- Foyer: This entry area welcomes you to the home and has a large coat closet.

- Kitchen: This L-shaped island kitchen has plenty of counter space and is open to the eating area and living room.

- Eating Area: This space can function as a casual family gathering area or a formal dining room.

- Master Bedroom: This private room has a large his-and-her closet.

- Garage: This large two-car garage has a door to the backyard.

Copyright by designer/architect.

Plan #251001

Dimensions: 61'3" W x 40'6" D
Levels: 1
Square Footage: 1,253
Bedrooms: 3
Bathrooms: 2
Foundation: Crawl space, slab
Materials List Available: Yes
Price Category: B

This charming country home has a classic full front porch for enjoying summertime breezes.

Features:

- Ceiling Height: 8 ft.

- Foyer: Guests will walk through the front porch into this foyer, which opens to the family room.

- Screened Porch: A second porch is screened and is located at the rear of the home off the dining room, so your guests can step out for a bit of fresh air after dinner.

- Family Room: Family and friends will be drawn to this large open space, with its handsome fireplace and sloped ceiling.

- Kitchen: This open and airy kitchen is a pleasure in which to work. It has ample counter space and a pantry.

- Master Bedroom: This master bedroom features a large walk-in closet. It has its own master bath with a single vanity, a tub, and a walk-in shower.

- Garage: This attached garage provides plenty of extra storage space, as well as parking for two cars.

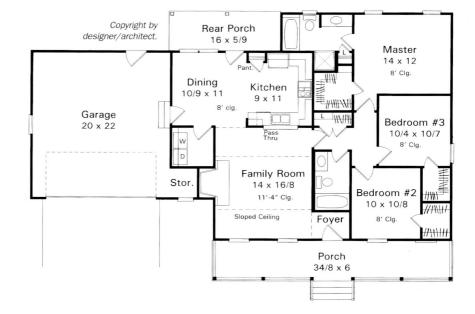

Plan #341022

Dimensions: 58'4" W x 31'10" D

Levels: 1

Square Footage: 1,281

Bedrooms: 3

Bathrooms: 2

Foundation: Crawl space, slab, or basement

Materials List Available: Yes

Price Category: B

Images provided by designer/architect.

CAD FILE AVAILABLE · CAD

Copyright by designer/architect.

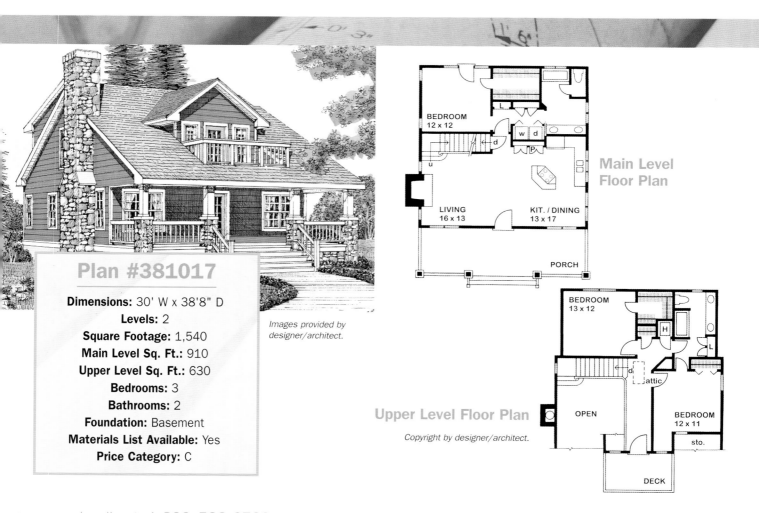

Plan #381017

Dimensions: 30' W x 38'8" D

Levels: 2

Square Footage: 1,540

Main Level Sq. Ft.: 910

Upper Level Sq. Ft.: 630

Bedrooms: 3

Bathrooms: 2

Foundation: Basement

Materials List Available: Yes

Price Category: C

Images provided by designer/architect.

Main Level Floor Plan

Upper Level Floor Plan

Copyright by designer/architect.

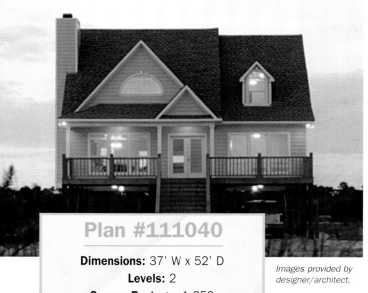

Plan #111040

Dimensions: 37' W x 52' D
Levels: 2
Square Footage: 1,650
Main Level Sq. Ft.: 1,122
Upper Level Sq. Ft.: 528
Bedrooms: 4
Bathrooms: 2
Foundation: Pier
Materials List Available: No
Price Category: C

Images provided by designer/architect.

Main Level Floor Plan

Upper Level Floor Plan

Copyright by designer/architect.

Plan #341035

Dimensions: 60' W x 28' D
Levels: 1
Square Footage: 1,680
Bedrooms: 4
Bathrooms: 2
Foundation: Crawl space, slab; basement option available for fee
Materials List Available: Yes
Price Category: C

Images provided by designer/architect.

CAD FILE AVAILABLE

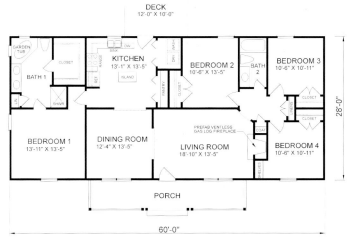

Copyright by designer/architect.

Plan #131001

Dimensions: 72'4" W x 32'4" D
Levels: 1
Square Footage: 1,615
Bedrooms: 3
Bathrooms: 2
Foundation: Crawl space, slab, basement, or walkout
Materials List Available: Yes
Price Category: D

Cathedral ceilings and illuminating skylights add drama and beauty to this practical ranch house.

Features:

• Ceiling Height: 8 ft.

• Front Porch: Watch the rain in comfort from the covered front porch.

• Foyer: The stone-tiled foyer flows into the living areas.

• Living Room: Oriented towards the front of the house, the living room opens to the dining room and shares a lovely three-sided fireplace with the family room.

• Family Room: Conveniently located to share the fireplace with the living room, this room is bright and cheery thanks to its skylights as well as the sliding glass doors that open onto the rear patio.

• Kitchen: An island makes this sunny room both efficient and attractive.

• Breakfast Nook: Located just off the kitchen, this area can serve double-duty as a spot for kitchen visitors to sit.

• Dining Room: The open design between the dining and living rooms adds to the spacious feeling that the cathedral ceiling creates in this area.

• Laundry Room: This area opens from the kitchen for convenience.

• Master Suite: A walk-in closet makes this room practical, but the master bathroom with a skylight, dual-sink vanity, soaking tub, and separate shower makes it luxurious.

• Bedrooms: The two additional bedrooms share a bathroom.

Plan #151749

Dimensions: 76' W x 50' D
Levels: 1
Square Footage: 1,616
Bedrooms: 3
Bathrooms: 2
Foundation: Crawl space
CompleteCost List Available: Yes
Price Category: C

Images provided by designer/architect.

Entertain your friends in this ranch-style log home plan with covered porches for enjoying the natural surroundings.

Features:

- **Foyer:** This entry space leads to the formal dining room, which has a pass-through window to the step-saver kitchen-perfect for entertaining.

- **Great Room:** This room features a fireplace, which is centered between French doors leading to the rear grilling porch. Guests can reside in the two bedrooms, which are located nearby.

- **Master Suite:** This suite is placed on the other side of the home and is complete with a walk-in closet, additional closet, and private bath.

- **Garage:** Through the laundry room just off the kitchen, you can reach this side-entry two-car garage.

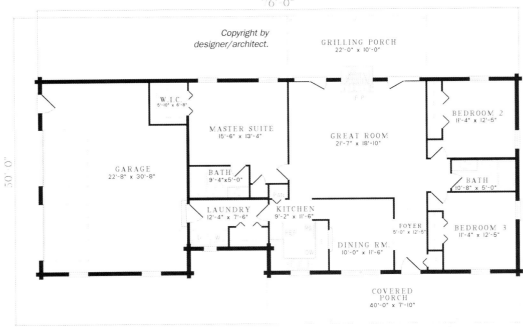

Copyright by designer/architect.

GRILLING PORCH
22'-0" x 10'-0"

W.I.C.
5'-10" x 6'-8"

MASTER SUITE
15'-6" x 13'-4"

GREAT ROOM
21'-7" x 18'-10"

BEDROOM 2
11'-4" x 12'-5"

GARAGE
22'-8" x 30'-8"

BATH
9'-4" x 5'-0"

BATH
10'-8" x 5'-0"

LAUNDRY
12'-4" x 7'-6"

KITCHEN
9'-2" x 11'-6"

FOYER
5'-0" x 12'-5"

BEDROOM 3
11'-4" x 12'-5"

DINING RM.
10'-0" x 11'-6"

COVERED PORCH
40'-0" x 7'-10"

76' 0"

50' 0"

Plan #281027

Dimensions: 52' W x 52' D
Levels: 1
Square Footage: 1,626
Bedrooms: 3
Bathrooms: 2
Foundation: Basement
Material List Available: Yes
Price Category: C

Images provided by designer/architect.

Beautiful on the outside, lovely and functional on the inside, best describes this home.

Features:

- Great Room: This large gathering area boasts a vaulted ceiling and cozy fireplace. Decorative columns frame the entry to the magnificent space.

- Kitchen: This central kitchen is close to the formal dining room and just a few convenient steps away from the laundry and garage. The raised bar adds additional seating and is open to the breakfast room.

- Master Suite: This luxurious suite is off by itself, well separated from the other two bedrooms, with its own well-appointed master bath. It also has access to the private rear patio.

- Bedrooms: The two additional bedrooms are tucked away on the far end of the house and share the hall bathroom.

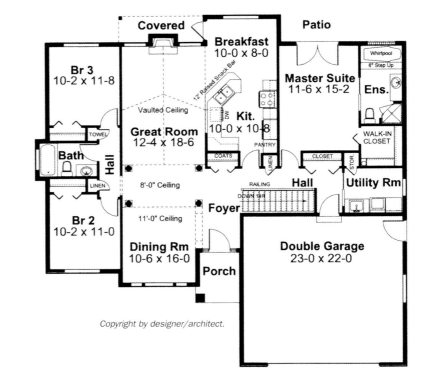

Copyright by designer/architect.

Rear Elevation

Left Side Elevation

Right Side Elevation

Plan #121008

Dimensions: 62' W x 56' D
Levels: 1
Square Footage: 1,651
Bedrooms: 2
Bathrooms: 2
Foundation: Basement
Materials List Available: Yes
Price Category: C

This elegant home is packed with amenities that belie its compact size.

Features:

- Ceiling Height: 8 ft.

- Dining Room: The foyer opens into a view of the dining room, with its distinctive boxed ceiling.

- Great Room: The whole family will want to gather around the fireplace and enjoy the views and sunlight streaming through the transom-topped window.

- Breakfast Area: Next to the great room and sharing the transom-topped windows, this cozy area invites you to linger over morning coffee.

- Covered Porch: When the weather is nice, take your coffee through the door in the breakfast area and enjoy this large covered porch.

- Master Suite: French doors lead to this comfortable suite featuring a walk-in. Enjoy long, luxurious soaks in the corner whirlpool accented with boxed windows.

Images provided by designer/architect.

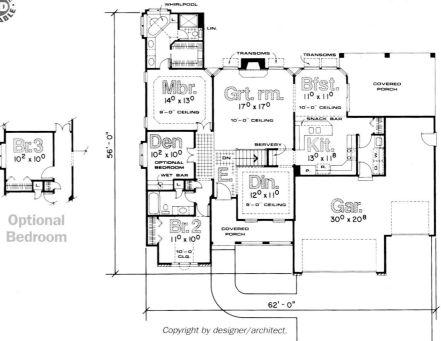

Optional Bedroom

Copyright by designer/architect.

SMARTtip
Finishing Your Fireplace with Tile

An excellent finishing material for a fireplace is tile. Luckily, there are reproductions of art tiles today. Most showrooms carry examples of Arts and Crafts, Art Nouveau, California, Delft, and other European tiles. Granite, limestone, and marble tiles are affordable alternatives to custom stone slabs.

Plan #181128

Dimensions: 36' W x 36' D
Levels: 2
Square Footage: 1,634
Main Level Sq. Ft.: 1,087
Second Level Sq. Ft.: 547
Bedrooms: 3
Bathrooms: 2
Foundation: Basement
Materials List Available: Yes
Price Category: C

This stone-accented rustic vacation home offers the perfect antidote to busy daily life.

Features:

- Ceiling Height: 8 ft. unless otherwise noted.
- Family Room: Family and friends will be unable to resist relaxing in this airy two-story family room, with its own handsome fireplace. French doors lead to the front deck.
- Kitchen: This eat-in kitchen features double sinks, ample counter space, and a pantry. It offers plenty of space for the family to gather for informal vacation meals.

- Master Suite: This first-floor master retreat occupies almost the entire length of the home. It includes a walk-in closet and a lavish bath.
- Secondary Bedrooms: On the second floor, two family bedrooms share a full bath.
- Mezzanine: This lovely balcony overlooks the family room.
- Basement: This full unfinished basement offers plenty of space for expansion.

Main Level Floor Plan

36'-0"
10,8 m

14'-0" X 12'-0"
4,20 X 3,60

20'-0" X 14'-0"
6,00 X 4,20

13'-0" X 17'-0"
3,90 X 5,10

36'-0"
10,8 m

Upper Level Floor Plan

10'-0" X 11'-8"
3,00 X 3,50

12'-0" X 11'-8"
3,60 X 3,50

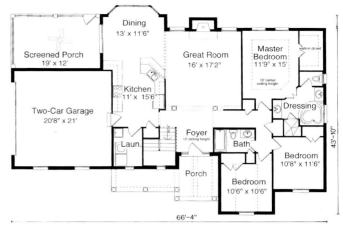

Plan #161007

Dimensions: 66'4" W x 43'10" D
Levels: 1
Square Footage: 1,611
Bedrooms: 3
Bathrooms: 2
Foundation: Basement
Materials List Available: Yes
Price Category: C

Images provided by designer/architect.

CAD FILE AVAILABLE

Copyright by designer/architect.

Rear Elevation

Plan #131038

Dimensions: 45' W x 43'2" D
Levels: 2
Square Footage: 1,629
Main Level Sq. Ft.: 1,098
Upper Level Sq. Ft.: 531
Bedrooms: 3
Bathrooms: 2
Foundation: Crawl space, slab, or basement
Materials List Available: Yes
Price Category: D

Images provided by designer/architect.

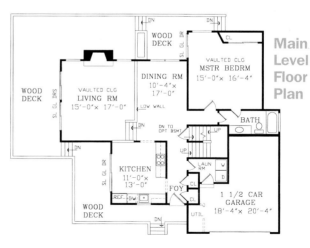

Main Level Floor Plan

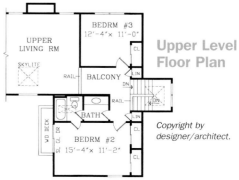

Upper Level Floor Plan

Copyright by designer/architect.

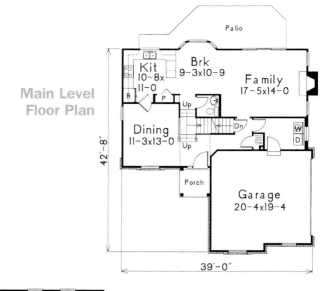

Main Level Floor Plan

Patio

Kit 10-8x 11-0

Brk 9-3x10-9

Family 17-5x14-0

Dining 11-3x13-0

Up

Dn

Up

W D

Porch

Garage 20-4x19-4

42'-8"

39'-0"

Images provided by designer/architect.

Plan #321058

Dimensions: 39' W x 42'8" D
Levels: 2
Square Footage: 1,700
Main Level Sq. Ft.: 896
Upper Level Sq. Ft.: 804
Bedrooms: 4
Bathrooms: 2½
Foundation: Basement
Materials List Available: Yes
Price Category: C

Br 3 11-3x10-10

Br 2 9-0x 10-10

MBr 14-2x12-4

Br 4 9-0x 9-9

open to below

Dn

L

Upper Level Floor Plan

Plan #281006

Dimensions: 34' W x 56' D
Levels: 2
Square Footage: 1,702
Main Level Sq. Ft.: 1,238
Upper Level Sq. Ft.: 464
Bedrooms: 3
Bathrooms: 2
Foundation: Walkout basement
Materials List Available: Yes
Price Category: C

Images provided by designer/architect.

BR 3 11-4 x 11-0

BR 2 14-0 x 11-6

lin

BATH

up

up

R F

KITCHEN 11-4 x 9-0

FOYER

DINING 11-4 x 9-0

dn

up

loft over

railing

LIVINGROOM 25-0 x 15-4

SUNDECK

Main Level Floor Plan

DECK

MASTER SUITE 14-0 x 11-6

attic

attic

Dressing

Bath

Walk-in Closet

dn

LOFT

railing

Livingroom below

Upper Level Floor Plan

Plan #131002

Dimensions: 70'1" W x 60'7" D
Levels: 1
Square Footage: 1,709
Bedrooms: 3
Bathrooms: 2½
Foundation: Crawl space, slab, or basement
Materials List Available: Yes
Price Category: D

Images provided by designer/architect.

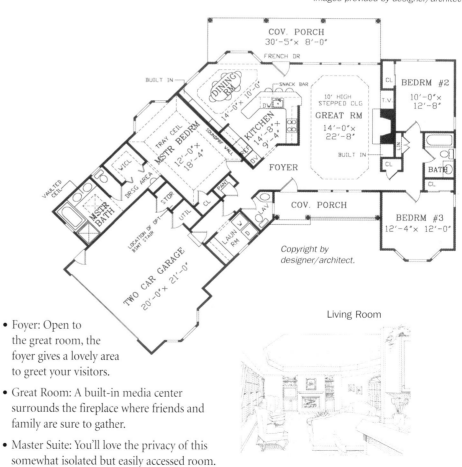

Copyright by designer/architect.

Living Room

Rear View

You'll love the way this angled ranch brings out the best in a corner lot or on a slope.

Features:

• Ceiling Height: 8 ft.

• Front Porch: Hang baskets of plants from the roof of this porch, which is just the right size for a couple of rockers and a side table.

• Dining Room: Well-placed windows flood this room with sunlight during the day and a built-in cabinet gives ample storage space for all your china, linens, and collectables.

• Foyer: Open to the great room, the foyer gives a lovely area to greet your visitors.

• Great Room: A built-in media center surrounds the fireplace where friends and family are sure to gather.

• Master Suite: You'll love the privacy of this somewhat isolated but easily accessed room. Decorate to show off the large bay window and tray ceiling, and enjoy the luxury of a compartmented bathroom.

Plan #401027

Dimensions: 44'8" W x 41'4" D
Levels: 2
Square Footage: 1,634
Main Level Sq. Ft.: 1,099
Upper Level Sq. Ft.: 535
Bedrooms: 3
Bathrooms: 2
Foundation: Basement
Materials List Available: Yes
Price Category: C

Images provided by designer/architect.

Features:

- Vaulted Ceilings: Inside, the open plan includes a vaulted great room with fireplace, a vaulted dining room, and a vaulted kitchen.

- Kitchen: This area has a pass-through to the dining room and large pantry for the ultimate in convenience and functionality.

- Master Suite: Located on the first floor for privacy this retreat contains a walk-in closet with dressing room, a sitting area, and full skylighted bath.

- Bedrooms: Two family bedrooms are on the second floor.

This design offers several different options to make the floor plan exactly as you like it. The exterior is graced by a wrapping veranda, round columns, stone facing with cedar-shingled accents, and a trio of dormers.

CAD FILE AVAILABLE

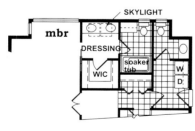

Optional Lower Level Floor Plan

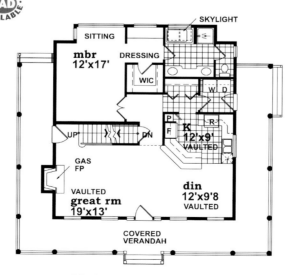

Main Level Floor Plan

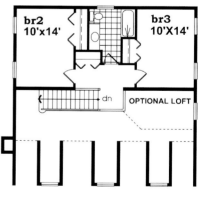

Upper Level Floor Plan

Copyright by designer/architect.

Plan #341057

Dimensions: 35' W x 44'4" D
Levels: 2
Square Footage: 1,642
Main Level Sq. Ft.: 762
Upper Level Sq. Ft.: 880
Bedrooms: 3
Bathrooms: 2½
Foundation: Crawl space
Materials List Available: Yes
Price Category: C

Images provided by designer/architect.

This two-story, three-bedroom home offers plenty for those who seek simple abundance in a comfortable and attractive home.

Features:

- **Family Room:** Just off the covered porch through the entry is this spacious gathering area with gas log fireplace and built-in bookcase.

- **Kitchen:** This L-shaped island kitchen is packed with cabinet and counter space. Step out the back door, and enjoy the fresh air on the screened porch.

- **Master Bedroom:** This sleeping area has large windows facing the front. The master bath features dual vanities.

- **Bedrooms:** The two secondary bedrooms, also located upstairs, share the common bathroom.

Main Level Floor Plan

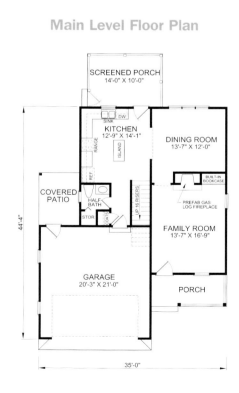

Upper Level Floor Plan

Copyright by designer/architect.

Plan #111041

Dimensions: 34' W x 32' D
Levels: 2
Square Footage: 1,743
Main Level Sq. Ft.: 912
Upper Level Sq. Ft.: 831
Bedrooms: 3
Bathrooms: 3
Foundation: Pier
Materials List Available: No
Price Category: C

You'll love the way this vacation home can accommodate a crowd or make a small family feel cozy and comfortable.

Features:

- **Living Area:** This easy-care living area is perfect for those times when you want to get away from it all—including extra housework.
- **Kitchen:** This kitchen is large enough for friends and family to chat with the cook or help with the dishes after a meal. You'll use the breakfast bar all day long for setting out drinks and snacks.

- **Master Suite:** Relax on the balcony off this master suit, and luxuriate in the bath with double vanities, a whirlpool tub, and a walk-in closet.
- **Study:** Adjacent to the master suite, this room lets you catch up on reading in a quiet spot.
- **Porch:** Let guests spill onto this convenient porch when you're hosting a party, or use it as outdoor space where the children can play.

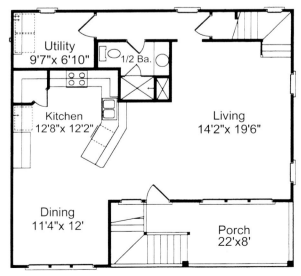

Main Level Floor Plan

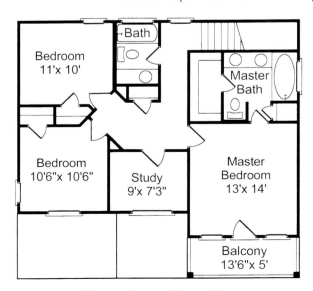

Upper Level Floor Plan

Plan #181245

Dimensions: 44' W x 44' D
Levels: 1
Square Footage: 1,707
Bedrooms: 3
Bathrooms: 1
Foundation: Basement
Materials List Available: Yes
Price Category: C

Images provided by designer/architect.

CAD FILE AVAILABLE

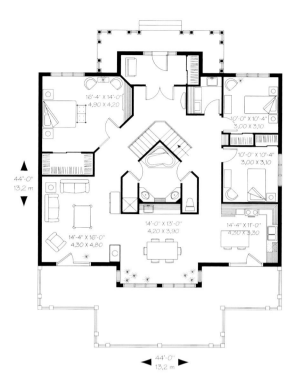

44'-0"
13,2 m

44'-0"
13,2 m

Copyright by designer/architect.

Plan #181017

Dimensions: 62' W x 43' D
Levels: 1
Square Footage: 1,736
Bedrooms: 3
Bathrooms: 2
Foundation: Full basement
Materials List Available: Yes
Price Category: C

Images provided by designer/architect.

CAD FILE AVAILABLE

Copyright by designer/architect.

43'-0"
12,9 m

62'-0"
18,9 m

SMARTtip
Simplify Your Deck Design

If your railing is an elaborate Chinese-Chippendale style, you may want to keep the design of benches, planters, and decking basic to prevent visual competition between the elements.

Plan #181116

Dimensions: 36' W x 34' D
Levels: 2
Square Footage: 1,872
Main Level Sq. Ft.: 1,078
Upper Level Sq. Ft.: 794
Bedrooms: 3
Bathrooms: 2
Foundation: Walkout or basement
Materials List Available: Yes
Price Category: D

Main Level Floor Plan

Copyright by designer/architect.

Images provided by designer/architect.

CAD FILE AVAILABLE

Basement Level Floor Plan

Upper Level Floor Plan

Plan #151007

Dimensions: 54'2" W x 56'2" D
Levels: 1
Square Footage: 1,787
Bedrooms: 3
Bathrooms: 2
Foundation: Crawl space, slab, basement, or walkout
CompleteCost List Available: Yes
Price Category: C

Images provided by designer/architect.

CAD FILE AVAILABLE

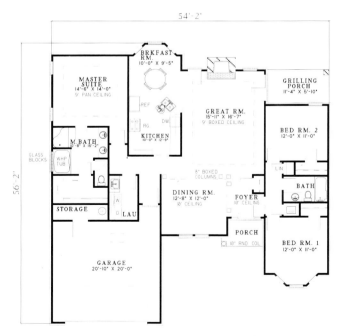

Copyright by designer/architect.

Plan #101015

Dimensions: 28' W x 46' D
Levels: 2
Square Footage: 1,647
Main Level Sq. Ft.: 1,288
Upper Level Sq. Ft.: 359
Bedrooms: 2
Bathrooms: 1
Foundation: Slab
Materials List Available: No
Price Category: C

This comfortable vacation retreat has handsome board-and-batten siding with stone accents..

CAD FILE AVAILABLE

Features:

- Ceiling Height: 20 ft. unless otherwise noted.

- Front Porch: This delightful front porch is perfect for spending relaxing vacation time in an old-fashioned rocker or porch swing.

- Great Room: From the porch you'll enter this enormous great room, where the whole family will enjoy spending time together under its 20-ft. vaulted ceiling.

- Kitchen: Within the great room is this open kitchen. An island provides plenty of food-preparation space, and there's a breakfast bar for casual vacation meals. The large pantry area provides space for a stacked washer and dryer.

- Bath: Also located downstairs is a compartmented bath with a 2-ft.-8-in. door that allows wheelchair access.

- Loft: Upstairs is an enormous loft with an 11-ft. ceiling. Use it to augment the two downstairs bedrooms or for recreation space.

...ges provided by designer/architect.

Main Level Floor Plan

BEDROOM 1
11'-10" x 10'-0"

BEDROOM 2
11'-4" x 10'-0"

COATS

LINEN

PANTRY

WD

46'-0"
• PORCH

GREAT ROOM
27'-4" x 29'-5"
20' HIGH CEILING

VAULT

VAULT

UP

DECK/PATIO
11'-6" x 18'-8"

DECK
7'-6" x 36'-0"

PORCH
24'-4" x 7'-6"

28'-0"
• DECKS/PATIO

Upper Level Floor Plan

VAULT

VAULT

LOFT
23'-1" x 15'-6"

40" KNEE WALL

DN

OPEN BELOW
20' HIGH CEILING

VAULT

VAULT

Copyright by designer/architect.

Plan #371072

Dimensions: 75'10" W x 38'8" D
Levels: 1
Square Footage: 1,772
Bedrooms: 3
Bathrooms: 2
Foundation: Crawl space, slab
Materials List Available: No
Price Category: C

This home, with its enclosed covered porch, defines country charm.

Features:

- Living Room: This large room has a 10-foot-high ceiling and large windows looking out onto a covered back porch. The cozy fireplace and built-in media center will be great for relaxing.

- Kitchen: This large country kitchen with breakfast nook features a raised bar.

- Dining Room: This beautiful room has large windows located in a boxed-out extension.

- Master Suite: This secluded suite has a large walk-in closet and a luxurious master bath.

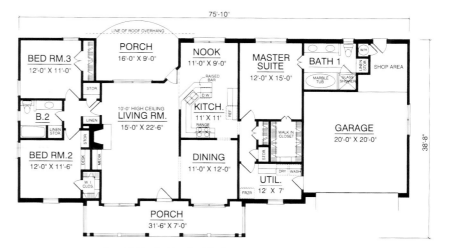

Copyright by designer/architect.

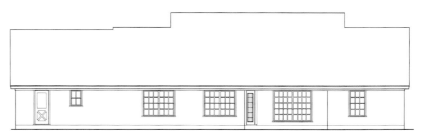

Rear Elevation

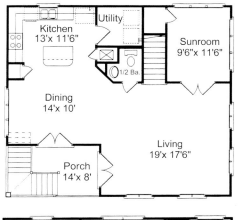

**Main
Level
Floor
Plan**

Kitchen
13'x 11'6"

Utility

Sunroom
9'6"x 11'6"

1/2 Ba.

Dining
14'x 10'

Living
19'x 17'6"

Porch
14'x 8'

Plan #111042

Dimensions: 34' W x 30' D

Levels: 2

Square Footage: 1,779

Main Level Sq. Ft.: 907

Upper Level Sq. Ft.: 872

Bedrooms: 3

Bathrooms: 2½

Foundation: Pier

Materials List Available: No

Price Category: C

*Images provided by
designer/architect.*

*Copyright by
designer/architect.*

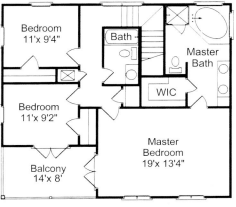

**Upper
Level
Floor
Plan**

Bedroom
11'x 9'4"

Bath

Master
Bath

WIC

Bedroom
11'x 9'2"

Master
Bedroom
19'x 13'4"

Balcony
14'x 8'

Plan #341029

Dimensions: 49' W x 57' D

Levels: 1

Square Footage: 1,737

Bedrooms: 3

Bathrooms: 2

Foundation: Crawl space, slab,
or basement

Materials List Available: Yes

Price Category: C

*Images provided by
designer/architect.*

CAD FILE
AVAILABLE

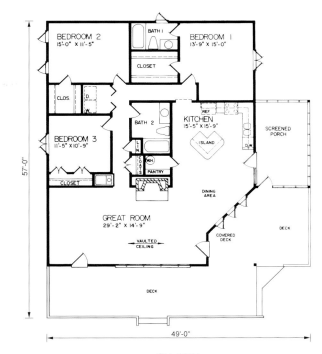

BEDROOM 2
15'-0" X 11'-5"

BATH 1

BEDROOM 1
13'-9" X 15'-0"

CLOSET

CLOS.

BEDROOM 3
11'-5" X 10'-9"

BATH 2

KITCHEN
15'-5" X 15'-9"

REF

SCREENED
PORCH

ISLAND

DW

DINING
AREA

CLOSET

WH

PANTRY

DECK

GREAT ROOM
29'-2" X 14'-9"

VAULTED
CEILING

COVERED
DECK

DECK

57'-0"

49'-0"

*Copyright by
designer/architect.*

Media Rooms

A successor to the low-tech TV rooms of the 1950s and '60s, today's media room can offer a multimedia experience. It can be outfitted with everything from DVD and VHS players to sophisticated home-theater setups complete with speakers inconspicuously mounted into walls and ceilings.

However, creating a media room means more than hooking up electronics. You'll need proper housing for all of the components, such as a big-screen TV, as well as comfortable, attractive furnishings. You can go the custom route, or check out what's on the market. Cabinetry that's designed specifically for the equipment is

readily available. So is movie-house-style row seating complete with cup holders and reclining chaises. You can also find floor-to-ceiling soundproofing systems that help hold and enhance the rich sound from digital equipment. It's your choice. It all depends on how much you want to spend.

A freestanding media cabinet, opposite, can be decorative and practical.

Semicustom kitchen cabinetry, above, can be outfitted and installed to suit your media-room needs.

Media-Wise Moves

No matter the size of your budget or the physical dimensions of your space, there are a full range of options that will make a media room look as good as it sounds.

Furniture

The focus here should be on functionality—enhancing your comfort and the entertainment experience. You can achieve both by furnishing the room with chairs, sectionals, and sofas that are upholstered in soft fabrics. Upholstery absorbs sound and can provide the comfort level you need when watching a two-hour movie. Add plush pillows to create an even cozier, more sound-friendly environment.

Leather furniture is always a fallback option. Although it does absorb sound better than hard materials, it can't compete with soft fabrics such as cotton, wool, and blended fabrics in terms of comfort or sound retention.

One smart option is a large upholstered storage ottoman, which can serve many purposes. It adds extra seating, serves as a coffee table, and provides a place for remote controls, DVDs, the television listings, and other media-room paraphernalia.

Cabinetry and Storage. Factor a lot of storage into your media-room plans. First, you need space for various components, such as a DVD player, VCR, receiver, CD player, and so forth. Next there's what will indeed be a growing collection of DVDs, videotapes, CDs, and remote controls. If you plan to order custom cabinetry for the space, buy your sound system and home-theater components first. Then have the cabinetmaker design the unit based on their specifications.

In terms of design, the cabinetry should accommodate components at eye level for easy operation. The topmost and lowest shelves can be reserved for lesser-used items. If you'll build the cabinet yourself, remember that there should be enough space around the components to "breathe;" built-in electronics need ventilation. Plus, you have to leave openings in the back to pull through any wires that have to be plugged into wall outlets.

In addition, be sure to include plenty of rollout drawers in the design to hold your library of favorite disks and tapes. Leave room for future purchases, too. Another option is to store tapes in a closet, a handsome trunk, or even a basket. Stockpiling tapes, CDs, and other clutter around the television screen can detract from the viewing experience.

When not in use, large TV monitors can look like big ugly boxes. Hide smaller televisions—27- or 32-inch—behind the handsome doors of a semicustom TV cabinet. Very large screens should probably be housed behind pocket, tambour, or concealed doors. Large cabinet doors that swing out into the room can obstruct traffic or even your view of the screen.

Walls, Floors, Ceilings, and Doors

Light-colored walls will reflect sunlight and artificial light and increase glare. Both can wash out the TV screen. For the same reason, mirrors and other shiny materials or glossy finishes in a media room don't make sense. Choose deep neutrals for walls, or even try a darker tone. Walls lined with corkboard, upholstered in fabric, or outfitted with high-tech sound-absorbing glass-

fiber panels covered in fashionable fabrics are all good options.

Acoustical ceiling tiles are a simple and effective solution to prevent sound from leaking into other areas. They come in a range of styles, one of which is bound to fit in with your decor.

One homeowner created a comfortable corner, above, for enjoying his collection of old recordings.

Stock cabinets, opposite, can be outfitted with optional features, such as drawers that neatly store CDs, DVDs, and VHS cassettes.

Carpeting is not only easy on the feet but also on the ear, preventing harsh echoes from bouncing around the room. Hard floor surfaces such as tile, stone, and marble can reflect and distort the sound coming from even the most expensive home-theater receiver and speakers. Cover the floor in a low-pile, low-maintenance Berber, sisal, or industrial carpet to keep sound true and pure.

Lighting

Indirect illumination that provides ambient light without on-screen glare is best for a media room. Lamps in a media room should have black or dark opaque lampshades that direct light up and down. Translucent shades radiate light in all directions. Rather than one or two bright-light sources, install several low-level lights. Dimmers will allow you to adjust lights for comfort. As a general rule, no light should be brighter than the TV screen. To avoid eyestrain and distraction, position light sources behind you and not between you and the screen.

If you want to create movie-house ambiance, install wall sconces like ones reminiscent of grand old theaters. Because you'll probably want to watch movies in a darkened room, make sure your plan includes aisle lighting, which you can plug into outlets. Wire them to one remote so you can dim them simultaneously.

Don't forget that you'll have to control natural light unless you plan to limit your home theater use to evenings. There are creative ways to reduce natural light as well. Shutters and blinds are easily adjustable window treatments. You can also check out the possibility of certain curtains that are made especially for home theaters.

Plugging into Your TV Options

Technology has clearly taken television to the next level. Even if you have an older standard model, you can improve the picture quality of broadcast viewing simply by adding cable, and even more by adding digital cable or digital satellite. But nothing beats DVD for watching movies.

HDTV, or high-definition television, has twice the picture clarity of standard TV, whether you're watching network or cable TV broadcasts or viewing a DVD. Ironically, most HDTVs don't contain high-definition tuners. So, although the picture may be better, you're not getting true HDTV unless you buy the tuning box, which is sold separately and costs around $700. Still, it's an improvement over the old versions.

Plasma and LCD TV Screens.

Thin TV is also a trend that is here to stay. Slimmed down flat-screen plasma TVs and LCD screens provide brilliant colors, better contrast and resolution, and a greater viewing angle. Because the screen is flat, there is no problem with glare. Having the lights on or off does not affect the picture. LCDs are smaller; screens range from 15 to 30 inches diagonally. Plasma TVs start at 32

Plump upholstered seating, opposite, arranged at the proper distance from the screen, lets you view TV and movies comfortably.

Ready-to-assemble furniture, above, is an affordable alternative to custom or semicustom cabinets.

inches and go up to big-screen size from there. Most of them accept HDTV signals, but they are usually not powerful enough to display all of the high resolution.

Rear Projection. The screen size of a rear-projection TV is large—40 to 82 inches—and can be viewed in natural light without sacrificing picture quality. In general, the picture is often inferior, unless it is an HDTV format. Another drawback: rear projection TVs must be watched at eye-level and straight-on for optimal viewing.

Front Projection. This system has a separate screen, which can either drop down from the ceiling or remain fixed on the wall, and a projector that is mounted at ceiling height across the room from the screen. It's akin to a movie-theater system. Front projection is expensive and requires a professional to install it. Although even minor light can wash out the picture, the image quality is unbeatable when the room is dark.

More Tips
If you're thinking of creating a home theater in your new house, here are a few pointers.
• Most home-theater designers recommend televisions screens that are at least 27 inches wide.
• Seating distance can add or subtract from the viewing quality. For optimal viewing,

there should be a distance between you and the TV that is 2 to 2½ times the width of the screen. That means placing sofa and chairs 54 to 68 inches from a 27-inch screen, for example. If your TV is a wide-screen high-definition model, place it a distance that is 1½ times the screen's diagonal width from your seating area.
• Five speakers will create a full-home theater sound. Place one speaker on each side of the TV screen, level with your ears when you are seated, and about 3 feet from the sidewalls. Place two speakers behind the sofa about 6 to 8 feet off the floor and at least as wide apart as the front speakers. Put the fifth speaker on top of the TV.
• Replace a collection of remote controls with a single universal model that can control everything from the DVD player to the lights (with a special receiver).

Plan #371053

Dimensions: 51'2" W x 66'7" D

Levels: 1

Square Footage: 1,654

Bedrooms: 3

Bathrooms: 2

Foundation: Slab

Materials List Available: No

Price Category: C

A cozy country porch and large inviting windows are the perfect way to say, "I'm home." This country charmer has everything you need.

Features:

- Kitchen: This large kitchen boasts a cathedral ceiling and a raised bar.

- Dining Room: This room has a cathedral ceiling and is open to the living room and kitchen.

- Living Room: The fireplace and cathedral ceiling give this room an inviting feeling.

- Master Suite: This private retreat features two walk-in closets. The old-fashioned bath with an antique tub is perfect for relaxing.

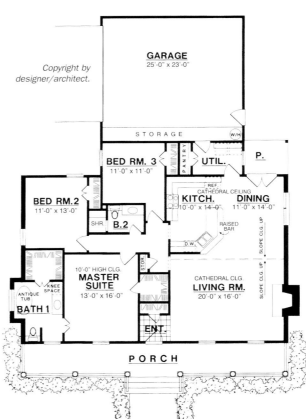

Plan #151801

Dimensions: 45'8" W x 41'8" D
Levels: 1.5
Square Footage: 1,658
Main Level Sq. Ft.: 1,002
Upper Level Sq. Ft.: 656
Bedrooms: 3
Bathrooms: 2
Foundation: Crawl space;
basement or walkout for fee
CompleteCost List Available: Yes
Price Category: C

Images provided by designer/architect.

This timeless log home is not only a complete design for a family but a work of art.

Features:

- **Open Plan:** The open gable with exposed log beams highlights an arched transom window, which allows plenty of natural light to pour into this two-story home plan.

- **Kitchen:** This island kitchen has access to the rear grilling porch and has a full bathroom nearby.

- **Master Suite:** Located on the first level for privacy, this suite features vaulted ceilings of log beams and includes a private master bath.

- **Upper Level:** As you travel up the beautifully hand-crafted stairs, you'll find the large loft with nearby bathroom and convenient laundry area. The two additional bedrooms here each have a quaint dormer window and private deck for late-night stargazing.

Upper Level Floor Plan

Copyright by designer/architect.

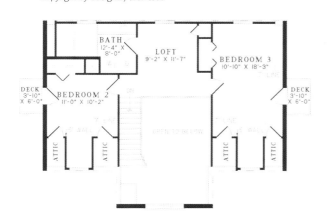

Main Level Floor Plan

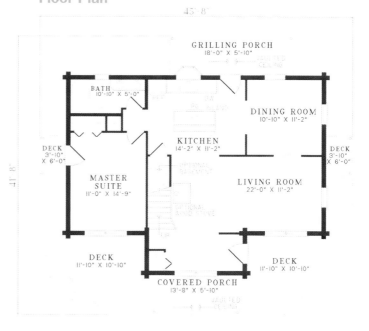

Plan #401035

Dimensions: 58' W x 32' D
Levels: 1½
Square Footage: 1,659
Main Level Sq.Ft.: 1,375
Upper Level Sq.Ft.: 284
Bedrooms: 3
Bathrooms: 2
Foundation: Basement
Materials List Available: Yes
Price Category: C

Images provided by designer/architect.

An expansive window wall across the great room of this home adds a spectacular view and accentuates the high ceiling.

CAD FILE AVAILABLE

Features:

- Kitchen: This open-plan workspace shares an eating bar with the dining room and features a convenient "U" shape. Sliding glass doors in the dining room lead to the deck.

- Bedrooms: Two family bedrooms sit to the back of the plan and share the use of a full bathroom.

- Master Suite: This retreat features a walk-in closet and private bathroom.

- Loft Area: Located on the upper level this loft adds living or sleeping space.

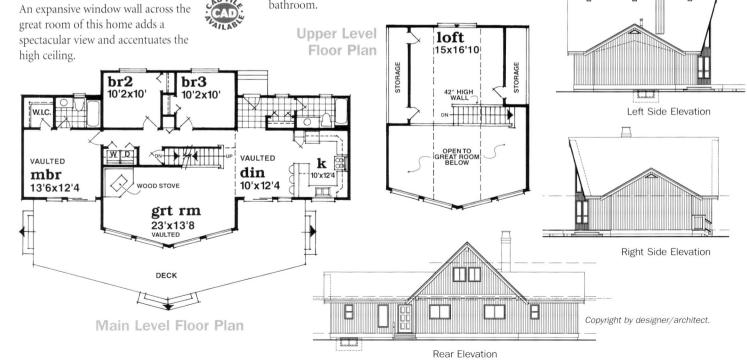

Upper Level Floor Plan

loft 15x16'10
STORAGE
STORAGE
42" HIGH WALL
DN
OPEN TO GREAT ROOM BELOW

Main Level Floor Plan

br2 10'2x10'
br3 10'2x10'
W.I.C.
VAULTED mbr 13'6x12'4
W D
DN UP
WOOD STOVE
VAULTED din 10'x12'4
k 10'x12'4
grt rm 23'x13'8 VAULTED
DECK

Left Side Elevation

Right Side Elevation

Rear Elevation

Copyright by designer/architect.

Plan #401006

Dimensions: 43' W x 35'4" D
Levels: 1½
Square Footage: 1,670
Main Level Sq.Ft.: 1,094
Upper Level Sq.Ft.: 576
Bedrooms: 3
Bathrooms: 2
Foundation: Crawl space
Materials List Available: Yes
Price Category: C

This vacation cottage's covered veranda (with a covered patio above) leads to French doors, which open to the living/dining area.

CAD FILE AVAILABLE

Features:

- Living/Dining Area: A masonry fireplace with a wood storage bin warms these rooms.

- Kitchen: This modified U-shaped kitchen serves the dining room; a laundry is just across the hall with access to a side veranda.

- Master Bedroom: Located on the first floor, this main bedroom has the use of a full bath. Sliding glass doors here and in the living room lead to still another veranda.

- Family Room: Located upstairs, this room has a fireplace, double doors to a deck, and a balcony overlooking the living and dining rooms. A large storage area on this level adds convenience.

- Bedrooms: The second floor also has two family bedrooms and a full bath.

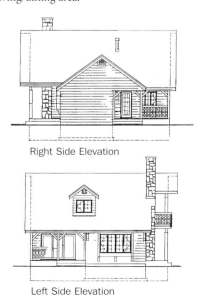

Right Side Elevation

Left Side Elevation

Main Level Floor Plan

Upper Level Floor Plan

Copyright by designer/architect.

Rear Elevation

Plan #151528

Dimensions: 41'4" W x 84'2" D
Levels: 1
Square Footage: 1,747
Bedrooms: 2
Bathrooms: 2
Foundation: Crawl space or slab
CompleteCost List Available: Yes
Price Category: C

This Craftsman-inspired design combines a rustic exterior with an elegant interior. The 10-ft.-high ceilings and abundance of windows enhance the family areas with plenty of natural lighting.

Features:

- Great Room: Featuring a fireplace and built-in computer center, this central gathering area is open to the breakfast room and has access to the rear covered porch.

- Kitchen: This combination kitchen and break fast room enjoys a bar counter for additional seating. Note the large laundry room with pantry, which is located between the kitchen and the garage.

- Master Suite: You'll spend many luxurious hours in this beautiful suite, with its 10-ft.-high boxed ceiling, his and her walk-in closets, and large bath with glass shower, whirlpool tub, and double vanity.

- Bedrooms: On the same side of the home as the master suite are these two other bedrooms, which have large closets and an adjoining bath room between them.

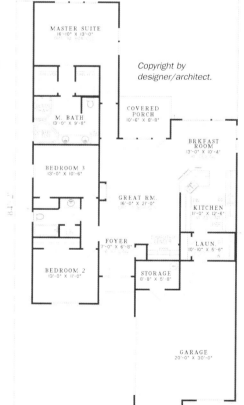

Front View

Plan #151196

Dimensions: 89' W x 49'4" D
Levels: 1
Square Footage: 1,800
Bedrooms: 3
Bathrooms: 2
Foundation: Crawl space, slab
CompleteCost List Available: Yes
Price Category: D

CAD FILE AVAILABLE

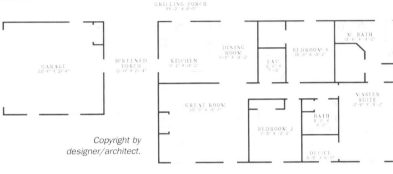

Images provided by designer/architect.

Copyright by designer/architect.

Plan #111010

Dimensions: 34' W x 38' D
Levels: 3
Square Footage: 1,804
Main Level Sq. Ft.: 731
Upper Level Sq. Ft.: 935
Third Level Sq.Ft.: 138
Bedrooms: 3
Bathrooms: 3
Foundation: Piers
Materials List Available: No
Price Category: D

Third Level Floor Plan

Look Out
9'x 15'

Images provided by designer/architect.

Main Level Floor Plan

Deck
14'x 10'

Kitchen
10'6"x 13'9"

Dining
9'x 13'8"

Living
14'x 19'

Screen Porch
19'6"x 10'

Copyright by designer/architect.

Side View

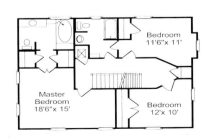

Bedroom
11'6"x 11'

Master Bedroom
18'6"x 15'

Bedroom
12'x 10'

Upper Level Floor Plan

©Alan Mascord Design Associates, Inc.

Images provided by designer/architect.

Plan #441017

Dimensions: 40' W x 53' D
Levels: 2
Square Footage: 1,707
Main Level Sq. Ft.: 1,230
Upper Level Sq. Ft.: 477
Bedrooms: 3
Bathrooms: 2½
Foundation: Crawl space; slab or basement available for fee
Materials List Available: No
Price Category: C

Features:

- **Kitchen:** The island, which adds work surface and storage, enhances this efficient kitchen. An open wall above the sink encourages conversation between here and the great room.

- **Breakfast Nook:** This angular breakfast nook is enclosed by windows and offers access to the backyard. Just steps away from the kitchen, the dining room and breakfast nook ease meal service.

- **Master Suite:** This suite provides a private getaway on the first floor. The attached master bath has a double-sink vanity and both a tub and a shower enclosure.

- **Upper Level:** From the walkway you can look down into the two-story great room as you pass the full bathroom and bonus room. The two secondary bedrooms complete this level.

The covered front entry, facade that's trimmed in brick, and tall mullioned windows give this home timeless appeal.

CAD FILE AVAILABLE

Main Level Floor Plan

NOOK
8/8 X 8/10

DINING
9/10 X 10/4

VAULTED MASTER
16/0 X 11/10

TWO STORY GREAT RM.
15/10 X 19/8

SPA

LINEN

GARAGE
19/4 X 21/8

UP

◄ 40' ►

▲ 53' ▼

Upper Level Floor Plan

BR. 3
12/6 X 12/2 +/-

BR. 2
10/8 X 12/2 +/-

LIN

OPEN TO GREAT RM. BELOW

DN

BONUS RM.
13/6 X 12/6

ATTIC STORAGE

Copyright by designer/architect.

N. Ibarra

Plan #371033

Dimensions: 73' W x 33' 4" D
Levels: 1
Square Footage: 1,724
Bedrooms: 3
Bathrooms: 2
Foundation: Slab
Materials List Available: No
Price Category: C

CAD FILE AVAILABLE

This beautiful brick-and-stone country home will be the envy of the neighborhood.

Features:

- Front Porch: This charming yet functional porch welcomes you home.

- Family Room: This large room, with its cathedral ceiling and cozy fireplace, is ideal for entertaining.

- Kitchen: This gourmet kitchen has all the necessities you will ever need, including a raised bar area.

- Master Suite: This cozy area features a stepped ceiling. The luxurious bath boasts a marble tub and two walk-in closets.

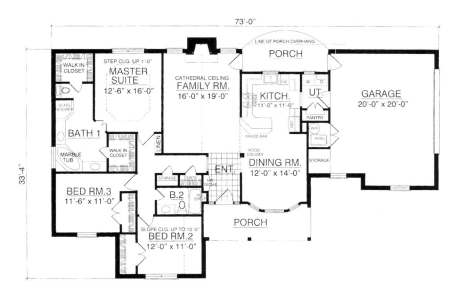

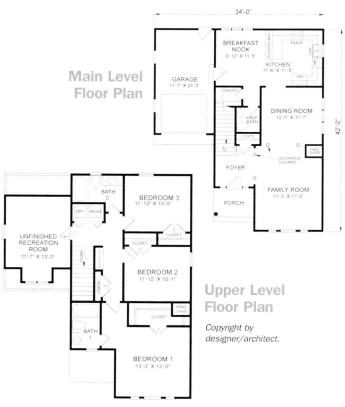

Main Level Floor Plan

Upper Level Floor Plan

Images provided by designer/architect.

Copyright by designer/architect.

Plan #341044

Dimensions: 34' W x 42' D
Levels: 2
Square Footage: 1,704
Main Level Sq. Ft.: 852
Upper Level Sq. Ft.: 852
Bedrooms: 3
Bathrooms: 2½
Foundation: Crawl space, slab; basement option available for fee
Materials List Available: Yes
Price Category: C

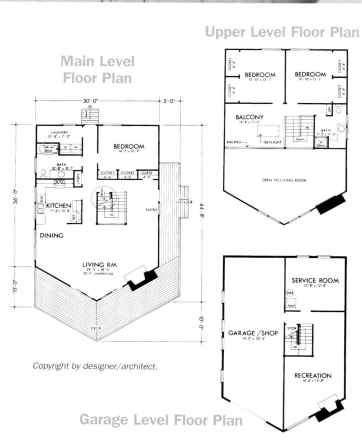

Main Level Floor Plan

Upper Level Floor Plan

Garage Level Floor Plan

Images provided by designer/architect.

Copyright by designer/architect.

Plan #271051

Dimensions: 30' W x 44'8" D
Levels: 2
Square Footage: 1,920
Main Level Sq. Ft.: 1,210
Upper Level Sq. Ft.: 710
Bedrooms: 3
Bathrooms: 2
Foundation: Crawl space or Walkout
Materials List Available: Yes
Price Category: D

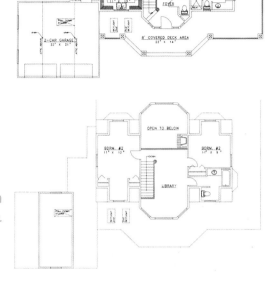

Main Level Floor Plan

Images provided by designer/architect.

Plan #451165

Dimensions: 62'2" W x 65'2" D
Levels: 2
Square Footage: 1,933
Main Level Sq. Ft.: 1,171
Upper Level Sq. Ft.: 762
Bedrooms: 3
Bathrooms: 2½
Foundation: Crawl space
Materials List Available: No
Price Category: D

Upper Level Floor Plan

Copyright by designer/architect.

Copyright by designer/architect.

Plan #371007

Dimensions: 72'10" W x 48'4½" D
Levels: 1
Square Footage: 1,944
Bedrooms: 4
Bathrooms: 2
Foundation: Slab;
crawl space option available for fee
Materials List Available: No
Price Category: D

Images provided by designer/architect.

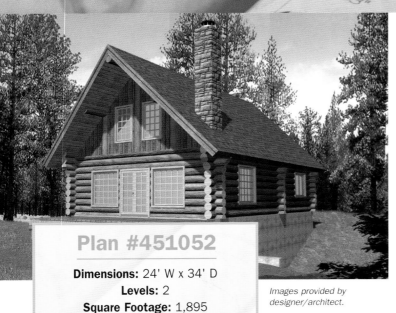

Main Level Floor Plan

BDRM. #1
11'4" X 11'0"

KITCHEN
10'8" X 11'4"

DN

GREAT ROOM
16'0" X 14'4"

DINING

DECK
24'8" X 8'0"

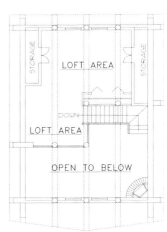

**Upper Level
Floor Plan**

STORAGE

LOFT AREA

STORAGE

DOWN

LOFT AREA

OPEN TO BELOW

*Copyright by
designer/architect.*

Plan #451052

Dimensions: 24' W x 34' D
Levels: 2
Square Footage: 1,895
Main Level Sq. Ft.: 720
Upper Level Sq. Ft.: 320
Basement Level Sq. Ft.: 855
Bedrooms: 2
Bathrooms: 1½
Foundation: Walkout basement
Material List Available: No
Price Category: D

*Images provided by
designer/architect.*

**Basement Level
Floor Plan**

BDRM. #2
12'3" X 14'5"

RECREATION
22'6" X 14'0"

Plan #271023

Dimensions: 60' W x 48'4" D
Levels: 1
Square Footage: 1,993
Bedrooms: 3
Bathrooms: 2
Foundation: Basement
Materials List Available: Yes
Price Category: D

*Images provided by
designer/architect.*

60'-0"

Master Suite
16-6x12-9
9 clg

Plant Shelf

Living Rm
14x21-6
12 vaulted clg

Dining
13-6x10

DN

Deck

Country Kitchen
28x13

Desk

Lndry
D W

48'-4"

DN

DN

Plant Shelf

Den
11x10-3

Br 2
10x11

Raised
Ceiling

Br 3
10x10-6

P

Garage
22x22

*Copyright by
designer/architect.*

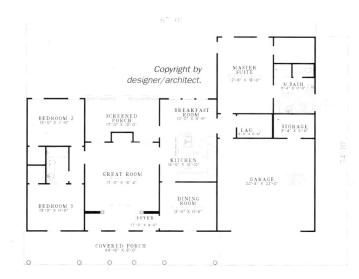

Images provided by designer/architect.

Plan #151054

Dimensions: 67' W x 54'10" D
Levels: 1
Square Footage: 1,746
Bedrooms: 3
Bathrooms: 2
Foundation: Crawl space or slab; basement option for fee
CompleteCost List Available: Yes
Price Category: C

CAD FILE AVAILABLE

SMARTtip
Mixing and Matching Windows

Windows, both fixed and operable, are made in various styles and shapes. While mixing styles should be carefully avoided, a variety of interesting window sizes and shapes may nevertheless be combined to achieve symmetry, harmony, and rhythm on the exterior of a home.

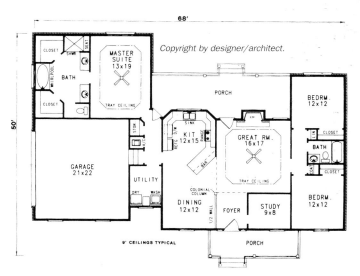

Images provided by designer/architect.

Plan #171009

Dimensions: 68' W x 50' D
Levels: 1
Square Footage: 1,771
Bedrooms: 3
Bathrooms: 2
Foundation: Crawl space, slab
Materials List Available: Yes
Price Category: C

SMARTtip
Deck Awnings

Awnings come in bright colors. As light filters through, it will cast a hue to anything under the deck. Warm colors, such as red or pink, will create a rosy glow; cool colors, such blues or greens, will enhance the shade.

Plan #371033

Dimensions: 73' W x 33' 4" D
Levels: 1
Square Footage: 1,724
Bedrooms: 3
Bathrooms: 2
Foundation: Slab
Materials List Available: No
Price Category: C

This beautiful brick-and-stone country home will be the envy of the neighborhood.

Features:

- Front Porch: This charming yet functional porch welcomes you home.

- Family Room: This large room, with its cathedral ceiling and cozy fireplace, is ideal for entertaining.

- Kitchen: This gourmet kitchen has all the necessities you will ever need, including a raised bar area.

- Master Suite: This cozy area features a stepped ceiling. The luxurious bath boasts a marble tub and two walk-in closets.

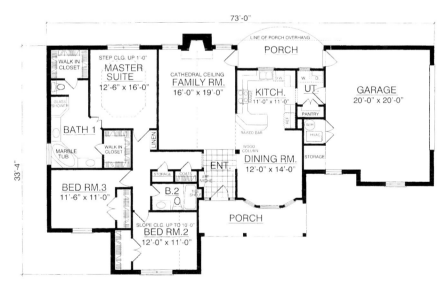

Images provided by designer/architect.

Plan #121031

Dimensions: 52' W x 51'4" D

Levels: 2

Square Footage: 1,772

Main Level Sq. Ft.: 1,314

Upper Level Sq. Ft.: 458

Bedrooms: 3

Bathrooms: 2½

Foundation: Basement

Materials List Available: Yes

Price Category: C

This home features architectural details reminiscence of earlier fine homes.

Features:

- Ceiling Height: 8 ft. unless otherwise noted.

- Foyer: This grand entry soars two-stories high. The U-shaped staircase with window leads to a second-story balcony.

- Great Room: You'll be drawn to the impressive views through the triple-arch windows at the front and rear of this room.

- Kitchen: Designed for maximum efficiency, this kitchen is a pleasure to be in. It features a center island, a full pantry, and a desk for added convenience.

- Breakfast Area: This area adjoins the kitchen. Both rooms are flooded with sunlight streaming from a shared bay window.

- Master Suite: The stylish bedroom includes a walk-in closet. Luxuriate in the whirlpool tub at the end of a long day .

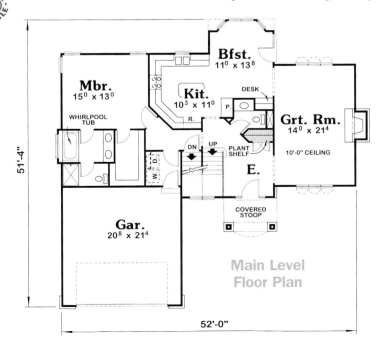

Main Level Floor Plan

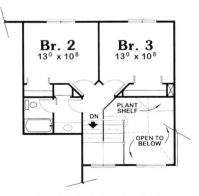

Copyright by designer/architect.

Upper Level Floor Plan

www.ultimateplans.com 125

Plan #271052

Dimensions: 57' W x 67' D
Levels: 2
Square Footage: 1,779
Main Level Sq. Ft.: 1,309
Upper Level Sq. Ft.: 470
Bedrooms: 3
Bathrooms: 2
Foundation: Crawl space, daylight basement
Materials List Available: Yes
Price Category: C

Images provided by designer/architect.

Designed for relaxation, this home offers a gigantic deck and an irresistible spa room.

Features:

• Great Room: A covered porch welcomes guests into the entry hall and this spectacular great room beyond. Outlined by windows and sliding glass doors, this great room offers panoramic views of scenic beauty. Step outside onto the deck to commune with nature one on one.

• Kitchen: This U-shaped kitchen flows into a cozy breakfast nook. A formal dining room is just steps away.

• Master Suite: This main-floor master suite features direct access to a passive-solar spa room and a sunning area beyond. A walk-in closet and a window seat round out the suite.

• Secondary Bedrooms: On the upper floor, a balcony hall overlooks the great room, while leading to these two good-sized bedrooms. A hall bath is located between them.

Basement Level Floor Plan

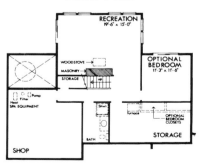

Copyright by designer/architect.

Main Level Floor Plan

Upper Level Floor Plan

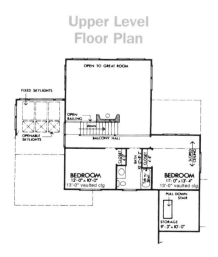

©Alan Mascord Design Associates, inc.

Plan #441017

Dimensions: 40' W x 53' D
Levels: 2
Square Footage: 1,707
Main Level Sq. Ft.: 1,230
Upper Level Sq. Ft.: 477
Bedrooms: 3
Bathrooms: 2½
Foundation: Crawl space; slab or basement available for fee
Materials List Available: No
Price Category: C

Images provided by designer/architect.

Features:

- **Kitchen:** The island, which adds work surface and storage, enhances this efficient kitchen. An open wall above the sink encourages conversation between here and the great room.

- **Breakfast Nook:** This angular breakfast nook is enclosed by windows and offers access to the backyard. Just steps away from the kitchen, the dining room and breakfast nook ease meal service.

- **Master Suite:** This suite provides a private getaway on the first floor. The attached master bath has a double-sink vanity and both a tub and a shower enclosure.

- **Upper Level:** From the walkway you can look down into the two-story great room as you pass the full bathroom and bonus room. The two secondary bedrooms complete this level.

The covered front entry, facade that's trimmed in brick, and tall mullioned windows give this home timeless appeal.

CAD FILE AVAILABLE

Main Level Floor Plan

NOOK 8/8 X 8/10
DINING 9/10 X 10/4
MASTER 16/0 X 11/10
TWO STORY GREAT RM. 15/10 X 19/8
GARAGE 19/4 X 21/8
SPA
UP

◄ 40' ►   ▲ 53' ▼

Upper Level Floor Plan

BR. 3 12/6 X 12/2 +/-
BR. 2 10/9 X 12/2 +/-
BONUS RM. 13/6 X 12/6
OPEN TO GREAT RM. BELOW
DN
ATTIC STORAGE

Copyright by designer/architect.

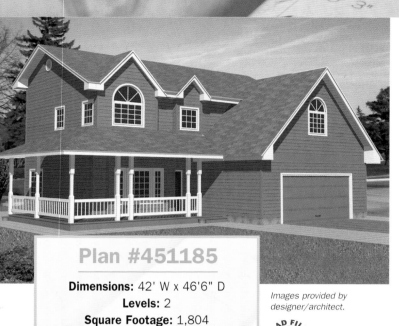

**Main Level
Floor Plan**

Plan #451185

Dimensions: 42' W x 46'6" D
Levels: 2
Square Footage: 1,804
Main Level Sq. Ft.: 992
Upper Level Sq. Ft.: 812
Bedrooms: 4
Bathrooms: 2½
Foundation: Crawl space
Materials List Available: No
Price Category: D

*Images provided by
designer/architect.*

**Upper Level
Floor Plan**

Copyright by designer/architect.

Plan #281029

Dimensions: 48' W x 59' D
Levels: 1
Square Footage: 1,833
Bedrooms: 3
Bathrooms: 2
Foundation: Basement
Materials List Available: Yes
Price Category: D

*Images provided by
designer/architect.*

Rear Elevation

Copyright by designer/architect.

Plan #121006

Dimensions: 46' W x 58' D
Levels: 1
Square Footage: 1,762
Bedrooms: 3
Bathrooms: 2
Foundation: Slab
Materials List Available: Yes
Price Category: C

Images provided by designer/architect.

The entry has a trio of arched openings that leads you to other areas of this amenity-packed home.

Features:

- Ceiling Height: 8 ft. except as noted.

- Eating Bar: Conveniently located between the kitchen and family room, this is sure to be a favorite spot for informal entertaining and family gatherings.

- Family room: A wall of windows, a fireplace, and a vaulted ceiling stretching to 11 ft. work together to make this a bright and warm room.

- Kitchen: There's no shortage of counter space in this well-planned kitchen that features a center island in addition to the eating bar.

- Master Suite: Luxuriate at the end of the day in this large bedroom with its decorative tray ceiling and walk-in closet. Enjoy the pampering bath with its sunlit corner whirlpool flanked by vanities.

- Garage: Two bays provide room for cars and plenty of storage as well.

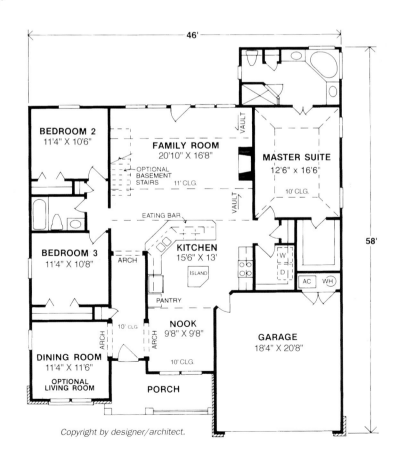

Copyright by designer/architect.

Images provided by designer/architect.

Plan #441021

Dimensions: 50' W x 44'6" D

Levels: 2

Square Footage: 1,760

Main Level Sq. Ft.: 941

Upper Level Sq. Ft.: 819

Bedrooms: 4

Bathrooms: 3

Foundation: Crawl space; slab or basement available for fee

Material List Available: No

Price Category: C

Add French country charm to any neighborhood with this great two-story home. A tall arched entry is adorned with stone. Varied window shapes add character to the façade.

Features:

- Great Room: Equipped with a fireplace, this vaulted room is a great place for the family to relax.

- Kitchen: This centralized kitchen features an island complete with a breakfast bar and sink. The spacious L-shape provides plenty of space for storage.

- Master Suite: Located upstairs, this suite features full amenities, with its spa bath, dual sinks, and a walk-in closet.

- Utility area: This laundry room—and more—is located on the second floor, eliminating trips up and down the stairs with laundry.

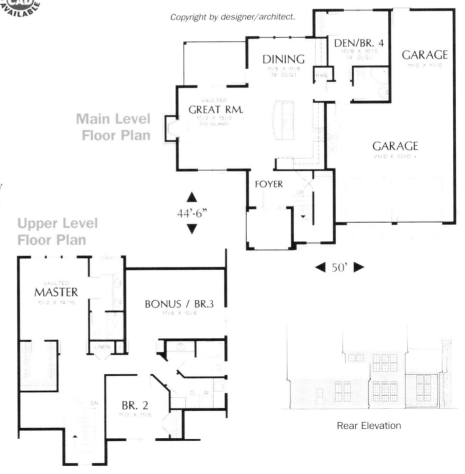

Copyright by designer/architect.

Main Level Floor Plan

Upper Level Floor Plan

Rear Elevation

Ibarra

Plan #371071

Dimensions: 73' W x 47'4" D

Levels: 1

Square Footage: 1,729

Bedrooms: 3

Bathrooms: 2

Foundation: Crawl space, slab

Materials List Available: No

Price Category: C

This beautiful brick-and-stone country home will be the envy of the neighborhood.

Features:

- Front Porch: This charming yet functional porch welcomes you home.

- Family Room: This large room, with its cathedral ceiling and cozy fireplace, is ideal for entertaining.

- Kitchen: This gourmet kitchen has all the necessities you will ever need, including a raised bar area.

- Master Suite: This master bedroom features a stepped ceiling. The luxurious bath boasts a marble tub and two walk-in closets.

Plan #321064

Dimensions: 34' W x 47' D
Levels: 2
Square Footage: 1,769
Main Level Sq. Ft.: 1,306
Upper Level Sq. Ft.: 463
Bedrooms: 3
Bathrooms: 2
Foundation: Basement
Materials List Available: Yes
Price Category: C

Images provided by designer/architect.

You'll love the way that this spacious A-frame home, with its distinctive interior design, complements any site.

Features:

- Living Room: With an elegant cathedral ceiling and a handsome fireplace, this room makes an ideal spot for entertaining in every season.

- Kitchen: The "U-shape" of this kitchen and adjoining dining area create a warm welcome for friends and family. This an ideal work spot, thanks to the thoughtful layout and ample counter and cabinet space.

- Master Suite: A sloped ceiling gives drama to this secluded suite. A walk-in closet adds practicality, and the amenities in the private bath provide the luxury that will make this area a true retreat.

- Secondary Bedrooms: The secondary bedrooms have large double closets for convenient storage space as well as access to natural lighting from their well-positioned windows.

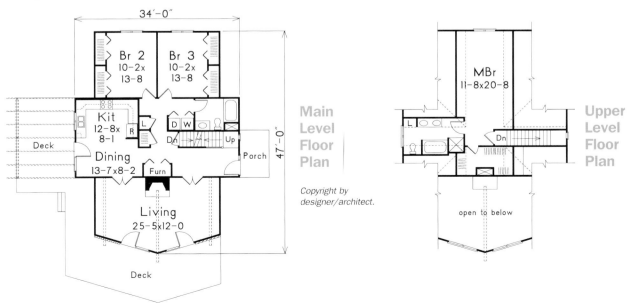

Main Level Floor Plan

Copyright by designer/architect.

Upper Level Floor Plan

Plan #151016

Dimensions: 60'2" W x 39'10" D
Levels: 2
Square Footage: 1,783;
2,107 with bonus
Main Level Sq. Ft.: 1,124
Upper Level Sq. Ft.: 659
Bonus Room Sq. Ft.: 324
Bedrooms: 3
Bathrooms: 2½
Foundation: Crawl space, slab,
or basement
CompleteCost List Available: Yes
Price Category: C

An open design characterizes this
spacious home built for family life
and entertaining.

Images provided by designer/architect.

Features:

- Great Room: Enjoy the fireplace in this spacious, versatile room.

- Dining Room: Entertaining is easy, thanks to the open design with the kitchen.

- Master Suite: Luxury surrounds you in this suite, with its large walk-in closet, double vanities, and a bathroom with a whirlpool tub and separate shower.

- Upper Bedrooms: Window seats make wonderful spots for reading or relaxing, and a nook between the windows of these rooms is a ready-made play area.

- Bonus Area: Located over the garage, this space could be converted to a home office, a studio, or a game room for the kids.

- Attic: There's plenty of storage space here.

Bonus Room Above Garage

Copyright by designer/architect.

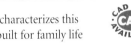

Main Level Floor Plan

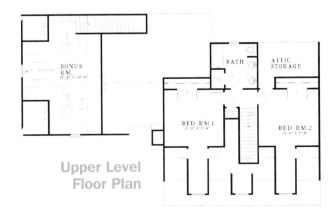

Upper Level Floor Plan

Plan #161001

Dimensions: 67'2" W x 47' D
Levels: 1
Square Footage: 1,782
Bedrooms: 3
Bathrooms: 2
Foundation: Basement
Materials List Available: Yes
Price Category: C

An all-brick exterior displays the solid strength that characterizes this gracious home.

Features:

- **Gathering Area:** A feeling of spaciousness permeates this gathering area, created by the foyer, great room, and dining room. Multiple windows provide natural light that dances along a sloped ceiling, spilling onto decorative columns and a fireplace.

- **Breakfast Area:** A continuation of the sloped ceiling leads to this breakfast area, where French doors open to a screened porch.

- **Kitchen:** An abundance of cabinets and counter space are the hallmarks of this large kitchen, with its easy access to a spacious laundry room and storage area.

- **Master Suite:** A tray ceiling and spacious walk-in closet in the master bedroom, along with a whirlpool tub and double-bowl vanity in the bathroom, enable you to pamper yourself.

CAD FILE AVAILABLE

Master Bedroom 14'5" x 14'5" — tray ceiling

Bath

Great Room 15'8" x 18'6"

Breakfast 11'7" x 9'6"

Screened-in Porch 10'6" x 17'4"

walk-in closet

Kitchen 11'7" x 13'4"

Bath

Hall

stairs dn

Foyer

Bedroom 13'10" x 9'11"

Study/ Bedroom 10'3" x 11'11"

Dining Room 10'8" x 11'9"

pantry

Laun.

Two-car Garage 20'2" x 20'1"

67'2"

47'

Copyright by designer/architect.

Great Room/Foyer

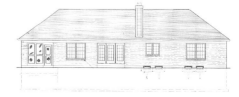

Rear Elevation

Main Level Floor Plan

53'- 4"

PORCH   NOOK 12'-0" × 9'-6"   MASTER SUITE 18'-0" × 12'-0"

DINING RM. 13'-2" × 9'-8"

KITCH. 13'-2" × 9'-8"

BATH 1

51'- 4"

LIVING RM. 11'-8" × 16'-2" CEILING OPEN 2 STORIES

STORAGE

ENT.

GARAGE 21'-8" × 22'-10"

PORCH

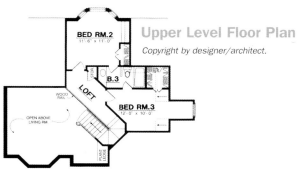

Upper Level Floor Plan

Copyright by designer/architect.

BED RM.2 11'-6" × 11'-0"

B.3

LOFT

OPEN ABOVE LIVING RM.

BED RM.3 12'-0" × 10'-0"

PLANT LEDGE

Plan #371094

Dimensions: 53'4" W x 51'4" D
Levels: 2
Square Footage: 1,875
Main Level Sq. Ft.: 1,345
Upper Level Sq. Ft.: 530
Bedrooms: 3
Bathrooms: 2½
Foundation: Crawl space, slab, or basement
Materials List Available: No
Price Category: D

Images provided by designer/architect.

CAD FILE AVAILABLE

Plan #321053

Dimensions: 35' W x 56' D
Levels: 2
Square Footage: 1,985
Main Level Sq. Ft.: 1,114
Upper Level Sq. Ft.: 871
Bedrooms: 4
Bathrooms: 3½
Foundation: Basement
Materials List Available: Yes
Price Category: D

Images provided by designer/architect.

Main Level Floor Plan

Copyright by designer/architect.

35'-0"

MBr 17-0x13-10

Deck

Kitchen 11-4x12-0

Great Rm 13-7x18-8 Sunken vaulted

56'-0"

Dining 11-4x12-0

Garage 18-4x21-4

Upper Level Floor Plan

Br 3 12-4x12-5

Br 2 11-0x12-5

open to below

Br 4 11-4x13-3

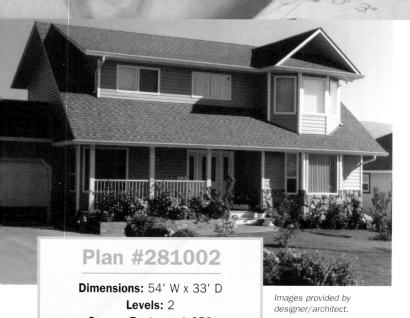

Upper Level
Floor Plan

Copyright by designer/architect.

BR 3
10-0 x 10-0

linen

BATH

ENS

W.I.C.

dn

MASTER SUITE
13-0 x 14-0

BR 2
10-0 x 12-4

STUDY

railing

Foyer below

TV/Books etc.

SITTING
9-0 x 7-6

Plan #281002

Dimensions: 54' W x 33' D
Levels: 2
Square Footage: 1,859
Main Level Sq. Ft.: 959
Second Level Sq. Ft.: 900
Bedrooms: 3
Bathrooms: 2½
Foundation: Basement
Materials List Available: Yes
Price Category: D

Images provided by designer/architect.

Front View

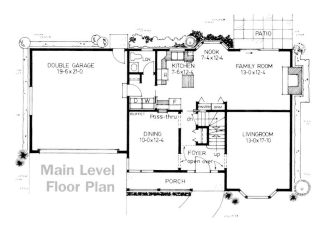

PATIO

DOUBLE GARAGE
19-6 x 21-0

Lav

KITCHEN
7-6 x 12-4

R

NOOK
7-4 x 12-4

FAMILY ROOM
13-0 x 12-4

D W

F

BUFFET

Pass-thru

PANTRY

BRM

dn

DINING
10-0 x 12-4

LIVINGROOM
13-0 x 17-10

FOYER

up

open over

Main Level
Floor Plan

PORCH

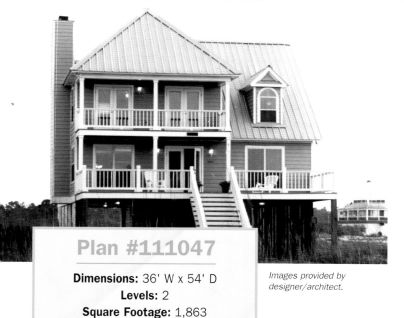

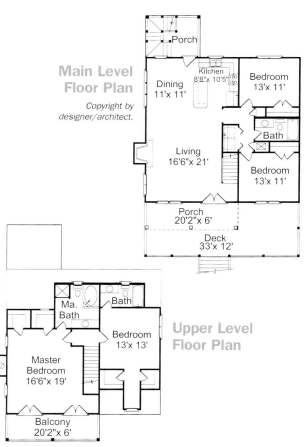

Porch

Main Level
Floor Plan

Copyright by designer/architect.

Kitchen
8'8"x 10'5"

Dining
11'x 11'

Bedroom
13'x 11'

Living
16'6"x 21'

Bath

Bedroom
13'x 11'

Porch
20'2"x 6'

Deck
33'x 12'

Plan #111047

Dimensions: 36' W x 54' D
Levels: 2
Square Footage: 1,863
Main Level Sq. Ft.: 1,056
Upper Level Sq. Ft.: 807
Bedrooms: 4
Bathrooms: 3
Foundation: Pier
Materials List Available: No
Price Category: D

Images provided by designer/architect.

Ma. Bath

Bath

Bedroom
13'x 13'

Upper Level
Floor Plan

Master Bedroom
16'6"x 19'

Balcony
20'2"x 6'

Plan #211039

Dimensions: 62' W x 64' D

Levels: 1

Square Footage: 1,868

Bedrooms: 3

Bathrooms: 2

Foundation: Slab

Materials List Available: Yes

Price Category: D

Images provided by designer/architect.

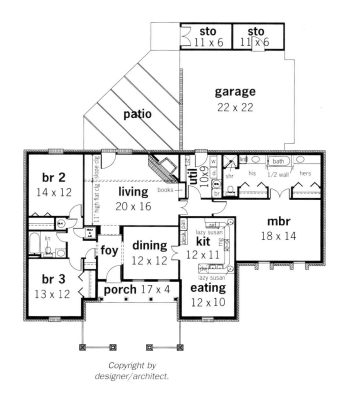

Copyright by designer/architect.

Plan #121051

Dimensions: 64' W x 44' D

Levels: 1

Square Footage: 1,808

Bedrooms: 3

Bathrooms: 2½

Foundation: Basement

Materials List Available: Yes

Price Category: D

Images provided by designer/architect.

CAD FILE AVAILABLE

Copyright by designer/architect.

SMARTtip
Cutting Molding

Using an bench-top table saw and a simple plywood jig is a safe, efficient, and foolproof way to cut many trim members at angles of less than 45 degrees.

**Main Level
Floor Plan**

*Images provided by
designer/architect.*

Plan #251008

Dimensions: 44'4" W x 73'2" D
Levels: 2
Square Footage: 1,808
Main Level Sq. Ft.: 1,271
Upper Level Sq. Ft.: 537
Bedrooms: 3
Bathrooms: 2½
Foundation: Basement
Materials List Available: Yes
Price Category: D

Upper Level Floor Plan

Copyright by designer/architect.

**Main Level
Floor Plan**

*Images provided by
designer/architect.*

Plan #181133

Dimensions: 38' W x 40' D
Levels: 2
Square Footage: 1,832
Main Level Sq. Ft.: 1,212
Second Level Sq. Ft. 620
Bedrooms: 3
Bathrooms: 2
Foundation: Walkout; crawl space,
slab, or basement for fee
Materials List Available: Yes
Price Category: D

Upper Level Floor Plan

Copyright by designer/architect.

Plan #121014

Dimensions: 52' W x 47'4" D
Levels: 2
Square Footage: 1,869
Main Level Sq. Ft.: 1,421
Upper Level Sq. Ft.: 448
Bedrooms: 3
Bathrooms: 2½
Foundation: Basement
Materials List Available: Yes
Price Category: D

Images provided by designer/architect.

Upper Level Floor Plan

Main Level Floor Plan

Copyright by designer/architect.

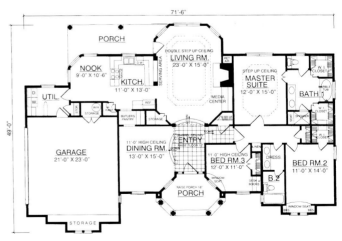

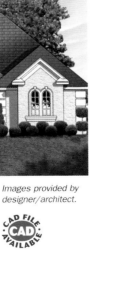

Plan #371042

Dimensions: 71'6" W x 49' D
Levels: 1
Square Footage: 1,999
Bedrooms: 3
Bathrooms: 2
Foundation: Slab
Materials List Available: No
Price Category: D

Images provided by designer/architect.

Copyright by designer/architect.

Plan #211002

Dimensions: 68' W x 62' D
Levels: 1
Square Footage: 1,792
Bedrooms: 3
Bathrooms: 2
Foundation: Crawl space
Materials List Available: Yes
Price Category: C

Arched windows on the front of this home give it a European style that you're sure to love.

Images provided by designer/architect.

SMARTtip

Water Features

Water features create the ambiance of a soothing oasis on a deck. A water-filled urn becomes a mirror that reflects the sky—making a small deck look larger. Fish flashing in an ornamental pool add color and act as a focal point for a deck with no view.

A water fountain introduces a pleasant rhythmical sound that helps drown out the background noises of traffic and nearby neighbors.

Features:

- Living Room: The 12-ft. ceiling in this large, open room enhances its spacious feeling. A fireplace adds warmth on chilly days and cool evenings.

- Dining Room: Decorate to accentuate the 12-ft. ceiling and formal feeling of this room.

- Kitchen: Designed for comfort and efficiency, this room also has a 12-ft. ceiling. The cozy breakfast bar is a natural gathering spot for friends and family.

- Master Suite: A split design guarantees privacy here. A sloped cathedral ceiling adds elegance, and a walk-in closet makes it practical. The bath has two vanities, a tub, and a walk-in shower.

- Garage: Park two cars here, and use the balance of this 520 sq. ft. area as a handy storage area.

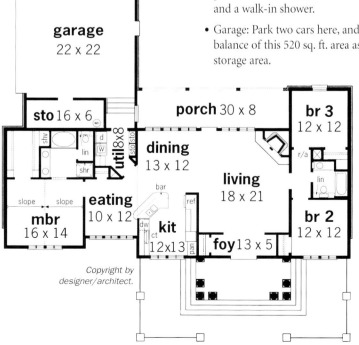

Copyright by designer/architect.

Plan #131047

Dimensions: 69'10" W x 51'8" D
Levels: 1
Square Footage: 1,793
Bedrooms: 3
Bathrooms: 2
Foundation: Crawl space, slab, or basement
Materials List Available: Yes
Price Category: C

The country charm of this well-designed home is mixed with the convenience and luxury normally reserved for more contemporary plans.

Images provided by designer/architect.

Features:

- Great Room: The spaciousness of this great room is enhanced by the 11-ft. stepped ceiling. A fireplace makes it cozy on cool evenings or on chilly winter days, and two sets of French sliding glass doors open to the back porch.

- Kitchen: In addition to the convenient layout of this design, you'll also love its bright, airy position. It includes an old-fashioned pantry,

a sink under a window, and a sunny breakfast area that opens to the wraparound porch.

- Master Suite: You'll find 11-ft. ceilings in both the master bedroom and the bayed sitting area that the suite includes. In the bath, the circular spa tub is surrounded by a glass-block wall.

- Bonus Space: A permanent staircase leads to an unfinished bonus space on the upper level.

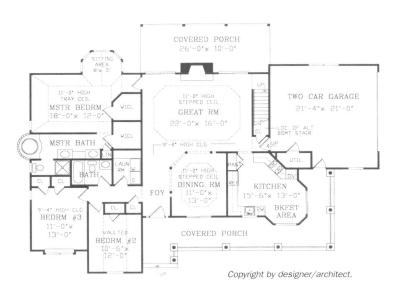

Copyright by designer/architect.

Rear Elevation

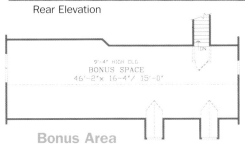

Bonus Area

Plan #401030

Dimensions: 36' W x 40' D
Levels: 1½
Square Footage: 1,795
Main Level Sq. Ft.: 1,157
Upper Level Sq. Ft.: 638
Bedrooms: 3
Bathrooms: 2½
Foundation: Crawl space
Materials List Available: Yes
Price Category: C

A sun deck is what makes this design so popular, but it is enhanced by views through an expansive wall of glass in the living and dining rooms.

CAD FILE AVAILABLE

Features:

- **Living Room:** Both this room and the dining room are warmed by a woodstove and enjoy vaulted ceilings.

- **Kitchen:** This area has a vaulted ceiling and a food-preparation island and breakfast bar. Behind the kitchen is a laundry room with side access.

Images provided by designer/architect.

- **Master Bedroom:** This master bedroom and its walk-in closet and private bath are conveniently located on the first floor.

- **Bedrooms:** Two bedrooms and a full bath room are found on the second floor.

Upper Level Floor Plan

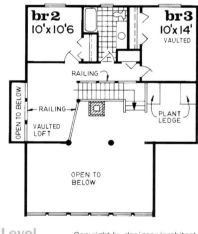

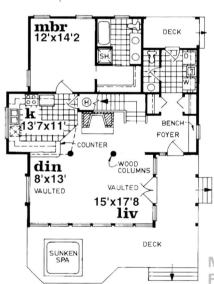

Main Level Floor Plan

Copyright by designer/architect.

Left Side Elevation

Rear Elevation

Right Side Elevation

Plan #121015

Dimensions: 52' W x 47'4" D
Levels: 2
Square Footage: 1,999
Main Level Sq. Ft.: 1,421
Upper Level Sq. Ft.: 578
Bedrooms: 4
Bathrooms: 2½
Foundation: Basement
Materials List Available: Yes
Price Category: D

This home, as shown in the photograph, may differ from the actual blueprints. For more detailed information, please check the floor plans carefully.

Hipped roofs and a trio of gables bring distinction to this plan.

Features:

• Ceiling Height: 8 ft.

• Open Floor Plan: The rooms flow into each other and are flanked by an abundance of windows. The result is a light and airy space that seems much larger than it really is.

• Formal Dining Room: Here is the perfect room for elegant entertaining.

• Breakfast Nook: This bright, bayed nook is the perfect place to start the day. It's also great for intimate get-togethers.

• Great Room: The family will enjoy gathering in this spacious area.

• Bedrooms: This large master bedroom, along with three secondary bedrooms and an extra room, provides plenty of room for a growing family.

• Attached Garage: The garage provides two bays of parking plus plenty of storage space.

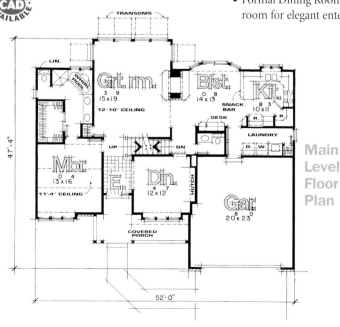

Main Level Floor Plan

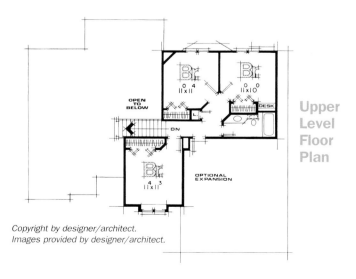

Upper Level Floor Plan

Copyright by designer/architect.
Images provided by designer/architect.

Plan #441032

Dimensions: 45' W x 55' D
Levels: 2
Square Footage: 1,944
Main Level Sq. Ft.: 1,514
Upper Level Sq. Ft.: 430
Bedrooms: 3
Bathrooms: 2½
Foundation: Crawl space; slab or basement available for fee
Materials List Available: No
Price Category: D

Images provided by designer/architect.

Main Level Floor Plan

Copyright by designer/architect.

Rear Elevation

Upper Level Floor Plan

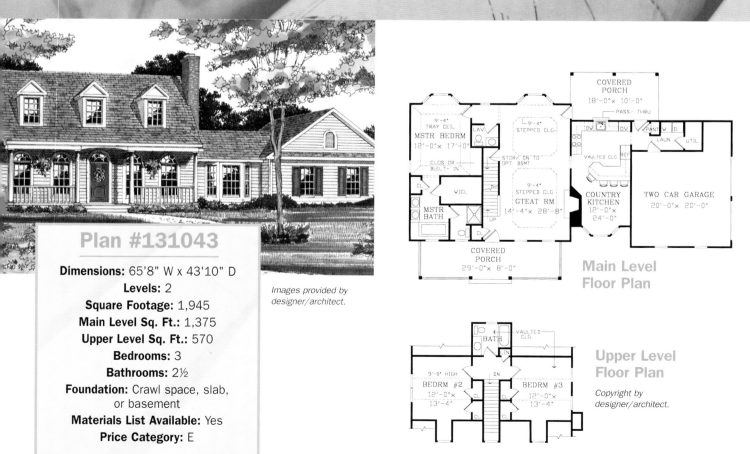

Plan #131043

Dimensions: 65'8" W x 43'10" D
Levels: 2
Square Footage: 1,945
Main Level Sq. Ft.: 1,375
Upper Level Sq. Ft.: 570
Bedrooms: 3
Bathrooms: 2½
Foundation: Crawl space, slab, or basement
Materials List Available: Yes
Price Category: E

Images provided by designer/architect.

Main Level Floor Plan

Upper Level Floor Plan

Copyright by designer/architect.

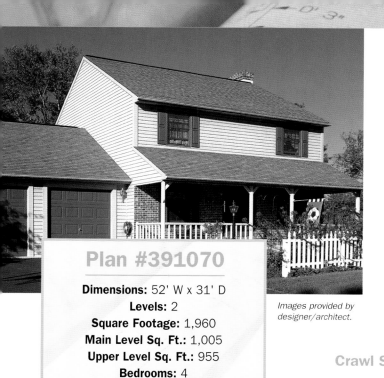

Plan #391070

Dimensions: 52' W x 31' D
Levels: 2
Square Footage: 1,960
Main Level Sq. Ft.: 1,005
Upper Level Sq. Ft.: 955
Bedrooms: 4
Bathrooms: 2½
Foundation: Crawl space, slab, or basement
Material List Available: Yes
Price Category: D

Images provided by designer/architect.

Main Level Floor Plan

Crawl Space/Slab Option

Upper Level Floor Plan

Copyright by designer/architect.

Plan #181062

Dimensions: 58' W x 55' D
Levels: 2
Square Footage: 1,953
Main Level Sq. Ft.: 1,301
Second Level Sq. Ft.: 652
Bedrooms: 3
Bathrooms: 2½
Foundation: Half basement, half crawl space
Materials List Available: Yes
Price Category: D

Images provided by designer/architect.

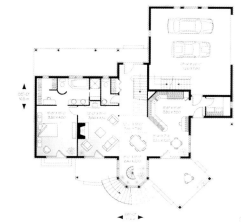

Main Level Floor Plan

Upper Level Floor Plan

Copyright by designer/architect.

Outdoor Living

M any homeowners treat their decks and patios as another room of the house. To gain the fullest use of these areas, homeowners often add cooking areas, outdoor lighting centers, and other features to their outdoor living areas.

Cooking Centers

As the trend toward outdoor entertaining gains popularity, many people are setting up complete, permanent outdoor cooking centers, which often become the focus of their decks. Others content themselves with a simple grill. In either case, practical planning makes outdoor cooking efficient and more enjoyable, whether it is for everyday family meals or for a host of guests.

Decide exactly what features you want in the outdoor kitchen area. If you prefer to keep it simple with just a grill, you'll still have some decisions to make. Do you want a charcoal, gas, or electric unit? A charcoal grill is the least expensive option; a natural gas grill will cost you the most because it must be professionally installed. (Check with your local building department beforehand. Some localities will require a permit or may not allow this installation.) Extra features and accessories, such as rotisseries, woks, burners, smoke ovens, and warming racks increase the cost, too. Just remember: if you intend to locate the grill in a wooden enclosure, choose a model designed for this application.

In addition to a grill, do you want an elaborate setup with a sink, countertop, or a refrigerator? If so, these amenities will need protection from the elements. However, some refrigerators designed specifically for outdoor use can withstand harsh weather conditions. These high-end units are vented from the front and can be built-in or freestanding on casters.

Typically, outdoor refrigerators are countertop height (often the same size as standard wine chilling units that mount underneath a kitchen countertop) and have shelving for food trays or drinks and indoor storage for condiments. Outdoor refrigerators intended strictly for cold beer storage come with a tap and can accommodate a half-keg.

More Entertainment Options

Do you entertain frequently? Think about including a custom-designed wet bar and countertop in your plans. Besides a sink, the unit can offer enclosed storage for beverages, ice, and glasses, and the countertop will be handy for serving or buffets. But if you can't handle the expense, consider a prefabricated open-air wet bar. It can be portable or built-in. Some portable wet-bars feature: a sink that you can hook up to the house plumbing or a garden hose (with a filter), ice bins with sliding lids, sectioned compartments for garnishes, a speed rail for bottles, and a beverage-chilling well. Deluxe models may come with extra shelves and side-mounted food warmers.

Practical Advantages

Integrating a cooking center with your deck provides easy access to the kitchen indoors. Remember, elaborate outdoor kitchens require gas, electricity, and plumbing; it is easier and less expensive to run those lines when the cooking area isn't at the other end of the yard. However, you'll have to carefully plan the cooktop so that it isn't too close to the house and so that the heat and smoke are directed away from seating areas.

In general, when arranging any outdoor cooking area, be sure that all accouterments—including serving platters, insulated mitts, basting brushes, spatulas, forks and knives, and long-handled tongs—are

readily at hand for the cook. And don't forget to plan enough surface room for setting down a tray of spices, condiments, sauces, and marinade or swiftly unloading a plate of hot grilled meats or vegetables. Because you'll have to juggle both uncooked and cooked foods, a roll-around cart may suffice. For safety's sake, always keep the pathway from the kitchen to the outdoor cooking area clear, and as a precaution, keep a fire extinguisher nearby.

Countertop Options

Any outdoor countertop should be able to withstand varying weather conditions. Rain, snow, and bright sunlight will pit and rot some materials, so choose carefully. Tile, concrete, or natural stone (such as slate) are the best options. Concrete can be tinted and inlaid for decorative effect but, like stone, it is porous and must be sealed. Avoid a surface laminate unless it's for use in a well-protected area because exposure to the weather causes the layers to separate. Solid-surfacing material is more durable, but it's better left to a sheltered location.

Think twice about using teak or other decay-resistant woods for a countertop. Although these woods weather handsomely, they are not sealed against bacteria, so you can't expose them directly to food. If you do select a wooden countertop, insert a tray or plate under any uncooked meats and vegetables. Decay-resistant woods such as redwood, cedar, teak, or mahogany are, however, good choices for outdoor cabinetry. Other types of wood will have to be sealed and stained or painted. Another option is oriented-strand board (OSB) that is weatherproof.

Side burners, opposite, help you prepare an entire meal at the grill.

Small, outdoor refrigerators, far right, save steps when entertaining outdoors.

What to Look for in a Grill

A grill cover should fit snugly. Some covers have adjustable lids, which allow airflow so that food cooks slowly and evenly.

Adjustable controls allow you to control the heat level of burners.

Side burners let you sauté toppings, simmer sauces, or fry side dishes. A side burner can come with a protective cover that also doubles as an extra landing surface for utensils.

A towel hook is a useful detail on a grill. Check for other extras, such as utility hooks for utensils, condiment compartments on side shelves, or warming racks.

Casters make the grill portable so that it is easy to reposition at your convenience. Keep in mind that a large stainless-steel grill can be as heavy as 230 pounds.

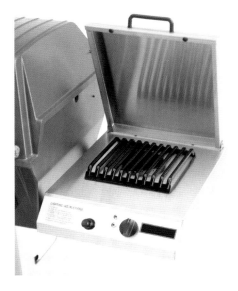

Grill Checklist

Look for these important features:

- **An electronic push-button ignition.** It starts better because it emits a continuous spark; knob igniters emit two to three sparks per turn.

- **Insulated handles.** These are convenient because they don't get hot. Otherwise you'll need a grilling mitt to protect yourself from burns when using the controls.

- **Easy access to the propane tank.** Some gas grills feature tilt-out bins, which make connecting and changing the tank a snap.

Safety Check

Hoses on gas grills can develop leaks. To check the hose on your gas grill, brush soapy water over it. If you see any bubbles, turn off the gas valve and disconnect the tank, then replace the hose.

Large grills, left, offer multiple, individually controlled burners, warming trays, and storage.

Selecting a Grill

It's not the size of the grill that counts; it's whether you have the space on the deck to accommodate it. Measure the intended cooking area before shopping, and take those measurements with you to the store or home center. Depending upon your budget, you may also want to consider one of the high-end units that luxury kitchen appliance manufacturers have introduced into the marketplace. They have lots of features and are built to last, but they are expensive and must be professionally installed. Serious cooks like them.

Think about the grill's location in relationship to the traffic, dining, and lounging zones. How far away will the grill be from the house? If your space is limited or if you expect a lot of activity—large crowds or kids underfoot—you may have to relegate the cooking area to someplace close, but not on the deck itself. Also consider how many people you typically cook for. Check out the grill's number of separate heating zones (there should be at least two) before buying it. If you have a large family or entertain frequently, you'll need a grill that can accommodate large quantities or different types of food at the same time.

Grill Features

Because you'll probably be using your new grill more often and with a greater variety of foods, buy one that has some important basic options. Are there any special features that you'd like with your grill? Extra burners, a rotisserie, a warming rack, or a smoker? What do you like to cook? Today, you can prepare more than hamburgers and barbecued chicken on your grill. In fact, tasty, healthy grilled food is popular year-round, and so you may be cooking outdoors from spring through late fall.

Many models now come with two burners, but larger ones have more. The burners should have adjustable temperature controls that will allow you to set the heat at high, medium, or low. Ideally, a unit should sustain an even cooking temperature and provide at least 33,000 Btu (British thermal units, the measurement for heat output) when burners are set on high. Generally, the larger the grill the higher the Btu output. A slow-roasting setting is optional on some models. Another good option is gauge that records the temperature when the lid is closed. If you enjoy sauces, make sure your grill comes with adjustable side burners, which can accommodate pots.

Outdoor Lighting

In terms of lighting and electricity, a deck can be as fully functional as any room inside your house. And if you add outdoor lighting, you will find that you get much more use out of your deck, patio, or outdoor living area. In addition to natural light, a pleasing combination of even, diffused general (also called "ambient") light, as well as accent and task lighting from artificial sources, can illuminate your deck for use after the sun goes down.

Developing an outdoor lighting plans differs from developing an interior lighting scheme. The basics are the same, but exterior lighting relies heavily on low-voltage systems. These operate on 12 volts as opposed to the 120 volts of a standard line system. A good outdoor plan will combine both types of lighting.

Developing a Lighting Planning

First decide how much light you need and where it should go. Besides general overall illumination, locate fixtures near activity zones: the food preparation and cooking area, the wet bar, or wherever you plan to set up drinks, snacks, or a buffet when you entertain. Be sure that there is adequate light near the dining table, conversation areas, and recreational spots, such as the hot tub, if you plan to use them in the evening. You may want separate switches for each one, and you might consider dimmers; you don't need or want the same intensity of light required for barbecuing as you do for relaxing in the hot tub.

What type of fixtures should you choose? That partly depends on the location. Near a wall or under a permanent roof, sconces and ceiling fixtures will provide light while staying out of the way. For uncovered areas, try post or railing lamps.

Lighting the Way

Walkways and staircases need lighting for safety. There are a number of practical options: path lights (if the walkway is ground level), brick lights that can be inserted into your walls near the steps, and railing fixtures that can be tucked under

deck railings or steps. Less-functional but more-decorative lighting such as post lamps can provide illumination for high traffic areas; sconces can be effective on stair landings or near doors. Walk lights also provide a needed measure of safety.

Don't forget about areas that may call for motion-sensitive floodlights, such as entrances into the house and garage, underneath a raised deck, and deep yards are all excellent locations for floodlights. Keep these fixtures on separate switches so that they don't interfere with the atmosphere you want to create while you are using the deck.

Railing- and bench-mounted lights, above, provide a subtle lighting option. They illuminate small areas without casting glare into the eyes of those on the deck.

Step lights, right, are a must for stairs leading down into the yard. Use these lights sparingly as shown. A little outdoor light goes a long way.

Provide a lighted backdrop to your outdoor living area by installing yard and garden light-ing, above. Use lights to line walks, accent flower beds, or highlight a fountain or pond.

Adding Accent Light

Are there any noteworthy plantings or objects in your garden that you can high-light? By using in-ground accent lighting or spotlights, you can create dramatic night-time effects or a focal point. Artful lighting can enhance the ambience of your deck by drawing attention to the shape of a hand-some tree, a garden statue, a fountain or pond, or an outdoor pool.

Choosing the Right Fixture

If your home is formal, traditional fixtures in brass or an antique finish will comple-ment the overall scheme nicely. For a mod-ern setting, choose streamlined fixtures with matte or brushed-metal finishes. Landscape lighting is often utilitarian, but it is intended to blend unobtrusively into the landscape; the light, not the fixture, is noticeable. Path and post lighting, however, can be decorative and comes in a variety of styles and finishes, from highly polished metals to antique and matte looks.

Depending on the lighting system you buy, you may be able to install the fixtures your-self. But working with electricity does pose technical, code, and safety concerns. It's probably best to hire a qualified profession-al for the installation. For complex projects, you may also want to consult a landscape lighting professional. Home centers some-times provide this type of expertise. If you decide to plot a design yourself, remember not to overlight the deck.

Other Considerations

As you plan to install deck lighting, think about the space's other electrical or wiring needs. If there is an outdoor kitchen, a grill area, or a bar, you may want outlets for a refrigerator or small appliances. You might include additional outlets for a stereo or speakers, or even a TV. Don't overlook a phone jack for the modem on your laptop computer. Some decking systems come prewired and are ready to be hooked up. So with forethought, you can incorporate everything you need into your outdoor liv-ing plans.

Water Features

There is nothing like the sight and sound of water to add a refreshing quality to your deck or patio. In fact, water can be a dynamic element in both the deck's design and its function. It can be in the form of one of the ultimate outdoor luxuries—a pool, spa, or hot tub—or in a water feature such as a fountain, waterfall, or pond. In any case, because of the relaxing qualities of water, you should consider integrating some form of it into your plans.

Planning a deck or patio near a pool requires taking the size and shape of the pool into consideration. In most cases, the pool will be a focal point in a landscape, so the design of the surrounding deck, including the flooring patterns, materials, and other details, can either enhance or detract

from its appeal. Aside from looks, think about how a pool deck will function.

Adding a Spa. Another way to enjoy water with your deck is with a soothing spa. Requiring less space than a pool, a spa uses hydrojets to move heated water. One type, a hot tub, is a barrel-like enclosure filled with water. It may or may not have jets and usually features an adjustable but simple bench. It offers a deeper soak—as much as 4 feet—than other types of spas, and many homeowners like the look of an aboveground hot tub's wood exterior. The tub comes with a vinyl or plastic liner.

A built-in spa is set into a deck or the ground (in-ground). It can be acrylic, or it can be constructed of poured concrete, gunite, or shotcrete. A spa can stand alone or be integrated with a large pool.

A portable spa is a completely self-contained unit that features an acrylic shell, a wooden surround, and all of the equipment needed to heat and move the water. A small portable spa costs less than an in-ground unit, and it runs on a standard 120-volt circuit. You can locate a portable spa on a concrete slab. But you can also install one on the deck. Just make sure there is proper structural support underneath the deck to sustain the additional weight of the unit, the water, and bathers.

Small, portable spas, opposite, are self-contained units that run on standard line-voltage electricity. Check weight restrictions if installing a spa on a deck.

Spas complete an outdoor living area, above. This sunken spa is a natural complement to the nearby pool and to the large multilevel deck.

Images provided by
designer/architect.

Plan #321006

Dimensions: 76' W x 45' D
Levels: 1, optional lower
Square Footage: 1,977
**Optional Basement Level
Sq. Ft.:** 1,416
Bedrooms: 4
Bathrooms: 2½
Foundation: Basement
Materials List Available: Yes
Price Category: D

Optional
Basement
Level
Floor Plan

Copyright by
designer/architect.

Plan #121050

Dimensions: 64' W x 50' D
Levels: 1
Square Footage: 1,996
Bedrooms: 2
Bathrooms: 2
Foundation: Basement
Materials List Available: Yes
Price Category: D

Images provided by
designer/architect.

CAD FILE AVAILABLE

Copyright by
designer/architect.

Plan #441006

Dimensions: 48' W x 64' D
Levels: 1
Square Footage: 1,891
Bedrooms: 3
Bathrooms: 2
Foundation: Crawl space
Materials List Available: No
Price Category: D

If you prefer the look of Craftsman homes, you'll love the details this plan includes. Wide-based columns across the front porch, Mission-style windows, and a balanced mixture of exterior materials add up to true good looks.

Features:

- Great Room: A built-in media center and a fireplace in this room make it distinctive.

- Kitchen: A huge skylight over an island eating counter brightens this kitchen. A private office space opens through double doors nearby.

- Dining Room: This room has sliding glass doors opening to the rear patio.

- Bedrooms: Two bedrooms with two bathrooms are located on the right side of the plan. One of the bedrooms is a master suite with a vaulted salon and a bath with a spa tub.

- Garage: You'll be able to reach this two-car garage via a service hallway that contains a laundry room, a walk-in pantry, and a closet.

Images provided by designer/architect.

Copyright by designer/architect.

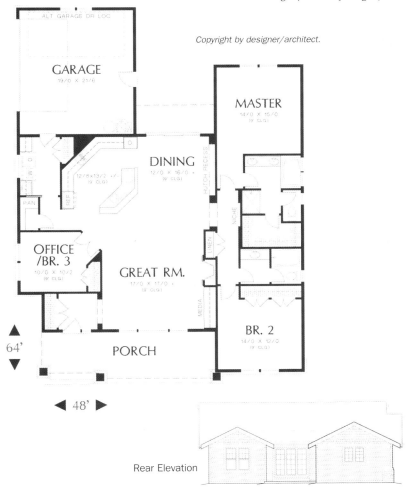

Rear Elevation

Plan #441001

Dimensions: 44' W x 68' D
Levels: 1
Square Footage: 1,850
Bedrooms: 3
Bathrooms: 2
Foundation: Crawl space
Materials List Available: No
Price Category: D

CAD FILE AVAILABLE
CAD

With all the tantalizing elements of a cottage and the comfortable space of a family-sized home, this Arts and Crafts-style one-story design is the best of both worlds. Exterior accents such as stone wainscot, cedar shingles under the gable ends, and mission-style windows just add to the effect.

Features:

- Great Room: A warm hearth lights this room—right next to a built-in media center.

- Dining Room: This area features a sliding glass door to the rear patio for a breath of fresh air.

- Den: This quiet area has a window seat and a vaulted ceiling, giving the feeling of openness and letting your mind wander.

- Kitchen: This open corner kitchen features a 42-in. snack bar and a giant walk-in pantry.

- Master Suite: This suite boasts a tray ceiling and a large walk-in closet.

Rear Elevation

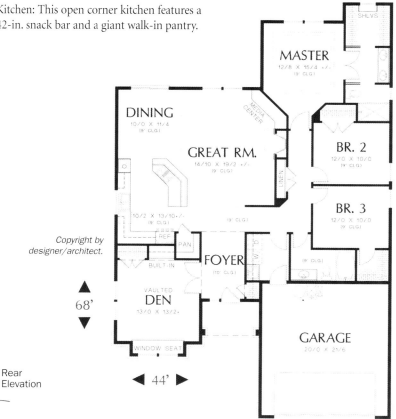

Copyright by designer/architect.

Plan #391068

Dimensions: 40' W x 27' D
Levels: 2
Square Footage: 1,855
Main Level Sq. Ft.: 913
Upper Level Sq. Ft.: 516
Basement Level Sq. Ft.: 426
Bedrooms: 3
Bathrooms: 2
Foundation: Basement
Materials List Available: No
Price Category: D

Images provided by designer/architect.

Wide windows on multiple levels infuse this home with the beauty of natural light.

Features:

- Great Room: This room with fireplace extends to the dining room, joining the camaraderie of an open kitchen.

- Master Suite: This suite with walk-in closet features a master bath with double vanities, a shower, and access to a terrace.

- Bedrooms: The second-floor loft embraces these two additional bedrooms and full bathroom as it overlooks the downstairs.

- Recreation Room: This fun area is located on the lower level with access to the lower patio. Close by is the mechanical room and an unfinished area for storage.

Main Level Floor Plan

Upper Level Floor Plan

Basement Level Floor Plan

Copyright by designer/architect.

Plan #441016

Dimensions: 50' W x 45' D
Levels: 2
Square Footage: 1,893
Main Level Sq. Ft.: 1,087
Upper Level Sq. Ft.: 806
Bedrooms: 3
Bathrooms: 2½
Foundation: Crawl space; slab or basement for fee
Materials List Available: No
Price Category: D

It's a classic: this two-story home delivers comfort and beauty that will serve your family for years to come.

Features:

- Den: Just off the foyer and through double doors is this cozy space, which features a view of the front yard.

- Kitchen: Equipped with an island, this L-shape kitchen hosts workstations for multiple cooks. The pantry stretches the storage space.

- Master Suite: This master suite includes a bedroom with ample wall space for positioning of furniture, a walk-in closet, and a private master bath with twin sinks, a tub, and a shower.

- Bedrooms: The two additional bedrooms boast large closets and share the other full-size bathroom.

Images provided by designer/architect.

Rear Elevation

Main Level Floor Plan

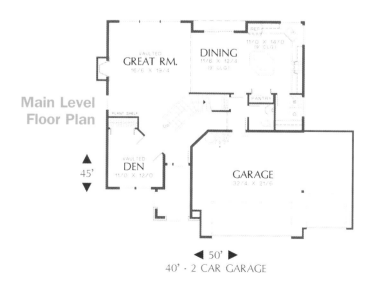

▲
45'
▼

◄ 50' ►
40' - 2 CAR GARAGE

Upper Level Floor Plan

Copyright by designer/architect.

Plan #321020

Dimensions: 58' W x 47'6" D

Levels: 1

Square Footage: 1,882

Bedrooms: 4

Bathrooms: 2

Foundation: Basement

Materials List Available: Yes

Price Category: D

Images provided by designer/architect.

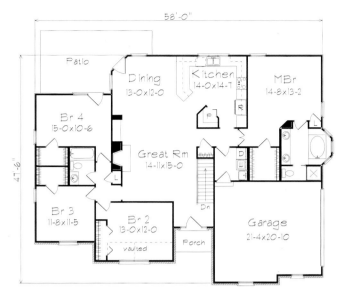

Copyright by designer/architect.

Plan #131035

Dimensions: 65'4" W x 45'10" D

Levels: 1

Square Footage: 1,892

Bedrooms: 3

Bathrooms: 2½

Foundation: Crawl space, slab, or basement

Materials List Available: Yes

Price Category: D

Images provided by designer/architect.

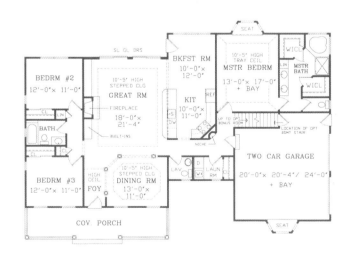

Bonus Area

Copyright by designer/architect.

Rear Elevation

Copyright by designer/architect.

Images provided by designer/architect.

Great Room

Plan #131016

Dimensions: 75' W x 45' D
Levels: 1
Square Footage: 1,902
Bedrooms: 3
Bathrooms: 2
Foundation: Crawl space, slab, or basement
Materials List Available: Yes
Price Category: E

Plan #271086

Dimensions: 56'6" W x 67'6" D
Levels: 2
Square Footage: 1,910
Main Level Sq. Ft.: 1,324
Upper Level Sq. Ft.: 586
Bedrooms: 3
Bathrooms: 2
Foundation: Crawl space, daylight basement
Materials List Available: Yes
Price Category: D

Images provided by designer/architect.

Copyright by designer/architect.

CAD FILE AVAILABLE

Plan #181063

Dimensions: 55' W x 41' D
Levels: 2
Square Footage: 2,037
Main Level Sq. Ft.: 1,347
Upper Level Sq. Ft.: 690
Bedrooms: 4
Bathrooms: 2
Foundation: Full basement
Materials List Available: Yes
Price Category: D

Images provided by designer/architect.

This home, as shown in the photograph, may differ from the actual blueprints. For more detailed information, please check the floor plans carefully.

Main Level Floor Plan

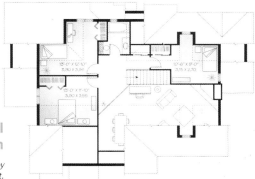

Upper Level Floor Plan

Copyright by designer/architect.

Plan #321045

Dimensions: 50' W x 36' D
Levels: 2
Square Footage: 2,058
Main Level Sq. Ft.: 1,098
Upper Level Sq. Ft.: 960
Bedrooms: 3
Bathrooms: 2½
Foundation: Crawl space, slab, or basement
Materials List Available: Yes
Price Category: D

Images provided by designer/architect.

Main Level Floor Plan

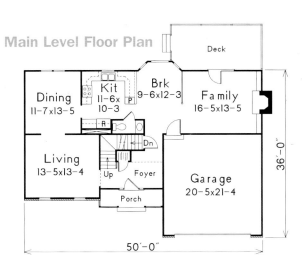

Upper Level Floor Plan

Copyright by designer/architect.

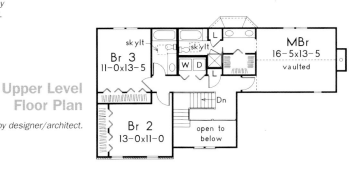

Main Level Floor Plan

Bedroom 12'x 11'
Bedroom 12'x 11'
Kitchen 12'x 13'
Living 21'x 19'2"
Dining 12'4"x 13'6"
Porch 21'x 8'

Images provided by designer/architect.

Upper Level Floor Plan

Copyright by designer/architect.

Study 10'x 10'
Sitting Area 10'9"x 10'
Master Bedroom 12'x 16'
Bedroom 12'4"x 13'
Balcony 21'x 8'

Plan #111021

Dimensions: 34' W x 44'0" D
Levels: 2
Square Footage: 2,221
Main Level Sq. Ft.: 1,307
Upper Level Sq. Ft.: 914
Bedrooms: 4
Bathrooms: 3
Foundation: Pier
Materials List Available: No
Price Category: E

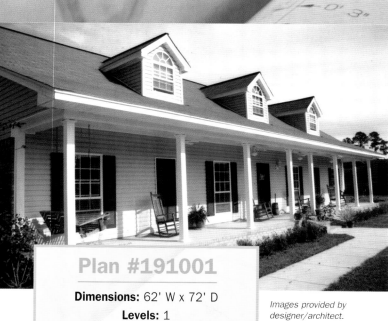

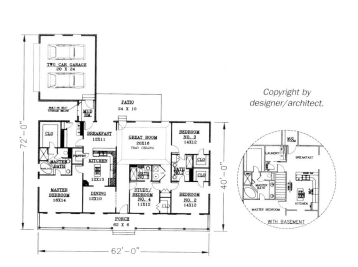

Copyright by designer/architect.

TWO CAR GARAGE 20 X 24
PATIO 24 X 10
MUD RM.
BUILT-IN SEAT STORAGE BELOW
CLO
BREAKFAST 12X11
GREAT ROOM 20X16 TRAY CEILING
BEDROOM NO. 3 14X12
CLO
MASTER BATH
PANTRY
KITCHEN 12X13
BATH RM.
BATH RM.
CLO
MASTER BEDROOM 16X14
DINING 12X10
STUDY/ BEDROOM NO. 4 11X12
BEDROOM NO. 2 14X12
PORCH 62 X 6
72'-0"
40'-0"
62'-0"

LAUNDRY
BREAKFAST
MASTER BATH
KITCHEN
MASTER BEDROOM
WITH BASEMENT

Images provided by designer/architect.

Plan #191001

Dimensions: 62' W x 72' D
Levels: 1
Square Footage: 2,156
Bedrooms: 4
Bathrooms: 3
Foundation: Crawl space, slab, or basement
Materials List Available: No
Price Category: D

Front View

Plan #441041

Dimensions: 49' W x 45' D
Levels: 2
Square Footage: 2,164
Main Level Sq. Ft.: 1,171
Upper Level Sq. Ft.: 993
Bedrooms: 3
Bathrooms: 2½
Foundation: Crawl space;
slab or basement available for fee
Material List Available: No
Price Category: D

Images provided by designer/architect.

The use of decorative brick or stone as the accent on the façade of this home adds a rich texture to an already inviting design.

CAD FILE AVAILABLE **CAD**

Features:

- Great Room: With large windows, which give a view of the backyard and allow natural light to flood the room, a vaulted ceiling, and a fireplace, this area is perfect for large gatherings.

- Kitchen: This kitchen has an abundance of cabinets and counter space as well as a pantry cabinet. The raised bar is open to the dining room.

- Dining Room: You can serve formal or informal meals here while you enjoy the view of the backyard. Step through the door, and you are on the rear porch.

- Bedrooms: All three bedrooms reside on the upper level. The master bedroom is vaulted and has a walk-in closet, and the master bath boasts a spa tub and double sinks. The family bedrooms share the full bathroom in the hallway.

- Garage: This large front-loading garage has room for tree cars or two cars and a shop area.

Rear Elevation

Upper Level Floor Plan

Main Level Floor Plan

Copyright by designer/architect.

Images provided by designer/architect.

Plan #161026

Dimensions: 67'6" W x 63'6" D
Levels: 1
Square Footage: 2,041
Bedrooms: 3
Bathrooms: 2
Foundation: Basement
Materials List Available: No
Price Category: D

You'll love the special features of this home, which has been designed for efficiency and comfort.

CAD FILE AVAILABLE

Features:

- Foyer: This raised foyer offers a view through the great room and beyond it to the covered deck.

- Great Room: Elegant windows allow versatility — decorate casually or more formally.

- Kitchen: You'll find ample counter space and cabinets in this spacious room, which adjoins the dining room and opens onto the rear yard.

- Library: Curl up on the window seat that wraps around the tower in this quiet spot.

- Laundry Room: A tub makes this large room practical for crafts as well as laundry.

- Master Suite: A vaulted ceiling gives grace to the sitting area, and the garden bath with a walk-in closet and whirlpool tub adds luxury.

Rear Elevation

Main Level Floor Plan

Basement Level Floor Plan

Copyright by designer/architect.

Plan #441034

Dimensions: 40' W x 40' D
Levels: 2
Square Footage: 2,262
Main Level Sq. Ft.: 1,302
Upper Level Sq. Ft.: 960
Bedrooms: 3
Bathrooms: 2½
Foundation: Slab
Materials List Available: No
Price Category: E

By locating the garage on the lower level, this design makes it possible to maximize use of a site that slopes to the front.

Images provided by designer/architect.

Features:

- Great Room: Two steps up lead to this two-story room, which is embellished with a built-in media center and shelves, an atrium door to a front deck, and a two-sided fireplace shared with the den.

- Kitchen: This kitchen with nook is located on the main level. It contains the walk-in pantry and winged island with cooktop. The nook makes great use of the bay-window bump out with sliding glass doors.

- Bedrooms: The master suite and two family bedrooms with shared bathroom reside on the upper level. The loft area connects the bedrooms. Look to the master bath for luxury appointments, including a walk-in closet, dual sinks, and a separate shower and spa tub.

- Garage: This large two-car garage is found, of course, on the lower level and contains extra space for a workshop.

Main Level Floor Plan

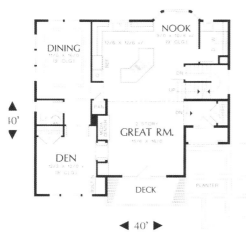

Upper Level Floor Plan

Garage Level Floor Plan

Copyright by designer/architect.

Plan #211006

Dimensions: 61' W x 77' D
Levels: 1
Square Footage: 2,177
Bedrooms: 3
Bathrooms: 2
Foundation: Crawl space or slab
Materials List Available: Yes
Price Category: D

This traditional home with a stucco exterior is distinguished by its 9-ft. ceilings throughout and its sleek, contemporary interior.

Features:

- **Living Room:** A series of arched openings that surround this room adds strong visual interest. Settle down by the fireplace on cold winter nights.

- **Dining Room:** Step up to enter this room with a raised floor that sets it apart from other areas.

- **Kitchen:** Ideal for cooking as well as casual socializing, this kitchen has a stovetop island and a breakfast bar.

- **Master Suite:** The sitting area in this suite is so big that you might want to watch TV here or make it a study. In the bath, you'll find a skylight above the angled tub with a mirror surround and well-placed plant ledge.

- **Rear Porch:** This 200-sq.-ft. covered porch gives you plenty of space for entertaining.

SMARTtip

DECK Furniture Style

Mix-and-match tabletops, frames, and legs are stylish. Combine materials such as glass, metal, wood, and mosaic tiles.

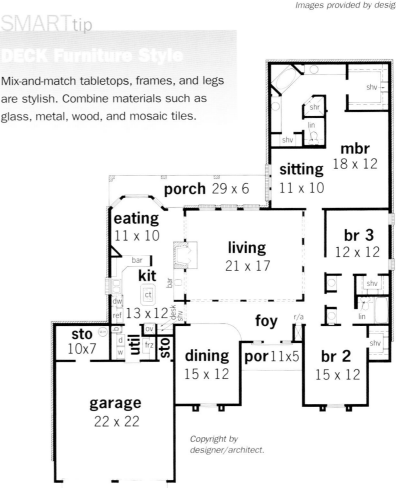

Copyright by designer/architect.

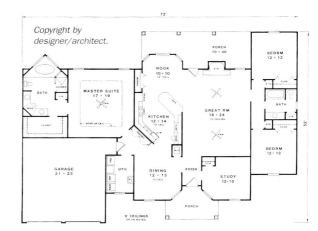

Images provided by
designer/architect.

Plan #171004

Dimensions: 72' W x 52' D
Levels: 1
Square Footage: 2,256
Bedrooms: 3
Bathrooms: 2
Foundation: Crawl space, slab
Materials List Available: Yes
Price Category: E

SMARTtip
Windows – Privacy

You can easily stencil a work of art onto a windowpane, perhaps only as a border around the edge. Choose or create a design that gives you as little or as much privacy and light control as you need. Use a ready-made stencil or a piece of openwork fabric such as lace, or mask a design onto the glass using tape and a razor knife. Then apply glass paint or frosted glass spray, referring to the instructions and guidelines that come with the product.

Plan #191034

Dimensions: 50'8" W x 38'6" D
Levels: 1
Square Footage: 1,551
Bedrooms: 3
Bathrooms: 2
Foundation: Slab
Materials List Available: No
Price Category: C

Images provided by
designer/architect.

Main Level Floor Plan

Images provided by designer/architect.

CAD FILE AVAILABLE

Upper Level Floor Plan

Copyright by designer/architect.

Plan #251014

Dimensions: 54' W x 61' D
Levels: 2
Square Footage: 2,210
Main Level Sq. Ft.: 1,670
Upper Level Sq. Ft.: 540
Bedrooms: 3
Bathrooms: 2½
Foundation: Crawl space, basement
Materials List Available: Yes
Price Category: E

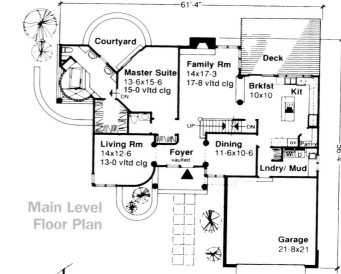

Images provided by designer/architect.

CAD FILE AVAILABLE

Main Level Floor Plan

Upper Level Floor Plan

Copyright by designer/architect.

Plan #271025

Dimensions: 61'4" W x 56'4" D
Levels: 2
Square Footage: 2,223
Main Level Sq. Ft.: 1,689
Upper Level Sq. Ft.: 534
Bedrooms: 3
Bathrooms: 2½
Foundation: Basement
Materials List Available: Yes
Price Category: E

Plan #181163

Dimensions: 38' W x 30' D
Levels: 2
Square Footage: 2,117
Main Level Sq. Ft.: 1,017
Upper Level Sq. Ft.: 384
Basement Level Sq. Ft.: 716
Bedrooms: 3
Bathrooms: 2
Foundation: Walkout basement
Materials List Available: Yes
Price Category: D

Images provided by designer/architect.

This lovely home, with its siding and stone accents, would be the perfect getaway or a full-time residence.

CAD FILE AVAILABLE

Features:

- Front Deck: On nice days, extend the size of the family room, relax, and enjoy the view on this deck.

- Main Level: This level features the master bedroom with walk-in closet and access to the full bathroom, kitchen with island/lunch counter and breakfast area, dining room, and family room with fireplace.

- Upper Level: Follow the stairs up to this upper level to find a cozy sitting area.

- Basement Level: This level features the foyer, with its coat closet and large storage, plus two bedrooms, a shower room, and a laundry area.

Main Level Floor Plan

Copyright by designer/architect.

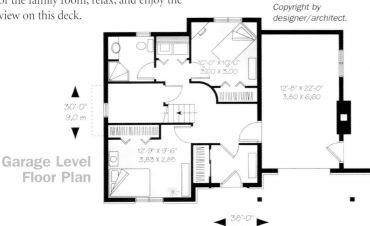

Garage Level Floor Plan

Upper Level Floor Plan

Images provided by designer/architect.

Plan #191032

Dimensions: 80'4" W x 52' D
Levels: 1
Square Footage: 2,091
Bedrooms: 3
Bathrooms: 2
Foundation: Slab
Materials List Available: No
Price Category: D

Copyright by designer/architect.

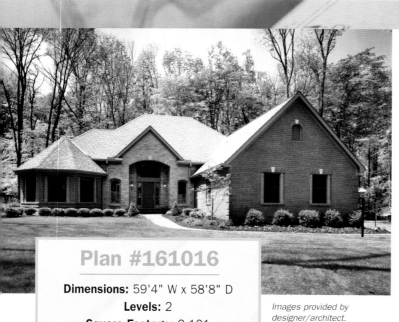

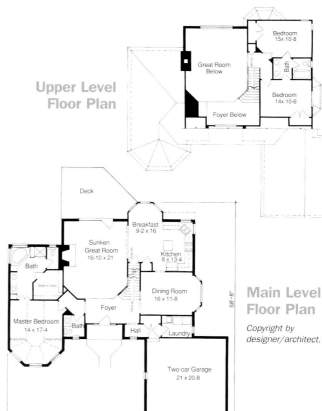

Plan #161016

Dimensions: 59'4" W x 58'8" D
Levels: 2
Square Footage: 2,101
Main Level Sq. Ft.: 1,626
Upper Level Sq. Ft.: 475
Bedrooms: 3
Bathrooms: 2½
Foundation: Basement;
crawl space option available for fee
Materials List Available: Yes
Price Category: D

Images provided by designer/architect.

Note: Home in photo reflects a modified garage entrance.

CAD FILE AVAILABLE

Upper Level Floor Plan

Main Level Floor Plan

Copyright by designer/architect.

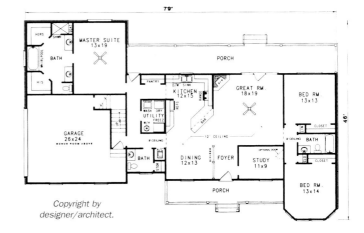

Images provided by
designer/architect.

Bonus Area

Plan #171015

Dimensions: 79' W x 52' D

Levels: 1

Square Footage: 2,089

Bedrooms: 3

Bathrooms: 2½

Foundation: Crawl space, slab

Materials List Available: Yes

Price Category: D

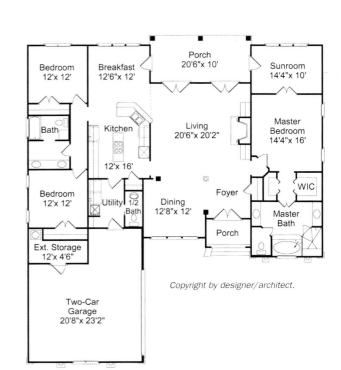

Images provided by
designer/architect.

Plan #111017

Dimensions: 61' W x 70' D

Levels: 1

Square Footage: 2,323

Bedrooms: 3

Bathrooms: 2½

Foundation: Monolithic slab

Materials List Available: No

Price Category: E

Multi-function Decks

Few decks are used for just one purpose. The trick is to plan for multiple uses before construction begins so that everyone is happy with the results. But don't go overboard. Unless you have unlimited space and budget, trying to cram too many ideas into one design will lead to disaster. You won't be happy with the results, and you will be way over budget. Start by planning for the one or two major activities that you and your family plan on enjoying on your deck, and work out from there. Here are some ideas to get you started.

The following article was reprinted from *Design Ideas For Decks* (Creative Homeowner 2003)

Here's a full-service deck design incorporating a spa, dining area, and inviting conversation pit.

Create Areas for Entertaining

The owners of this deck, right, designed a cooking and serving area for those times when they entertain. The lower counter comes in handy for serving. Improve outdoor cooking areas by including electrical service and a small refrigerator.

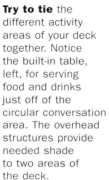

Try to tie the different activity areas of your deck together. Notice the built-in table, left, for serving food and drinks just off of the circular conversation area. The overhead structures provide needed shade to two areas of the deck.

Decks need not have complex designs to be great for entertaining. The area in front of this pool house at left is welcoming and inviting.

Plan Space for a Soothing Soak

This spa is paired, right, with a unique fountain to complete this deck. If installing a spa on a deck, be aware that you will need to drain the spa periodically and should make arrangements to remove the extra water.

The platform, left, surrounding this spa provides seating and a space for people to lie down and sunbathe. Place your spa so that equipment hatches are accessible for repairs and maintenance. It is also a good idea to keep the spa out of high-traffic areas.

Before ordering the spa, right, check with your deck builder to make sure that the structure can handle the weight of a spa filled with water and people. In many cases, you will place the spa on a concrete pad that is installed on the ground and then build the deck even with the top of the spa.

The owners, of this yard, right, used decking materials to build a walkway off of the main deck to the spa located in the corner of the yard.

Plan #191016

Dimensions: 113' W x 56' D

Levels: 1

Square Footage: 2,421

Bedrooms: 3

Bathrooms: 2

Foundation: Crawl space or slab

Material List Available: No

Price Category: E

Images provided by designer/architect.

Copyright by designer/architect.

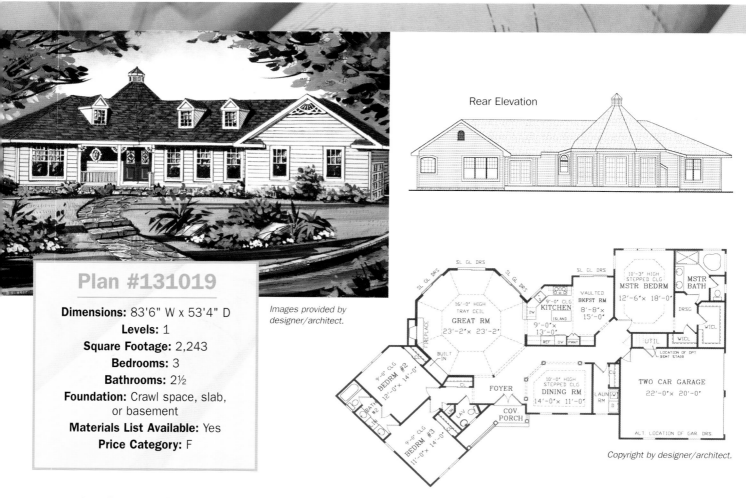

Plan #131019

Dimensions: 83'6" W x 53'4" D

Levels: 1

Square Footage: 2,243

Bedrooms: 3

Bathrooms: 2½

Foundation: Crawl space, slab, or basement

Materials List Available: Yes

Price Category: F

Images provided by designer/architect.

Rear Elevation

Copyright by designer/architect.

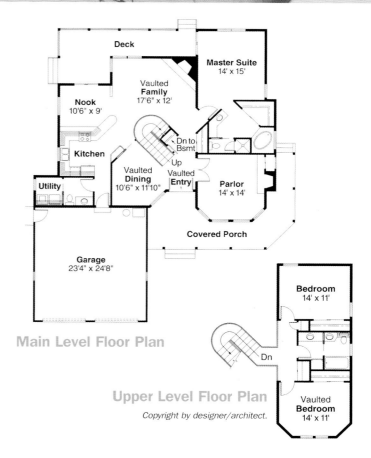

Plan #361104

Dimensions: 55' W x 64' D
Levels: 2
Square Footage: 2,094
Main Level Sq. Ft.: 1,544
Upper Level Sq. Ft.: 550
Bedrooms: 3
Bathrooms: 2½
Foundation: Crawl space
Materials List Available: No
Price Category: D

Images provided by designer/architect.

CAD FILE AVAILABLE

Main Level Floor Plan

Upper Level Floor Plan

Copyright by designer/architect.

Deck

Master Suite
14' x 15'

Nook
10'6" x 9'

Vaulted Family
17'6" x 12'

Kitchen

Dn to Bsmt

Up

Vaulted Entry

Vaulted Dining
10'6" x 11'10"

Parlor
14' x 14'

Utility

Covered Porch

Garage
23'4" x 24'8"

Bedroom
14' x 11'

Dn

Vaulted Bedroom
14' x 11'

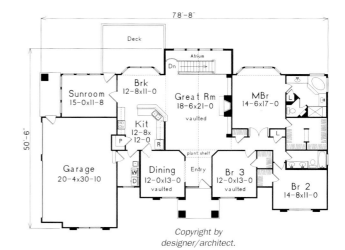

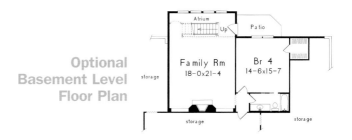

Plan #321037

Dimensions: 78'8" W x 50'6" D
Levels: 1
Square Footage: 2,397
Bedrooms: 3
Bathrooms: 2
Foundation: Basement or walkout
Materials List Available: Yes
Price Category: E

Images provided by designer/architect.

Copyright by designer/architect.

78'-8"

Deck

Atrium

Dn

Sunroom
15'-0x11-8

Brk
12-8x11-0

Great Rm
18-6x21-0
vaulted

MBr
14-6x17-0

50'-6"

Kit
12-8x 12-0

Garage
20-4x30-10

Dining
12-0x13-0
vaulted

Entry

plant shelf

Br 3
12-0x13-0
vaulted

Br 2
14-8x11-0

Optional Basement Level Floor Plan

Atrium

Up

Patio

Family Rm
18-0x21-4

Br 4
14-6x15-7

storage

storage

storage

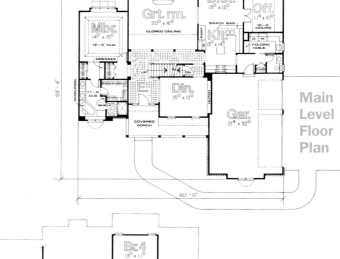

Main Level Floor Plan

Upper Level Floor Plan

Copyright by designer/architect.

Plan #121025

Dimensions: 60' W x 59'4" D
Levels: 2
Square Footage: 2,562
Main Level Sq. Ft.: 1,875
Upper Level Square Footage: 687
Bedrooms: 4
Bathrooms: 2½
Foundation: Basement
Materials List Available: Yes
Price Category: E

Images provided by designer/architect.

Copyright by designer/architect.

Plan #321009

Dimensions: 55'8" W x 46'4" D
Levels: 1
Square Footage: 2,295
Bedrooms: 3
Bathrooms: 2
Foundation: Basement
Materials List Available: Yes
Price Category: E

Images provided by designer/architect.

Rear View

Optional Basement Level Floor Plan

Plan #151530

Dimensions: 38'10" W x 70'4" D
Levels: 2
Square Footage: 2,146
Main Level Sq. Ft.: 1,654
Upper Level Sq. Ft.: 492
Bedrooms: 3
Bathrooms: 2½
Foundation: Crawl space or slab
CompleteCost List Available: Yes
Price Category: D

Images provided by designer/architect.

Gables, columns, and architectural detailing give this home a warm feeling reminiscent of your grandmother's house.

Features:

- **Foyer:** The cozy porch gently welcomes you into this column-lined foyer, which separates the formal dining room from the large great room with fireplace.

- **Kitchen:** This kitchen with breakfast room is centrally located and looks out at the lovely courtyard patio, which is perfect for entertaining.

- **Master Suite:** Your perfect hideaway awaits you in this spacious suite, with its large walk-in closet and master bath packed with amenities.

- **Upper Level:** The upstairs has two bedrooms, each with private access to the full bathroom, as well as future bonus space when desired.

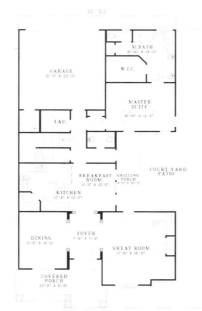

Main Level Floor Plan

Copyright by designer/architect.

Upper Level Floor Plan

Front View

Plan #441039

Dimensions: 50' W x 56' D
Levels: 2
Square Footage: 2,120
Main Level Sq. Ft.: 1,603
Upper Level Sq. Ft.: 517
Bedrooms: 3
Bathrooms: 2½
Foundation: Crawl space; slab or basement for fee
Materials List Available: No
Price Category: D

Images provided by designer/architect.

Forget the comfortable livability of this plan (if you can)-it's just plain charming.

Features:

• Great Room: This gathering area features a vaulted ceiling and a cozy fireplace. Take note of the optional built-in.

• Kitchen: This peninsula kitchen has a built-in pantry and raised bar open to the dining room and great room. The laundry room is nearby.

• Master Suite: Located on the main level, this retreat features a vaulted ceiling in the sleeping area. The master bath boasts a spa tub, dual vanities, and a separate shower and lavatory area.

• Upper Level: Upstairs you will find the two secondary bedrooms, which share the common bathroom. There is a view down into the great room.

CAD FILE AVAILABLE

Upper Level Floor Plan

Main Level Floor Plan

Copyright by designer/architect.

Rear Elevation

Plan #441049

Dimensions: 50' W x 47'6" D
Levels: 2
Square Footage: 2,124
Main Level Sq. Ft.: 1,157
Upper Level Sq. Ft.: 967
Bedrooms: 3
Bathrooms: 2½
Foundation: Crawl space; slab or basement for fee
Materials List Available: No
Price Category: D

Take a quaint cottage design, and expand naturally with a second-floor addition over the garage-the result is a comfortable home with all the charm of bungalow style.

Features:

• Foyer: Enter the home through the covered entry porch, with Arts and Crafts columns, into this foyer brightened by sidelights and a transom at the front door. The half-bathroom and coat closet make the entry area convenient.

• Great Room: This gathering area features a vaulted ceiling and a fireplace. Tall windows allow the room to be flooded with natural light, giving a warm and airy feeling.

• Kitchen: This island kitchen boasts long counters lined with cabinetry, making it a gourmet's delight to prepare meals in the area. The raised bar is open to the great room and dining room.

• Upper Level: This upper level is devoted to sleeping space. There is the vaulted master salon with private master bath and walk-in closet, plus the two family bedrooms, which that share the other full bathroom. Note the large linen closet in the upper-level hall.

Images provided by designer/architect.

Rear Elevation

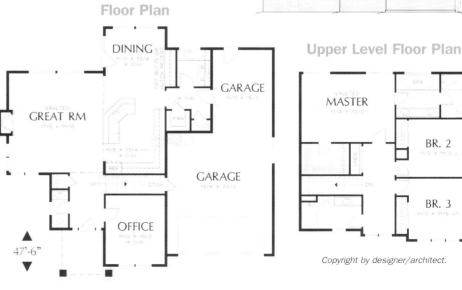

Main Level Floor Plan

Upper Level Floor Plan

Copyright by designer/architect.

Plan #181151

Dimensions: 50' W x 46' D
Levels: 2
Square Footage: 2,283
Main Level Sq. Ft.: 1,274
Second Level Sq. Ft.: 1,009
Bedrooms: 3
Bathrooms: 2½
Foundation: Basement
Materials List Available: Yes
Price Category: E

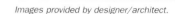

Images provided by designer/architect.

- **Kitchen:** This efficient and well-designed kitchen has double sinks and offers a separate eating area for those impromptu family meals.

- **Master Bedroom:** This master retreat has a walk-in closet and its own sumptuous bath.

- **Home Office:** Whether you work at home or just need a place for the family computer and keeping track of family finances, this home office fills the bill.

Multiple porches, stately columns, and arched multi-paned windows adorn this country home.

Features:

- Ceiling Height: 8 ft. unless otherwise noted.

- Great Room: The second-floor mezzanine overlooks this great room. With its soaring ceiling, this dramatic room is the centerpiece of a spacious and flowing design that is just as suited to entertaining as it is to family life.

- Dining Area: Guests will naturally flow into this dining area when it is time to eat. After dinner they can step directly out onto the porch to enjoy coffee and dessert when the weather is fair.

Main Level Floor Plan

21'-0" X 20'-8"
8,30 X 6,20

17'-0" X 11'-8"
5,10 X 3,50

9'-8" X 8'-8"
2,90 X 2,60

9'-0" X 10'-0"
2,70 X 3,00

10'-0" X 12'-0"
3,00 X 3,60

9'-8" X 9'-4"
2,90 X 2,80

12'-0" X 20'-8"
3,60 X 6,20

46'-0"
13,8 m

50'-0"
15,0 m

Upper Level Floor Plan

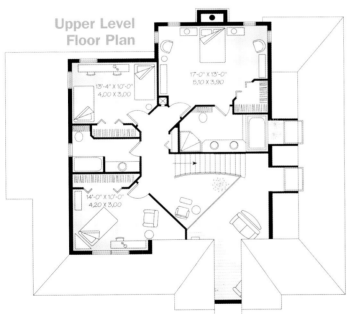

13'-4" X 10'-0"
4,00 X 3,00

17'-0" X 13'-0"
5,10 X 3,90

14'-0" X 10'-0"
4,20 X 3,00

Copyright by designer/architect.

Dining Room

Living Room

Master Bath

SMARTtip

Coping Chair Rails

If the teeth of your rasp tend to break out thin edges of the cope, try wrapping the rasp with sandpaper to make fine adjustments.

Plan #161042

Dimensions: 59'4" W x 65' D
Levels: 2
Square Footage: 2,198
Main Level Sq. Ft.: 1,706
Upper Level Sq. Ft.: 492
Bedrooms: 3
Bathrooms: 2½
Foundation: Basement
Materials List Available: Yes
Price Category: D

Images provided by designer/architect.

Upper Level Floor Plan

Main Level Floor Plan

Copyright by designer/architect

Bedroom 15' x 10'7"
Great Room Below
Bath
Bedroom 13'10" x 10'7"
Foyer Below

Breakfast 9' x 16'
Kitchen 8'4" x 15'4"
Great Room 16'10" x 21'
Dressing
walk in closet
Dining Room 13'8" x 11'8"
Master Bedroom 14' x 17'4"
Hall
Foyer
Bath
Porch
Laun.
FIRST FLOOR
Two-car Garage 21' x 29'8"
59'4"

Main Level Floor Plan

Upper Level Floor Plan

Copyright by designer/architect.

Plan #181053

Dimensions: 56' W x 53'2" D
Levels: 2
Square Footage: 2,353
Main Level Sq. Ft.: 1,606
Upper Level Sq. Ft.: 747
Bedrooms: 3
Bathrooms: 2½
Foundation: Crawl space, basement
Materials List Available: Yes
Price Category: E

Images provided by designer/architect.

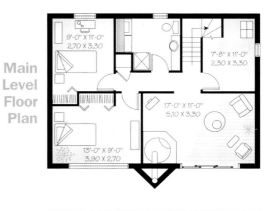

Plan #181106

Dimensions: 32'4" W x 24'4" D
Levels: 2
Square Footage: 1,574
Main Level Sq. Ft.: 787
Upper Level Sq. Ft.: 787
Bedrooms: 3
Bathrooms: 2
Foundation: Finished basement
Materials List Available: Yes
Price Category: E

Images provided by designer/architect.

CAD FILE AVAILABLE

Main Level Floor Plan

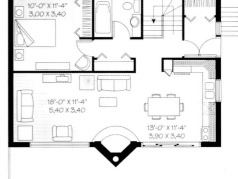

24'-4"
7,3 m

Upper Level Floor Plan

Copyright by designer/architect.

32'-4"
9,7 m

Plan #181125

Dimensions: 39'8" W x 36'8" D
Levels: 3
Square Footage: 2,392
Main Level Sq. Ft.: 967
Upper Level Sq. Ft.: 1,076
Third Level Sq. Ft.: 349
Bedrooms: 4
Bathrooms: 3½
Foundation: Pillars
Materials List Available: Yes
Price Category: E

Images provided by designer/architect.

CAD FILE AVAILABLE

Main Level Floor Plan

36'-8"
11,0 m

39'-8"
11,9 m

Top Level Floor Plan

Copyright by designer/architect.

Upper Level Floor Plan

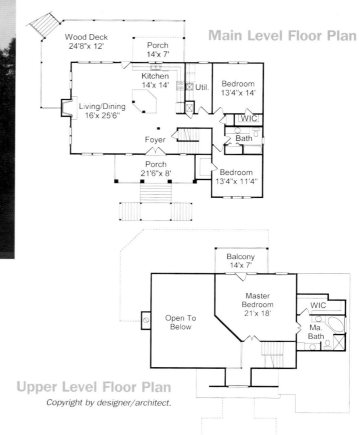

Main Level Floor Plan

Wood Deck 24'8"x 12'
Porch 14'x 7'
Kitchen 14'x 14'
Util.
Bedroom 13'4"x 14'
Living/Dining 16'x 25'6"
WIC
Bath
Foyer
Porch 21'6"x 8'
Bedroom 13'4"x 11'4"

Balcony 14'x 7'
Master Bedroom 21'x 18'
WIC
Open To Below
Ma. Bath

Upper Level Floor Plan

Copyright by designer/architect.

Plan #111049

Dimensions: 60' W x 50' D
Levels: 2
Square Footage: 2,205
Main Level Sq. Ft.: 1,552
Upper Level Sq. Ft.: 653
Bedrooms: 3
Bathrooms: 2
Foundation: Pier
Materials list available: No
Price Code: E

Images provided by designer/architect.

OPTIONAL 2 CAR GARAGE LINE
3 CAR GARAGE 24'-0" X 36'-4"
WITH 3 CAR GARAGE 90'-8"
WITH 2 CAR GARAGE 77'-0"
STORAGE
STORAGE
COVERED PORCH 2 32'-4" X 9'-6"
HOBBY ROOM 16'-0" X 12'-4"
CLOSET
BREAKFAST AREA 12'-0" X 11'-0"
GREAT ROOM 20'-0" X 16'-0"
BEDROOM 3 14'-0" X 14'-0"
LAUNDRY
MASTER BATH
KITCHEN 12'-0" X 13'-8"
BATH
HALL
CLOSET
CLOSET
54'-10"
MASTER BEDROOM 16'-0" X 16'-0"
DINING 12'-0" X 14'-0"
FOYER
BEDROOM 2 11'-0" X 14'-0"
BEDROOM 4 14'-0" X 14'-0"
COVERED PORCH 1 62'-0" X 6'-0"
62'-0"

Copyright by designer/architect.

Plan #191014

Dimensions: 62' W x 90'8" D
Levels: 1
Square Footage: 2,435
Bedrooms: 4
Bathrooms: 2
Foundation: Crawl space or slab
Material List Available: No
Price Category: E

Images provided by designer/architect.

Plan #321019

Dimensions: 70'8" W x 70' D
Levels: 1
Square Footage: 2,452
Bedrooms: 4
Bathrooms: 2½
Foundation: Basement
Materials List Available: Yes
Price Category: E

Images provided by designer/architect.

Copyright by designer/architect.

Plan #121073

Dimensions: 70' W x 52' D
Levels: 2
Square Footage: 2,579
Main Level Sq. Ft.: 1,933
Upper Level Sq. Ft.: 646
Bedrooms: 4
Bathrooms: 2½
Foundation: Basement
Materials List Available: Yes
Price Category: E

Images provided by designer/architect.

CAD FILE AVAILABLE

Main Level Floor Plan

Upper Level Floor Plan

Copyright by designer/architect.

Plan #441040

Dimensions: 45' W x 52' D
Levels: 2
Square Footage: 2,079
Main Level Sq. Ft.: 1,109
Upper Level Sq. Ft.: 970
Bedrooms: 3
Bathrooms: 2½
Foundation: Crawl space; slab or basement available for fee
Material List Available: No
Price Category: D

This two-story home truly maximizes usable space on a lot.

Features:

• Entry: This angled entry opens to a foyer that contains a half-bath, a coat closet, and the stairway to the upper level.

• Great Room: The fireplace keeps gatherings cozy in this room, with its vaulted ceiling.

• Dining Room: A covered porch off this formal area makes room for alfresco meals. The vaulted ceiling gives a feeling of openness.

• Master Suite: This suite is on the upper level, along with two family bedrooms. A vaulted master bedroom joins the deluxe bath, with its spa tub and compartmented toilet.

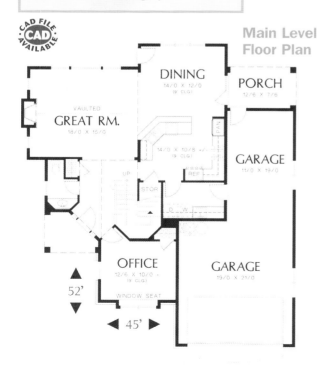

Main Level Floor Plan

Upper Level Floor Plan

Copyright by designer/architect.

Rear Elevation

Plan #441035

Dimensions: 50' W x 56' D
Levels: 2
Square Footage: 2,196
Main Level Sq. Ft.: 1,658
Upper Level Sq. Ft.: 538
Bedrooms: 4
Bathrooms: 2½
Foundation: Crawl space;
slab or basement available for fee
Materials List Available: No
Price Category: D

Features:

- Great Room: Containing a fireplace and double doors to the rear yard, this large room is further enhanced by a vaulted ceiling.

- Kitchen: This cooking center has an attached nook with corner windows overlooking the backyard.

- Master Suite: This suite is well designed with a vaulted ceiling and Palladian window. Its bath sports a spa tub.

- Bonus Space: This huge space, located on the second level, provides for a future bedroom, game room, or home office. Two dormer windows grace it.

- Garage: A service hall, with laundry alcove, opens to this garage. There is space enough here for three cars or two and a workshop.

This home's stone-and-cedar-shingle facade is delightfully complemented by French Country detailing, dormer windows, and shutters at the large arched window and its second-story sister.

Rear Elevation

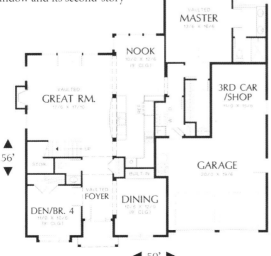

Main Level Floor Plan

Upper Level Floor Plan

Copyright by designer/architect.

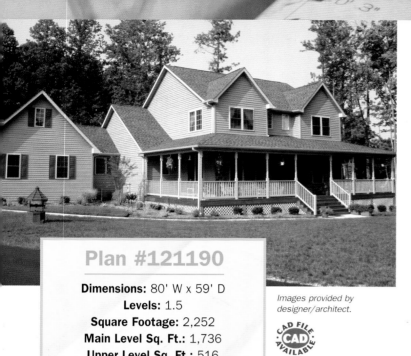

Main Level Floor Plan

Plan #121190

Dimensions: 80' W x 59' D
Levels: 1.5
Square Footage: 2,252
Main Level Sq. Ft.: 1,736
Upper Level Sq. Ft.: 516
Bedrooms: 4
Bathrooms: 3
Foundation: Slab; crawl space for fee
Materials List Available: Yes
Price Category: E

Images provided by designer/architect.

Upper Level Floor Plan

Copyright by designer/architect.

CAD FILE AVAILABLE

Front View

Plan #321041

Dimensions: 64' W x 34' D
Levels: 2
Square Footage: 2,286
Main Level Sq. Ft.: 1,283
Upper Level Sq. Ft.: 1,003
Bedrooms: 4
Bathrooms: 2½
Foundation: Crawl space, slab, or basement
Materials List Available: Yes
Price Category: E

Images provided by designer/architect.

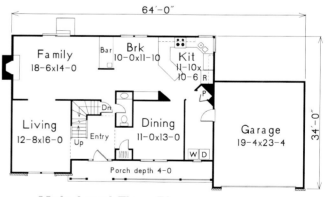

Main Level Floor Plan

Upper Level Floor Plan

Copyright by designer/architect.

Plan #151756

Dimensions: 54' W x 52' D
Levels: 1.5
Square Footage: 2,137
Main Level Sq. Ft.: 1,556
Upper Level Sq. Ft.: 581
Bedrooms: 3
Bathrooms: 2½
Foundation: Crawl space
CompleteCost List Available: Yes
Price Category: D

Images provided by designer/architect.

An 8-ft.-deep deck wraps around this spectacular log home design and gives shelter to the patios below.

Features:

• Great Room: This room includes a fireplace and French doors to the sun deck as well as a bay-window sitting area.

• Kitchen: The long eat-at bar in this kitchen can also serve as a buffet while you're entertaining in the adjoining dining room.

• Master Suite: This well-planned suite has a double vanity area and separate bath.

• Upper Level: This upper level has two large bedrooms, one with a French door entry, plus a loft area for a world of different uses.

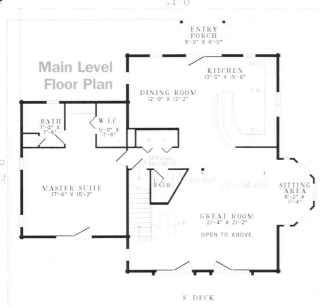

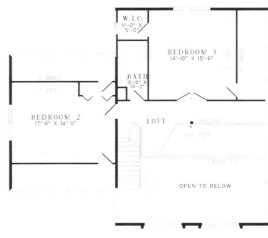

Copyright by designer/architect.

Plan #151795

Dimensions: 97'4" W x 51'10" D
Levels: 1.5
Square Footage: 2,181
Bedrooms: 3
Bathrooms: 2½
Foundation: Crawl space
CompleteCost List Available: Yes
Price Category: B

This old-fashioned yet updated log home plan has storage galore.

Features:

- **Living Room:** Upon entering the home you arrive in this room, which has a coat closet and a cozy fireplace. The dining room, with its access to the rear deck, is open to this area.

- **Kitchen:** This fully equipped kitchen will please the chef in the family with its abundance of cabinets and counter space. Just a step away is the mudroom, which houses the washer and dryer.

- **Master Suite:** Enjoy the solitude of this main-level suite and private bathroom, which has a linen closet and a window for ventilation.

- **Upper Level:** Adding to the wonderful home are the two additional bedrooms upstairs, which share the full bathroom, and the much-desired loft area for family movie time and popcorn.

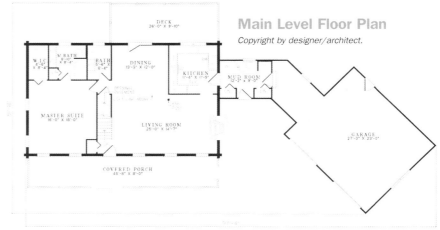

Main Level Floor Plan
Copyright by designer/architect.

Upper Level Floor Plan

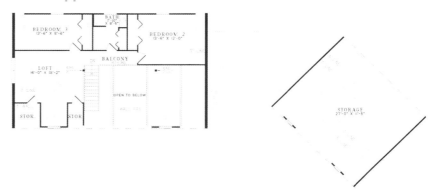

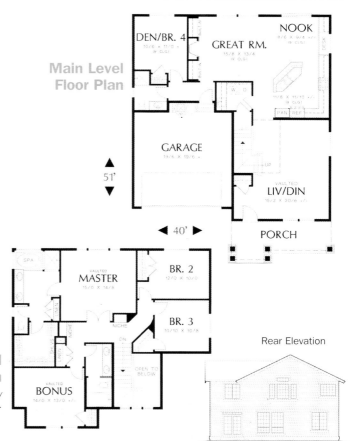

Main Level Floor Plan

DEN/BR. 4
NOOK
GREAT RM.
GARAGE
LIV/DIN
PORCH

51'

40'

Images provided by designer/architect.

CAD FILE AVAILABLE

Plan #441037

Dimensions: 40' W x 51' D
Levels: 2
Square Footage: 2,237
Main Level Sq. Ft.: 1,252
Upper Level Sq. Ft.: 985
Bedrooms: 4
Bathrooms: 3
Foundation: Crawl space; slab or basement for fee
Material List Available: No
Price Category: E

Upper Level Floor Plan

MASTER
BR. 2
BR. 3
BONUS

Copyright by designer/architect.

Rear Elevation

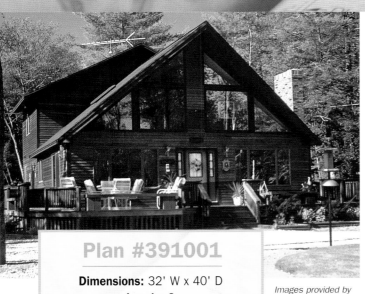

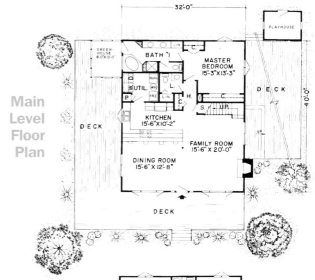

Main Level Floor Plan

32'-0"
PLAYHOUSE
GREEN-HOUSE
BATH #1
MASTER BEDROOM 15'-3"X13'-3"
DECK
UTIL
KITCHEN 15'-6"X10'-2"
FAMILY ROOM 15'-6"X 20'-0"
DECK
DINING ROOM 15'-6"X 12'-8"
DECK

Images provided by designer/architect.

Plan #391001

Dimensions: 32' W x 40' D
Levels: 2
Square Footage: 2,015
Main Level Sq. Ft.: 1,280
Upper Level Sq. Ft.: 735
Bedrooms: 3
Bathrooms: 2½
Foundation: Crawl space
Materials List Available: Yes
Price Category: D

Upper Level Floor Plan

Copyright by designer/architect.

BEDROOM #2 13'-0"X 13'-3"
BEDROOM #3 11'-4"X 13'-3"
LOFT 15'-9" X 12'-0"
OPEN TO MAIN FLOOR

Plan #141014

Dimensions: 72' W x 38' D

Levels: 2

Square Footage: 2,091

Main Level Sq. Ft.: 1,362

Upper Level Sq. Ft.: 729

Bedrooms: 3

Bathrooms: 2½

Foundation: Basement

Materials List Available: Yes

Price Category: D

Images provided by designer/architect.

The wraparound front porch and front dormers evoke an old-fashioned country home.

Features:

- Ceiling Height: 8 ft. unless otherwise noted.

- Living Room: This spacious area has an open flow to the dining room, so you can graciously usher guests when it is time to eat.

- Dining Room: This elegant dining room has a bay that opens to the sun deck.

- Kitchen: This warm and inviting kitchen looks out to the front porch. Its bayed breakfast area is perfect for informal family meals.

- Master Suite: The bedroom enjoys a view through the front porch and features a master bath with all the amenities.

- Flexible Room: A room above the two-bay garage offers plenty of space that can be used for anything from a home office to a teen suite.

- Study Room: The two second-floor bedrooms share a study that is perfect for homework.

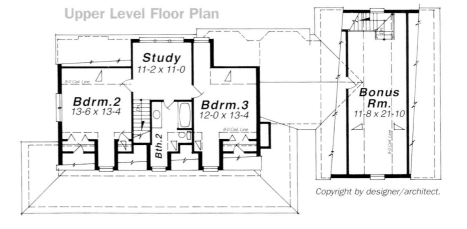

Copyright by designer/architect.

Images provided by designer/architect.

Plan #181085

Dimensions: 56'4" W x 44' D
Levels: 2
Square Footage: 2,183
Main Level Sq. Ft.: 1,232
Second Level Sq. Ft.: 951
Bedrooms: 3
Bathrooms: 2½
Foundation: Basement
Materials List Available: Yes
Price Category: D

This country home features an inviting front porch and a layout designed for modern living.

Features:

- Ceiling Height: 8 ft.

- Solarium: Sunlight streams through the windows of this solarium at the front of the house.

- Living Room: Walk through French doors, and you will enter this inviting living room. Family and friends will be drawn to the corner fireplace.

- Formal Dining Room: Usher your guests directly from the living room into this formal dining room. The kitchen is located on the

other side of the dining room for convenient service.

- Kitchen: This generously sized kitchen is a delight, it offers a center island, separate eat-in area, and access to the back deck.

- Bonus Room: This room just off the entry hall can become a family room, a bedroom, or an office.

- Master Suite: Curl up by the corner fireplace in this master retreat, with its walk-in closet and lavish bath with separate shower and tub.

Main Level Floor Plan

Upper Level Floor Plan

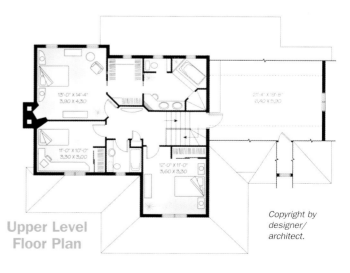

Copyright by designer/architect.

Plan #151002

Dimensions: 67' W x 66' D
Levels: 1
Square Footage: 2,444
Bedrooms: 3
Bathrooms: 2½
Foundation: Crawl space, slab, or basement
CompleteCost List Available: Yes
Price Category: E

Images provided by designer/architect.

This gracious, traditional home is designed for practicality and convenience.

Features:

- Ceiling Height: 9 ft. except as noted below.

- Great Room: This room is ideal for entertaining, thanks to its lovely fireplace and French doors that open to the covered rear porch. Built-in cabinets give convenient storage space.

- Family Room: With access to the kitchen as well as the rear porch, this room will become your family's "headquarters."

- Study: Enjoy the quiet in this room with its 12-ft. ceiling and doorway to a private patio on the side of the house.

- Dining Room: Take advantage of the 8-in. wood columns and 12-ft. ceilings to create a formal dining area.

- Kitchen: An eat-in bar is a great place to snack, and the handy computer nook allows the kids to do their homework while you cook.

- Breakfast Room: Opening from the kitchen, this area gives added space for the family to gather any time.

- Master Suite: Featuring a 10-ft. boxed ceiling, the master bedroom also has a door way that opens onto the covered rear porch. The master bathroom has a step-up whirlpool tub, separate shower, and twin vanities with a makeup area.

Copyright by designer/architect.

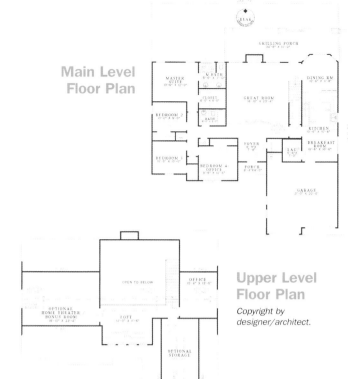

Main Level Floor Plan

Upper Level Floor Plan

Images provided by designer/architect.

Copyright by designer/architect.

Plan #151730

Dimensions: 56' W x 63'8" D
Levels: 1.5
Square Footage: 2,266
Main Level Sq. Ft.: 1,895
Upper Level Sq. Ft.: 371
Bedrooms: 4
Bathrooms: 2
Foundation: Crawl space or slab
CompleteCost List Available: Yes
Price Category: D

Images provided by designer/architect.

Main Level Floor Plan

Copyright by designer/architect.

Basement Level Floor Plan

Upper Level Floor Plan

Plan #451231

Dimensions: 53' W x 42' D
Levels: 2
Square Footage: 2,281
Main Level Sq. Ft.: 1,436
Upper Level Sq. Ft.: 845
Bedrooms: 3
Bathrooms: 2½
Foundation: Walk-out basement
Materials List Available: No
Price Category: E

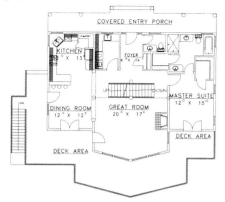

Main Level Floor Plan

Copyright by designer/architect.

Upper Level Floor Plan

Basement Level Floor Plan

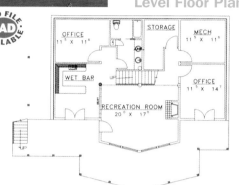

Plan #451249

Dimensions: 52' W x 54'8" D
Levels: 2
Square Footage: 2,281
Main Level Sq. Ft.: 1,436
Upper Level Sq. Ft.: 845
Bedrooms: 3
Bathrooms: 3
Foundation: Walkout basement
Materials List Available: No
Price Category: E

CAD FILE AVAILABLE

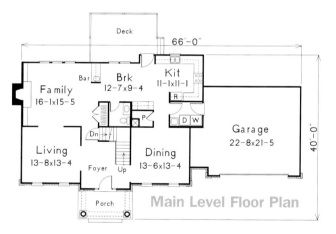

Main Level Floor Plan

Upper Level Floor Plan

Copyright by designer/architect.

Plan #321046

Dimensions: 66' W x 40' D
Levels: 2
Square Footage: 2,411
Main Level Sq. Ft.: 1,293
Upper Level Sq. Ft.: 1,118
Bedrooms: 3
Bathrooms: 2½
Foundation: Basement
Materials List Available: Yes
Price Category: E

Plan #441048

Dimensions: 48' W x 40' D
Levels: 2
Square Footage: 2,453
Main Level Sq. Ft.: 1,118
Upper Level Sq. Ft.: 1,335
Bedrooms: 4
Bathrooms: 2½
Foundation: Crawl space
Materials List Available: No
Price Category: E

Images provided by designer/architect.

The perfect-size plan and a pretty facade add up to a great home for your family. The combination of wood siding and stone complements a carriage-style garage door and cedar-shingle detailing on the outside of this home.

CAD FILE AVAILABLE

Features:

- Entry: The interior opens though this angled front entry, with the den on the left and a half-bathroom on the right. The den has a comfortable window seat for dreaming and gazing.

- Kitchen: The dining area adjoins this island kitchen, which has a roomy pantry and built-in desk.

- Master Suite: This vaulted suite features a spa bath, walk-in closet with window seat, and separate tub and shower.

- Upper Level: All bedrooms are located on this level. Bedroom 3 has a walk-in closet. The laundry area is also located here to make wash day trouble free.

Rear Elevation

Copyright by designer/architect.

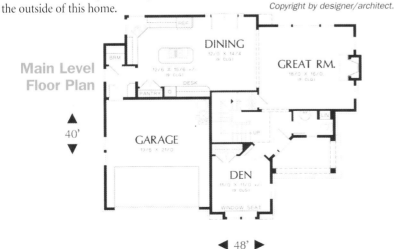

Main Level Floor Plan

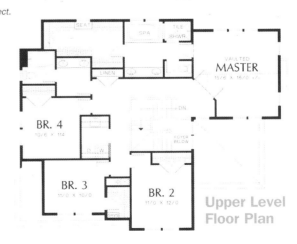

Upper Level Floor Plan

Plan #161037

Dimensions: 46' W x 59'4" D
Levels: 2
Square Footage: 2,469
Main Level Sq. Ft.: 1,462
Basement Level Sq. Ft.: 1,007
Bedrooms: 2
Bathrooms: 2½
Foundation: Walkout; basement for fee
Materials List Available: Yes
Price Category: E

Images provided by designer/architect.

A brick-and-stone facade welcomes you into this lovely home, which is designed to fit into a narrow lot.

Features:

- **Foyer:** This entrance, with vaulted ceiling, introduces the graciousness of this home.

- **Great Room:** A vaulted center ceiling creates the impression that this large great room and dining room are one space, making entertaining a natural in this area.

- **Kitchen:** Designed for efficiency with ample storage and counter space, this kitchen also allows casual dining at the counter.

- **Master Suite:** A tray ceiling sets this room off from the rest of the house, and the lavishly equipped bathroom lets you pamper yourself.

- **Lower Level:** Put extra bedrooms or a library in this finished area, and use the wet bar in a game room or recreation room.

Dining Room

Rear Elevation

Main Level Floor Plan

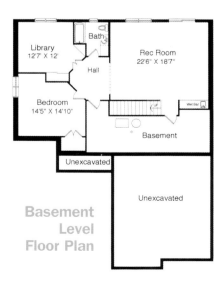

Basement Level Floor Plan

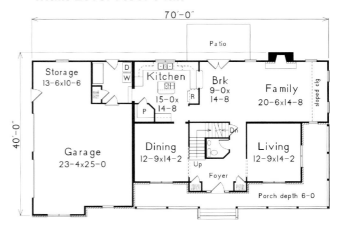

70'-0"

Patio

40'-0"

Storage
13-6x10-6

Kitchen
15-0x
14-8

Brk
9-0x
14-8

Family
20-6x14-8

sloped clg

Garage
23-4x25-0

Dining
12-9x14-2

Up

Dn

Living
12-9x14-2

Foyer

Porch depth 6-0

Images provided by designer/architect.

Plan #321055

Dimensions: 70' W x 40' D
Levels: 2
Square Footage: 2,505
Main Level Sq. Ft.: 1,436
Upper Level Sq. Ft.: 1,069
Bedrooms: 3
Bathrooms: 2½
Foundation: Basement
Materials List Available: Yes
Price Category: E

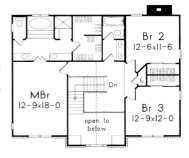

Upper Level Floor Plan

Copyright by designer/architect.

Br 2
12-6x11-6

MBr
12-9x18-0

Dn

Br 3
12-9x12-0

open to
below

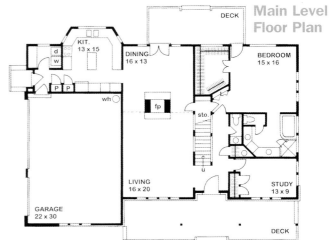

Main Level Floor Plan

DECK

KIT.
13 x 15

DINING
16 x 13

BEDROOM
15 x 16

wh

fp

sto.

LIVING
16 x 20

STUDY
13 x 9

GARAGE
22 x 30

DECK

Images provided by designer/architect.

Plan #381019

Dimensions: 62' W x 49'6" D
Levels: 2
Square Footage: 2,535
Main Level Sq. Ft.: 1,740
Upper Level Sq. Ft.: 795
Bedrooms: 3
Bathrooms: 2½
Foundation: Crawl space
Materials List Available: Yes
Price Category: E

Upper Level Floor Plan

LOFT
15 x 15

BEDROOM
17 x 20

OPEN

BEDROOM
15 x 20

OPEN

Copyright by designer/architect.

As Your Landscape Grows

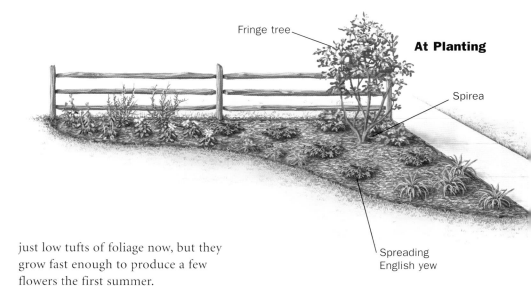

At Planting

Fringe tree

Spirea

Spreading
English yew

Landscapes change over the years. As plants grow, the overall look evolves from sparse to lush. Trees cast cool shade where the sun used to shine. Shrubs and hedges grow tall and dense enough to provide privacy. Perennials and ground covers spread to form colorful patches of foliage and flowers. Meanwhile, paths, arbors, fences, and other structures gain the patina of age.

Constant change over the years—sometimes rapid and dramatic, sometimes slow and subtle—is one of the joys of landscaping. It is also one of the challenges. Anticipating how fast plants will grow and how big they will eventually get is difficult, even for professional designers, and was a major concern in formulating the designs for this book.

To illustrate the kinds of changes to expect in a planting, these pages show one of the designs at three different "ages." Even though a new planting may look sparse at first, it will soon fill in. And because of careful spacing, the planting will look as good in ten to fifteen years as it does after three to five. It will, of course, look different, but that's part of the fun.

At Planting—Here's how the corner might appear in spring immediately after planting. The fence and mulch look conspicuously fresh, new, and unweathered. The fringe tree is only 4 to 5 ft. tall, with trunks no thicker than broomsticks. (With this or other trees, you can buy bigger specimens to start with, but they're a lot more expensive and sometimes don't perform as well in the long run.) The spireas and spreading English yews, transplanted from 2-gal. nursery containers, spread 12 to 18 in. wide. The perennials, transplanted from quart- or gallon-size containers, are

just low tufts of foliage now, but they grow fast enough to produce a few flowers the first summer.

Three to Five Years—The fringe tree has grown about 6 in. taller every year but is still quite slender. Some trees would grow faster, as much as 1 to 2 ft. a year. The spireas, like many fast-growing shrubs, have reached almost full size. From now on, they'll get thicker but not much taller. The slower-growing English yews make a series of low mounds; you still see them as individuals, not a continuous patch. Most perennials, such as the coneflowers, Shasta daisies, daylilies, and dianthus shown here, grow so crowded after a few years that they need to be divided and replanted.

Ten to Fifteen Years—The fringe tree is becoming a fine specimen, 10 to 12 ft. wide and tall. Unless you prune away enough of its lower limbs to let some sunlight in, the spireas will gradually stop blooming, get weaker, and need to be replaced with shade-tolerant shrubs such as more English yews or with shade-loving perennials and ferns. The original English yews will have formed a continuous ground cover by now and may have spread enough to limit the space available for perennials. Since the perennials get divided every few years anyway, it's no trouble to rearrange or regroup them, as shown here.

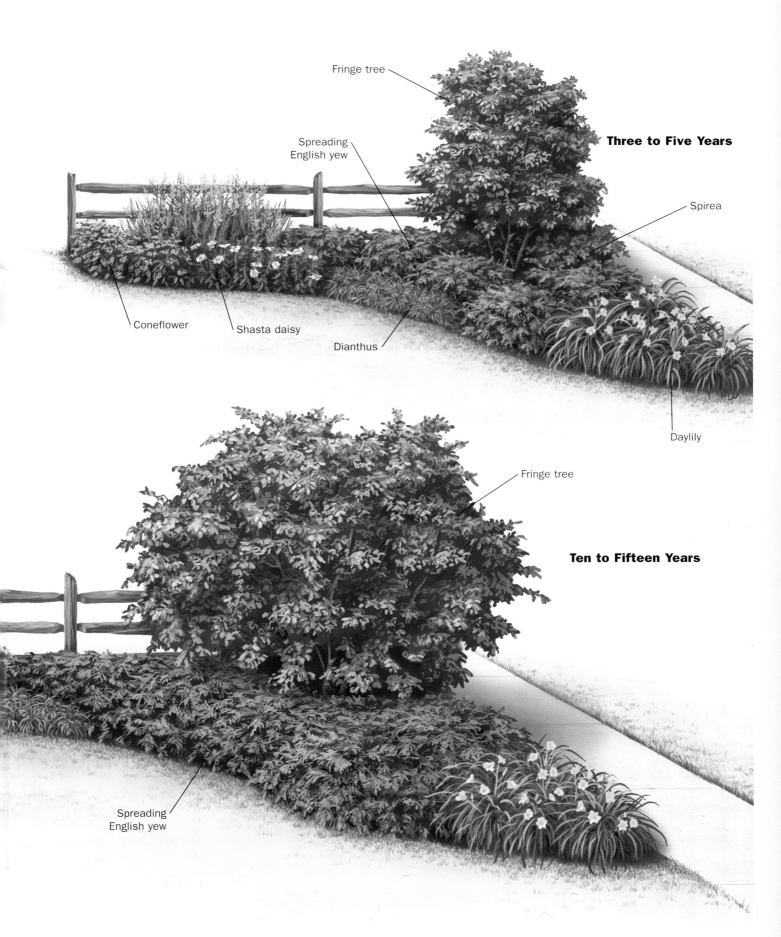

Fringe tree

Spreading
English yew

Three to Five Years

Spirea

Coneflower

Shasta daisy

Dianthus

Daylily

Fringe tree

Ten to Fifteen Years

Spreading
English yew

A Shady Hideaway
Create a fragrant oasis

A 'Emerald' American arborvitae

B Goldflame honeysuckle

M Arbor

C Sweet autumn clematis

E Oakleaf hydrangea

G Russian sage

J Bigroot geranium

H 'Sarah Bernhardt' peony

K 'Bath's Pink' dianthus

L Flagstone paving

H 'Sarah Bernhardt' peony

J Bigroot geranium

K 'Bath's Pink' dianthus

If your property is long on lawn and short on shade, a bench under a leafy arbor can provide a cool respite from the heat or the cares of the day. Tucked into a corner of the property and set among attractive shrubs, vines, and perennials, the arbor shown here is a desirable destination even when the day isn't sizzling. While all the plants are lovely to look at, the main attraction of this garden is fragrance, supplied by flowers and foliage alike.

There's something in the air in every season. Late spring is most varied, with the scented flowers of lilacs, dianthus, honeysuckle, and peonies. You'll enjoy the roses all summer and the clematis in the fall. Pluck a leaf off the geraniums, Russian sage, or catmint anytime for an olfactory pick-me-up. And if you venture to the arbor in winter, the arborvitae will supply a bracing woodland fragrance.

Plants & Projects

The arbor requires more muscle than finesse to build—recruit some sturdy assistants to help out. After the vines are established on the arbor, they'll need annual pruning, as will several of the shrubs.

D 'Miss Kim' lilac

F 'Angel Face' rose

Mowing strip

I 'Six Hills Giant' catmint

A 'Emerald' American arborvitae
Thuja occidentalis (use 2 plants)
These slender evergreen shrubs at the back of the arbor create a cozy enclosure. The glossy bright green foliage has a piney fragrance.

B Goldflame honeysuckle
Lonicera x heckrottii (use 1)
A fast-growing semievergreen vine that will cover its side of the arbor in a few years. From spring through fall, pink-and-yellow flowers produce the classic honeysuckle scent.

C Sweet autumn clematis
Clematis terniflora (use 1)
This vigorous deciduous vine climbs the other side of the arbor, offering welcome shade and small white honey-scented flowers in late summer.

D 'Miss Kim' lilac
Syringa patula (use 2)
Anchoring one end of the planting, this midsize, compact deciduous shrub has clusters of fragrant pale lilac flowers in May. Its leaves turn a pretty purple in autumn.

E Oakleaf hydrangea
Hydrangea quercifolia (use 1)
A four-season asset, this deciduous shrub offers handsome foliage with bright fall colors, long-lasting white flowers, and attractive peeling cinnamon-colored bark.

F 'Angel Face' rose
Rosa (use 1)
All summer long, a rich spicy aroma wafts from the double mauve flowers clustered on this bushy shrub.

G Russian sage
Perovskia atriplicifolia (use 3)
You get an olfactory treat when you brush up against the silvery foliage of this shrubby perennial. Tiers of blue flowers cover the upright stems for weeks in late summer.

H 'Sarah Bernhardt' peony
Paeonia (use 3)
This old-fashioned favorite produces large, fragrant, double pink flowers in late spring. Dark glossy foliage showcases flowers and is a distinct contrast to the neighboring Russian sage.

I 'Six Hills Giant' catmint
Nepeta x faassenii (use 2)
Loose spikes of purple flowers rise above the soft gray, aromatic foliage of this bushy perennial off and on through the summer.

J Bigroot geranium
Geranium macrorrhizum (use 7)
Within easy reach of the bench, this perennial's semi-evergreen leaves release a musky aroma when touched. Pinkish purple flowers bloom in June.

K 'Bath's Pink' dianthus
Dianthus (use 3)
This perennial's sweetly fragrant, clear pink flowers rise above a mat of slender evergreen leaves in late spring.

L Flagstone paving
Flagstones lead to the bench and edge the beds as a mowing strip.

M Arbor
With a little help, you can build this simple design in a weekend or two.

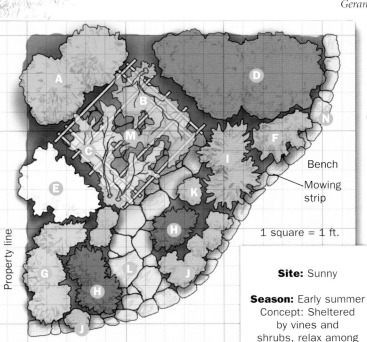

Property line

Bench

Mowing strip

1 square = 1 ft.

Site: Sunny

Season: Early summer
Concept: Sheltered by vines and shrubs, relax among a potpourri of fragrant plants.

Note: All plants are appropriate for USDA Hardiness *Zones 5, 6, and 7.*

Under the Old Shade Tree

Create a cozy garden in a cool spot

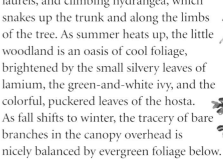

This planting is designed to help home-owners blessed with a large shade tree make the most of their good fortune. A bench is provided, of course. There's no better spot to rest on a hot summer day. But why stop there? The tree's high wide canopy provides an ideal setting for a planting of understory shrubs, perennials, and ferns. The result is a woodland garden that warrants a visit any day of the year.

The planting roughly coincides with the pool of shade cast by the tree. A selection of medium to large deciduous and ever-green shrubs extends about halfway around the perimeter. You can position these to provide privacy, screen a view from the bench, or block early-morning or late-afternoon sun. Smaller plants (ferns, hostas, and perennial ground covers) are placed nearer the path and bench, where they can be appreciated at close range.

The planting blooms for weeks in spring and early summer. White flowers cover the buckeyes, Korean spice viburnums, cherry laurels, and climbing hydrangea, which snakes up the trunk and along the limbs of the tree. As summer heats up, the little woodland is an oasis of cool foliage, brightened by the small silvery leaves of lamium, the green-and-white ivy, and the colorful, puckered leaves of the hosta. As fall shifts to winter, the tracery of bare branches in the canopy overhead is nicely balanced by evergreen foliage below.

Site: Shady

Season: Summer
Concept: Woodland understory plants make lovely shade garden for sitting or strolling.

Plants & Projects

For best results, thin the tree canopy, if necessary, to produce dappled rather than deep shade. Also remove limbs to a height of 8 ft. or more to provide headroom. The tree's roots compete for moisture with anything planted nearby. The plants here do well in these drier conditions, but judicious supplemental watering and moisture-conserving mulch will improve their performance.

A **Climbing hydrangea**
Hydrangea petiolaris (use 1 plant)
A vining relative of the common shrub, it has clusters of lacy white flowers in June, glossy dark green leaves, and a stout trunk with flaky cinnamon-colored bark.

B **Bottlebrush buckeye**
Aesculus parviflora (use 2)
A sizable deciduous shrub that forms a mound of large, medium green leaves. Slender spikes of white flowers stand like birthday candles above the foliage in early summer.

C **Korean spice viburnum**
Viburnum carlesii (use 4)
These deciduous shrubs frame the entrance to the path with dense green foliage from spring through fall. In May, pretty pink buds open into clusters of fragrant white flowers.

D **'Otto Luyken' cherry laurel**
Prunus laurocerasus (use 6)

These beautiful shrubs form spreading mounds of glossy evergreen foliage. Its sweet-scented small white flowers brighten the shady scene in late spring.

E **Mountain laurel**
Kalmia latifolia (use 4)
Large evergreen shrubs with shiny oblong leaves make a hand-some screen. Striking clusters of cuplike white or pink flowers appear in late spring.

F **Dwarf Hinoki cypress**
Chamaecyparis obtusa
'Nana Gracilis' (use 2)
The dense curly foliage of these small slow-growing evergreen trees screens the bench.

G **'Frances Williams' hosta**
Hosta (use 18)
A popular perennial valued for its stately size and exotic foliage. Large, heavily textured leaves have a blue-green center and irregular green-gold edges. White flowers in mid- to late summer.

H **Japanese autumn fern**
Dryopteris erythrosora (use 19)
A clump-forming fern. New fronds are a coppery color, turning glossy dark green by midsummer and lasting partway into the winter.

I **Lenten rose**
Helleborus orientalis (use 32)
A long-lived perennial with very early, very lovely nodding flowers

in shades of white to dusky pink to rose. Leaves are evergreen.

J **'Beacon Silver' lamium**
Lamium maculatum (use 25)
This perennial ground cover brightens the path with green-edged silver leaves and pink flowers in early summer. The foliage is evergreen where winters are mild.

K **European wild ginger**
Asarum europaeum (use 24)
A splendid ground cover for shade, this perennial spreads slowly to form a glossy evergreen carpet of elegant heart-shaped leaves.

L **'Glacier' English ivy**
Hedera helix (use 40)
A hardy, ground-covering vine. Pale evergreen leaves are mottled with white and gray in summer and turn pinkish in winter.

M **Path**
A 4-in. layer of wood chips is serviceable and attractive in this situation.

Korean spice viburnum **C**

'Glacier' **L**
English ivy

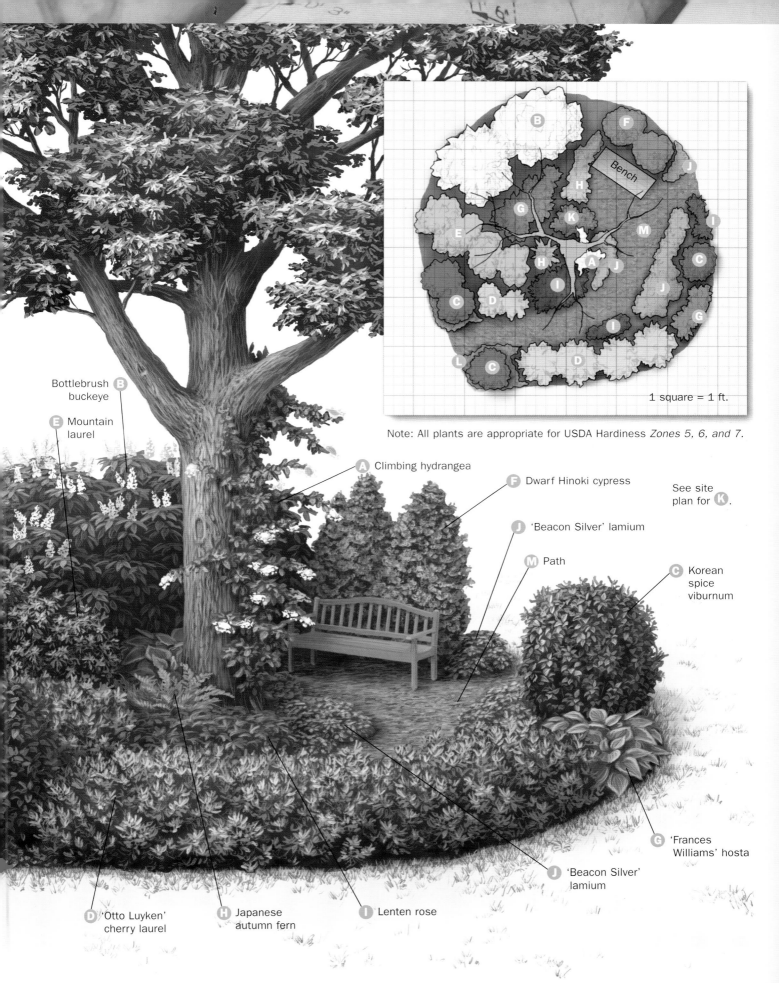

B Bottlebrush buckeye

E Mountain laurel

Bench

1 square = 1 ft.

Note: All plants are appropriate for USDA Hardiness *Zones 5, 6, and 7.*

A Climbing hydrangea

F Dwarf Hinoki cypress

J 'Beacon Silver' lamium

M Path

See site plan for K.

C Korean spice viburnum

G 'Frances Williams' hosta

J 'Beacon Silver' lamium

I Lenten rose

D 'Otto Luyken' cherry laurel

H Japanese autumn fern

A Woodland Link

Create a shrub border for nearby woods

'Arnold Promise' witch hazel **B**

'Sibirica' Siberian dogwood **E**

Oakleaf hydrangea **G**

The woodlands and forests of the Mid-Atlantic are treasured by all who live in the region. Many subdivisions, both new and old, incorporate woodland areas, with homes bordering landscapes of stately trees and large shrubs. (In some older neighborhoods, mature trees on adjacent lots create almost the same woodland feeling.)

The planting shown here integrates a domestic landscape with a woodland at its edge. It makes a pleasant transition between the open area of lawn, with its sunny entertainments, and the cool, secluded woods beyond. The design takes inspiration from the border of small trees and shrubs nature provides at the sunny edge of a wood, and it should have the same attraction to birds and wildlife.

Small deciduous native trees, growing to about 20 ft., mingle with shrubs varying in height from 8 ft. to 18 in., imitating natural layered growth. A curving path disappears between tall shrubs into the adjacent woods, adding a hint of mystery.

Whether viewed from the path or the distant house, the planting is attractive all year. From late winter to early summer, there is a procession of flowers in whites, yellows, and magenta, some very fragrant. Handsome foliage and a variety of berries carry through summer into fall, when this largely deciduous planting blazes with color. In winter, a few well-placed evergreens complement patterns of bare branches, including the eye-catching red stems of the dogwood.

Plants & Projects

Trees and large shrubs give the planting a solid structure. Three witch hazels form a small copse at one corner, balanced by two large viburnums at the other. Winterberry holly and the buckeye are large presences at the back of the planting, and the serviceberry anchors a casual arrangement of smaller shrubs extending to the lawn. Once the plants are established, in a year or so, just devote a weekend each spring and fall to mulching and basic pruning, then sit back and enjoy.

A **Serviceberry**
Amelanchier x grandiflora (use 1 plant)
This small deciduous multi-trunked tree earns its place in front with white flowers in April, purple fruits in July, and pretty fall color.

B **'Arnold Promise' witch hazel**
Hamamelis x intermedia (use 3)
In early spring these deciduous multitrunked trees repay a stroll to their corner of the planting with sweet-scented yellow flowers. Leaves turn gold in fall.

C **Bottlebrush buckeye**
Aesculus parviflora (use 1)
This forms a mounded thicket with attractive large leaves, brushy white flowers in early summer, and leathery seedpods. A wide-spreading shrub, it may eventually crowd out nearby azaleas.

D **'Shasta' double-file viburnum**
Viburnum plicatum var. *tomentosum* (use 3)
A stately deciduous shrub with tiers of horizontal branches whose rich green leaves turn purple in fall. Clusters of lovely white flowers in spring are followed by bright red fruits.

E **'Sibirica' Siberian dogwood**
Cornus alba (use 6)
Bright red stems in winter, white flowers in spring, bluish berries in summer, and crimson foliage in fall—this deciduous shrub has it all.

F **'Sparkleberry' winterberry holly**
Ilex verticillata (use 5)
An upright or vase-shaped deciduous shrub. Thousands of tiny bright red berries line the twigs in fall and winter and make a sparkling display until the birds eat them all.

G **Oakleaf hydrangea**
Hydrangea quercifolia (use 1)
A deciduous shrub that is striking in every season: showy white flowers in spring, handsome leaves with good fall color, and attractive flaking bark for the winter months.

H **'PJM' rhododendron**
Rhododendron (use 6)
A narrow, upright evergreen shrub with stunning clusters of magenta flowers in early spring. Small leathery leaves are green in summer, turning maroon in winter.

I **'Gold Dust' azalea**
Rhododendron: Deciduous azaleas (use 5)
A deciduous shrub with striking clusters of fragrant yellow flowers in spring. Fall foliage is also colorful.

J **Pink evergreen azalea**
Rhododendron (use 3)
An attractive small shrub with year-round presence, perfect for edging the path. Try 'Pink Gumpo', which has clusters of large pink flowers in spring.

K **Korean beautyberry**
Callicarpa dichotoma (use 7)

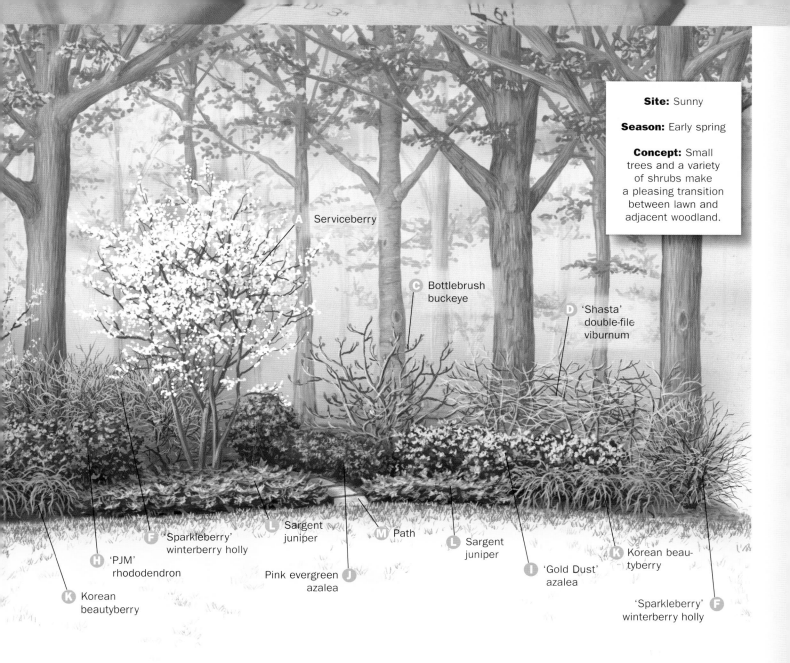

Site: Sunny

Season: Early spring

Concept: Small trees and a variety of shrubs make a pleasing transition between lawn and adjacent woodland.

A Serviceberry

C Bottlebrush buckeye

D 'Shasta' double-file viburnum

F 'Sparkleberry' winterberry holly

H 'PJM' rhododendron

K Korean beautyberry

L Sargent juniper

J Pink evergreen azalea

M Path

L Sargent juniper

I 'Gold Dust' azalea

K Korean beautyberry

F 'Sparkleberry' winterberry holly

Spectacular lilac-colored berries line the arching branches of this deciduous shrub in autumn. Foliage blends into the background the rest of the season.

L Sargent juniper
Juniperus chinensis var. *sargentii* (use 7)
This low-growing evergreen shrub forms a fine-textured green carpet edging the lawn and path at the foot of the serviceberry.

M Path
Flagstone steppingstones, 18 in. square, curve through the planting.

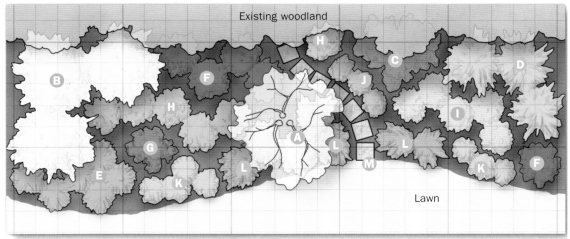

Existing woodland

Lawn

Note: All plants are appropriate for USDA Hardiness *Zones 5, 6, and 7.*

Plan #131027

Dimensions: 62'4" W x 53'6" D
Levels: 2
Square Footage: 2,567
Main Level Sq. Ft.: 2,017
Upper Level Sq. Ft.: 550
Bedrooms: 4
Bathrooms: 3
Foundation: Crawl space, slab, or basement
Materials List Available: Yes
Price Category: F

This home, as shown in the photograph, may differ from the actual blueprints. For more detailed information, please check the floor plans carefully.

The features of this home are so good that you may have trouble imagining all of them at once.

Features:

- **Great Room:** Imagine a stepped ceiling, corner fireplace, built-media center, and wall of windows with a glass door to the backyard—in one room.

- **Dining Room:** A stepped ceiling and server with a sink add to the elegance of this formal room.

- **Breakfast Room:** Eat at the bar this room shares with the island kitchen, and admire the 12-ft. cathedral ceiling and bayed group of 8- and 9-ft. windows. Or go through the sliding glass door to the covered side porch.

- **Master Suite:** The bedroom has a tray ceiling and cozy sitting area, and a whirlpool tub, shower, and walk-in closet are in the skylighted bath.

- **Optional Study:** The private bath in bedroom 2 makes it ideal for a study or home office.

- **Bonus Room:** Enjoy the extra 300 sq. ft.

Main Level Floor Plan

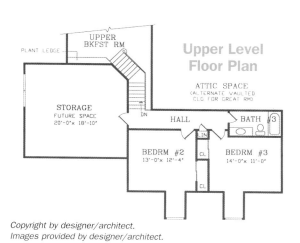

Upper Level Floor Plan

Copyright by designer/architect.
Images provided by designer/architect.

Images provided by designer/architect.

Plan #441042

Dimensions: 52' W x 45' D
Levels: 2
Square Footage: 2,538
Main Level Sq. Ft.: 1,342
Upper Level Sq. Ft.: 1,196
Bedrooms: 3
Bathrooms: 2½
Foundation: Crawl space;
slab or basement available for fee
Materials List Available: No
Price Category: E

It's never too late to have a happy childhood—or the exact home you want.

Features:

- Foyer: This entry soars up two stories with a view to the open hallway above.

- Family Room: This large informal gathering area has large windows with a view to the backyard. It also has a two-sided fireplace, which it shares with the den.

- Kitchen: This fully equipped island kitchen has a built-in pantry and desk. The nook and family room are open to it.

- Master Suite: This private retreat includes a sitting area in the master bedroom that

provides ample space for a comfortable lounge in front of its fireplace. The master bath features a compartmentalized lavatory, spa tub, large shower, and his and her vanities.

- Bedrooms: The two additional bedrooms are located on the upper level with the master suite. Both rooms have large closets and share a common bathroom.

Rear Elevation

Main Level Floor Plan

◀ 52' ▶

Upper Level Floor Plan

Copyright by designer/architect.

Main Level Floor Plan

Plan #181081

Dimensions: 58' W x 33' D
Levels: 2
Square Footage: 2,350
Main Level Sq. Ft.: 1,107
Second Level Sq. Ft.: 1,243
Bedrooms: 3
Bathrooms: 2½
Foundation: Basement
Materials List Available: Yes
Price Category: E

Images provided by designer/architect.

CAD FILE AVAILABLE

Upper Level Floor Plan

Copyright by designer/architect.

Plan #391058

Dimensions: 44' W x 58'4" D
Levels: 1.5
Square Footage: 2,477
Main Level Sq. Ft.: 1,448
Basement Level Sq. Ft.: 1,029
Bedrooms: 4
Bathrooms: 2½
Foundation: Slab
Materials List Available: Yes
Price Category: E

Images provided by designer/architect.

Main Level Floor Plan

Basement Level Floor Plan

Copyright by designer/architect.

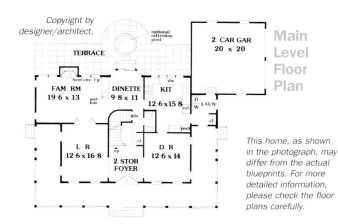

Copyright by designer/architect.

Main Level Floor Plan

TERRACE

2 CAR GAR
20 x 20

FAM. RM
19·6 x 13

DINETTE
9·8 x 11

KIT
12·6 x 15·8

LAUN

L. R
12·6 x 16·8

2 STOR
FOYER

D. R
12·6 x 14

This home, as shown in the photograph, may differ from the actual blueprints. For more detailed information, please check the floor plans carefully.

Plan #131051

Dimensions: 64'4" W x 53'4" D
Levels: 2
Square Footage: 2,431
Main Level Sq. Ft.: 1,293
Upper Level Sq. Ft.: 1,138
Bedrooms: 4
Bathrooms: 2½
Foundation: Crawl space, slab, or basement
Materials List Available: Yes
Price Category: F

Images provided by designer/architect.

Optional 3rd Level Floor Plan

ALL PURPOSE RM

Upper Level Floor Plan

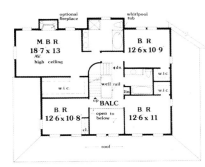

M. B. R
18·7 x 13
AV. high ceiling

B. R
12·6 x 10·9

B. R
12·6 x 10·8

BALC
open to below

B. R
12·6 x 11

Main Level Floor Plan

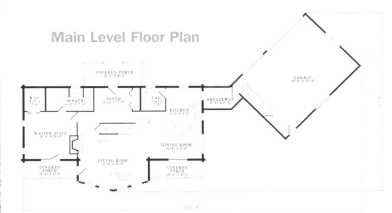

COVERED PORCH

GARAGE

M. BATH

FOYER

LAU.

KITCHEN

BREEZEWAY

MASTER SUITE

DINING ROOM

COVERED PORCH

LIVING ROOM

COVERED PORCH

Plan #151789

Dimensions: 106'4" W x 57'8" D
Levels: 1.5
Square Footage: 2,521
Main Level Sq. Ft.: 1,645
Upper Level Sq. Ft.: 876
Bedrooms: 3
Bathrooms: 2
Foundation: Crawl space
CompleteCost List Available: Yes
Price Category: E

Images provided by designer/architect.

CAD FILE AVAILABLE

Upper Level Floor Plan
Copyright by designer/architect.

ATTIC SPACE

BATH

ATTIC SPACE

OPTIONAL BONUS

BEDROOM 3

LOFT

BEDROOM 2

ATTIC SPACE

ATTIC SPACE

ATTIC SPACE

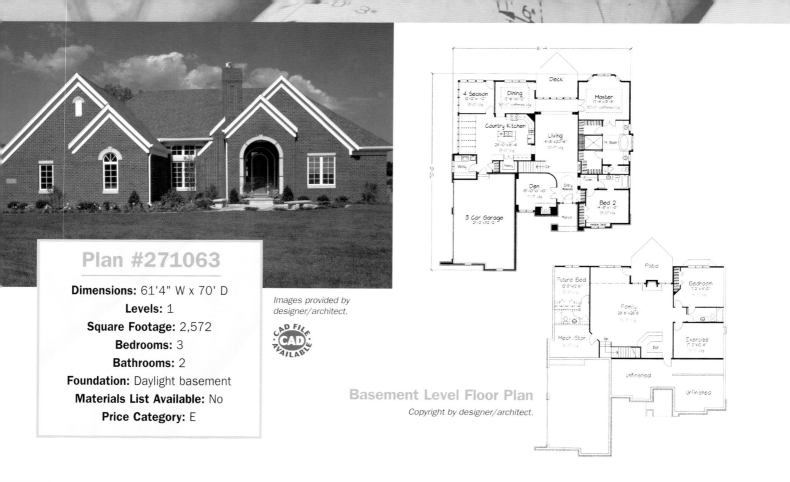

Plan #271063

Dimensions: 61'4" W x 70' D
Levels: 1
Square Footage: 2,572
Bedrooms: 3
Bathrooms: 2
Foundation: Daylight basement
Materials List Available: No
Price Category: E

Images provided by designer/architect.

CAD FILE AVAILABLE

Basement Level Floor Plan

Copyright by designer/architect.

Plan #131046

Dimensions: 68' W x 57'6" D
Levels: 2
Square Footage: 2,245
Main Level Sq. Ft.: 1,720
Upper Level Sq. Ft.: 525
Bedrooms: 3
Bathrooms: 2½
Foundation: Crawl space, slab, or basement
Materials List Available: Yes
Price Category: F

Images provided by designer/architect.

Main Level Floor Plan

Upper Level Floor Plan

Copyright by designer/architect.

Plan #151752

Dimensions: 58' W x 40' D
Levels: 1.5
Square Footage: 2,402
Main Level Sq. Ft.: 1,584
Upper Level Sq. Ft.: 818
Bedrooms: 3
Bathrooms: 2½
Foundation: Crawl space
CompleteCost List Available: Yes
Price Category: E

Images provided by designer/architect.

CAD FILE AVAILABLE

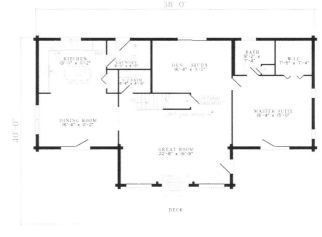

Main Level Floor Plan

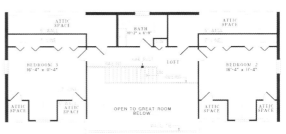

Upper Level Floor Plan

Copyright by designer/architect.

Plan #151754

Dimensions: 64' W x 51' D
Levels: 2
Square Footage: 2,412
Main Level Sq. Ft.: 1,892
Upper Level Sq. Ft.: 520
Bedrooms: 3
Bathrooms: 2½
Foundation: Crawl space
CompleteCost List Available: Yes
Price Category: E

Images provided by designer/architect.

CAD FILE AVAILABLE

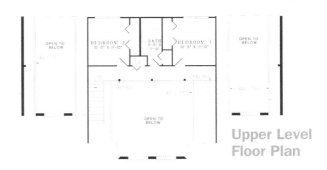

Upper Level Floor Plan

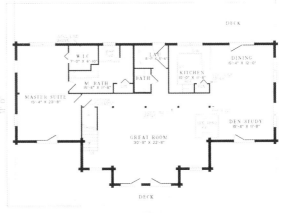

Main Level Floor Plan

Copyright by designer/architect

Plan #131032

Dimensions: 69'2" W x 46' D
Levels: 2
Square Footage: 2,455
Main Level Sq. Ft.: 1,499
Upper Level Sq. Ft.: 956
Bedrooms: 4
Bathrooms: 3
Foundation: Crawl space, slab, or basement
Materials List Available: Yes
Price Category: F

If you love Victorian styling, you'll be charmed by the ornate, rounded front porch and the two-story bay that distinguish this home.

Images provided by designer/architect.

Features:

• Living Room: You'll love the 13-ft. ceiling in this room, as well as the panoramic view it gives of the front porch and yard.

• Kitchen: Sunlight streams into this room, where an angled island with a cooktop eases both prepping and cooking.

• Breakfast Room: This room shares an eating bar with the kitchen, making it easy for the family to congregate while the family chef is cooking.

• Guest Room: Use this lovely room on the first level as a home office or study if you wish.

• Master Suite: The dramatic bayed sitting area with a high ceiling has an octagonal shape that you'll adore, and the amenities in the private bath will soothe you at the end of a busy day.

Rear View

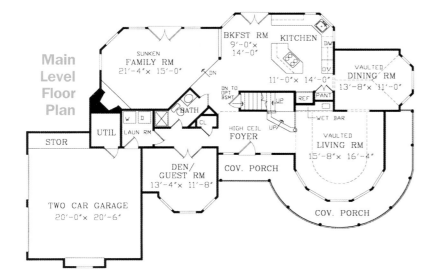

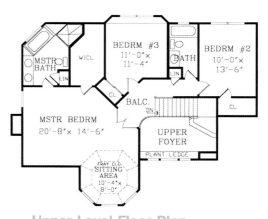

Upper Level Floor Plan
Copyright by designer/architect.

Plan #441038

Dimensions: 59' W x 51'6" D
Levels: 2
Square Footage: 2,518
Main Level Sq. Ft.: 1,464
Upper Level Sq. Ft.: 1,054
Bedrooms: 4
Bathrooms: 3
Foundation: Crawl space;
slab or basement available for fee
Materials List Available: No
Price Category: E

Images provided by designer/architect.

Features:

- Kitchen: This kitchen contains gourmet appointments with an island countertop, a large pantry, and a work desk built in.
- Dining Room: This formal room connects directly to the kitchen for convenience.
- Master Suite: This suite features a fine bath with a spa tub and separate shower.

- Bedrooms: A bedroom (or make it a home office) is tucked away behind the two-car garage and has the use of a full bathroom across the hall. Three additional bedrooms are found on the upper level, along with a large bonus space that could be developed later into bedroom 5.

Victorians are such a cherished style; it's impossible not to admire them. This one begins with all the classic details and adds a most up-to-date floor plan.

CAD FILE AVAILABLE

Main Level
Floor Plan

Upper Level
Floor Plan

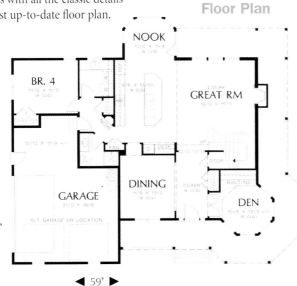

Copyright by designer/architect.

Plan #131030

Dimensions: 51' W x 41'10" D
Levels: 2
Square Footage: 2,470
Main Level Sq. Ft.: 1,290
Upper Level Sq. Ft.: 1,180
Bedrooms: 4
Bathrooms: 2½
Foundation: Crawl space, slab, basement, or walkout basement
Materials List Available: Yes
Price Category: F

This home, as shown in the photograph, may differ from the actual blueprints. For more detailed information, please check the floor plans carefully.

If high ceilings and spacious rooms make you happy, you'll love this gorgeous home.

Features:

• **Family Room:** An 18-ft. vaulted ceiling that's open to the balcony above, a corner fireplace, and a wall of windows make this room feel special.

• **Dining Room:** This formal room, which flows into the living room, also opens to the front porch and optional backyard deck.

• **Kitchen:** A bright breakfast room joins with this kitchen and opens to the backyard deck.

• **Master Suite:** You'll smile when you see the 11-ft. vaulted ceiling, stunning arched window, and two walk-in closets in the bedroom. A skylight lets natural light into the private bath, with its spa tub, separate shower, and dual-sink vanity.

• **Bedrooms:** To reach these three charming bedrooms, you'll admire the view into the family room below as you walk along the balcony hall.

Main Level Floor Plan

Copyright by designer/architect.

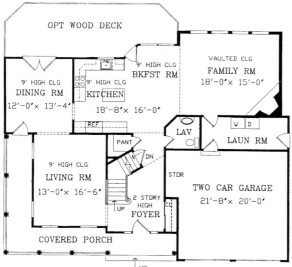

Upper Level Floor Plan

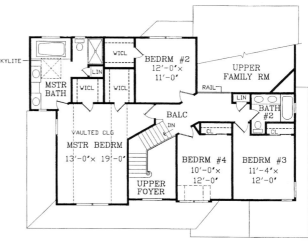

Images provided by designer/architect.

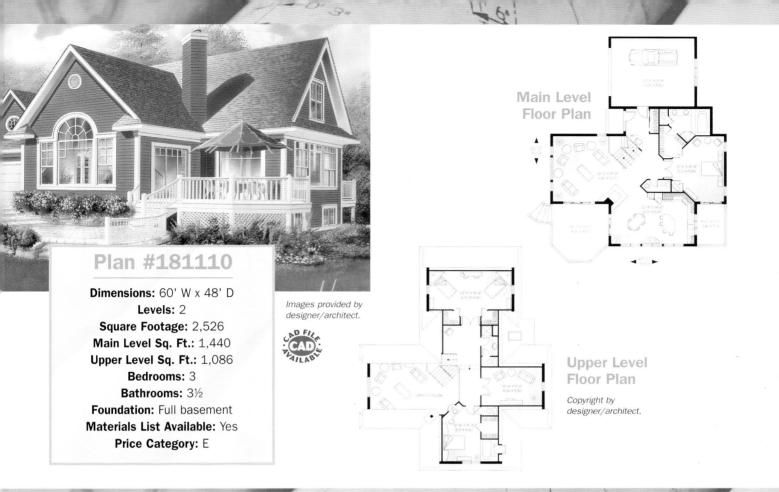

Plan #181110

Dimensions: 60' W x 48' D
Levels: 2
Square Footage: 2,526
Main Level Sq. Ft.: 1,440
Upper Level Sq. Ft.: 1,086
Bedrooms: 3
Bathrooms: 3½
Foundation: Full basement
Materials List Available: Yes
Price Category: E

Images provided by designer/architect.

CAD FILE AVAILABLE

Main Level Floor Plan

Upper Level Floor Plan

Copyright by designer/architect.

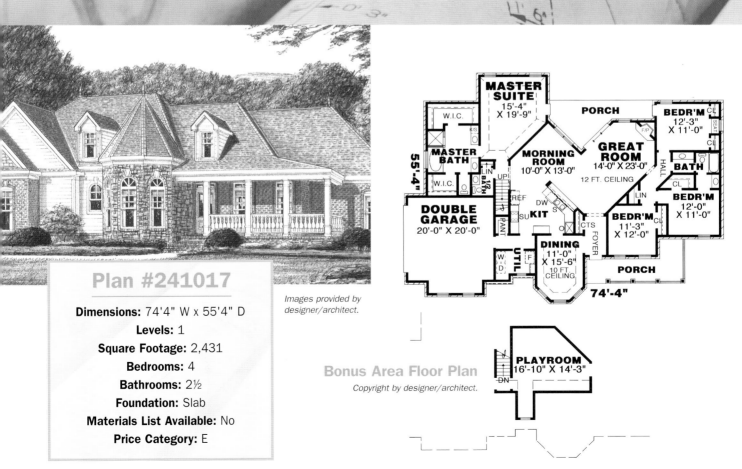

Plan #241017

Dimensions: 74'4" W x 55'4" D
Levels: 1
Square Footage: 2,431
Bedrooms: 4
Bathrooms: 2½
Foundation: Slab
Materials List Available: No
Price Category: E

Images provided by designer/architect.

MASTER SUITE
15'-4" X 19'-9"

W.I.C.

MASTER BATH

W.I.C.

PORCH

MORNING ROOM
10'-0" X 13'-0"

GREAT ROOM
14'-0" X 23'-0"
12 FT. CEILING

BEDR'M
12'-3" X 11'-0"

BATH

BEDR'M
12'-0" X 11'-0"

DOUBLE GARAGE
20'-0" X 20'-0"

KIT

BEDR'M
11'-3" X 12'-0"

FOYER

UTIL

DINING
11'-0" X 15'-6"
10 FT. CEILING

PORCH

55'-4"

74'-4"

Bonus Area Floor Plan

PLAYROOM
16'-10" X 14'-3"

Copyright by designer/architect.

Main Level Floor Plan

Dining 12'8"x 12'

Bedroom 13'x 12'

Living 18'6"x 22'

Bedroom 13'x 11'9"

Porch

Deck

Plan #111027

Dimensions: 48' W x 57' D
Levels: 2
Square Footage: 2,601
Main Level Sq. Ft.: 1,623
Upper Level Sq. Ft.: 978
Bedrooms: 3
Bathrooms: 2
Foundation: Pier
Materials List Available: No
Price Category: F

Upper Level Floor Plan

Master Bedroom 18'6"x 20'

Study 13'x 15'6"

Balcony

Main Level Floor Plan

SUNDECK

Covered Deck

NOOK 13-0x11-0

KITCHEN 12-0x13-0

desk

Gas FP

FAMILY ROOM 17-0 x 12-6

Powder Rm

China

DINING 13-0x12-0

Hall

STUDY 13-0 x 10-0

FOYER

LIVINGROOM 13-0 x 17-0

Gas FP

vaulted tray clg

Covered Deck

Covered Porch

roof line

SUNDECK

Plan #281028

Dimensions: 43' W x 56' D
Levels: 2
Square Footage: 2,643
Main Level Sq. Ft.: 1,464
Upper Level Sq. Ft.: 1,179
Bedrooms: 4
Bathrooms: 2½
Foundation: Basement
Materials List Available: Yes
Price Category: F

Rear Elevation

BR 2 13-0 x 13-0

Bath

BR 3 13-0 x 13-0

Hall

ENS

WIC

railing

BR 4 13-0 x 10-4

whirlpool

MBR 13-0 x 16-0

Foyer below

Upper Level Floor Plan

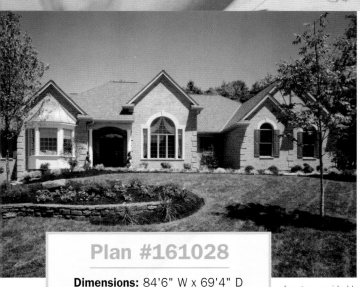

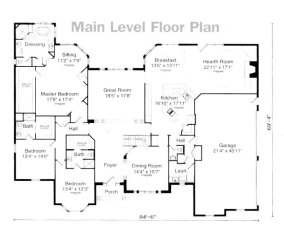

Main Level Floor Plan

Copyright by designer/architect.

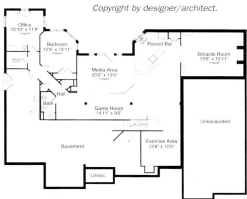

Optional Basement Level Floor Plan

Plan #161028

Dimensions: 84'6" W x 69'4" D
Levels: 1
Square Footage: 3,570
Optional Finished Basement
Sq. Ft.: 2,367
Bedrooms: 3
Bathrooms: 3½
Foundation: Basement
Materials List Available: Yes
Price Category: H

Images provided by designer/architect.

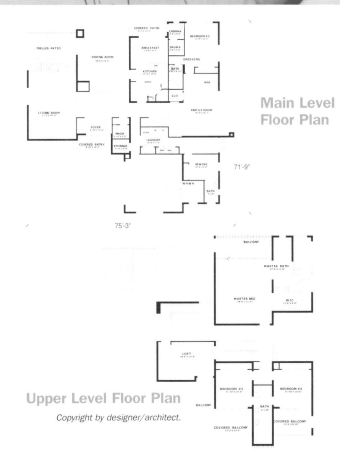

Main Level Floor Plan

Upper Level Floor Plan

Copyright by designer/architect.

Plan #151251

Dimensions: 75'3" W x 71'9" D
Levels: 2
Square Footage: 4,855
Main Level Sq. Ft.: 3,048
Upper Level Sq. Ft.: 1,807
Bedrooms: 4
Bathrooms: 4 full, 2 half
Foundation: Slab
CompleteCost List Available: Yes
Price Category: I

Images provided by designer/architect.

Plan #441047

Dimensions: 50' W x 42' D
Levels: 2
Square Footage: 2,605
Main Level Sq. Ft.: 1,142
Upper Level Sq. Ft.: 1,463
Bedrooms: 3
Bathrooms: 2½
Foundation: Crawl space;
slab or basement available for fee
Material List Available: No
Price Category: F

A touch of European styling dresses the façade of this comfortable two-story home. Stone detailing on the main level and around the entryway complements board-and-batten siding above.

Images provided by designer/architect.

Features:

- Foyer: A side-lighted entry gains admittance to this central foyer with half-bathroom on the left. Beyond the foyer lies open living space, with the great room, dining room, and kitchen.
- Great Room: This room is open upward for the full two stories and is graced by the hearth and media center.
- Dining Room: This room has a wall of windows on one side and sliding glass doors leading to the rear yard on the other.

- Master Suite: On the upper level is this vaulted suite, with its vaulted bathroom. The compartmented toilet, walk-in closet, and spa tub are just a few of the coveted amenities here.
- Bedrooms: Bedroom 3 has a vaulted ceiling and shares the full bathroom on the other side of the stairs with Bedroom 2.

Rear Elevation

Copyright by designer/architect.

Plan #441046

Dimensions: 50' W x 42' D
Levels: 2
Square Footage: 2,606
Main Level Sq. Ft.: 1,216
Upper Level Sq. Ft.: 1,390
Bedrooms: 4
Bathrooms: 2½
Foundation: Crawl space; slab or basement for fee
Materials List Available: No
Price Category: F

Little things mean a lot, and in this design it's the little details that add up to a marvelous plan.

Features:

- Great Room: If you like, you might include a corner media center in this room to complement the fireplace.

- Den: This vaulted room lies just off the entry and opens through double doors.

- Kitchen: Both formal and casual dining spaces are included and flank this open kitchen, which overlooks the great room.

- Upper Level: Sleeping quarters are upstairs and include three family bedrooms and the master suite. Look for a spa tub, separate shower, dual sinks, and a walk-in closet in the master bath. The family bedrooms share the full bathroom, which has double sinks.

Images provided by designer/architect.

Main Level Floor Plan

Rear Elevation

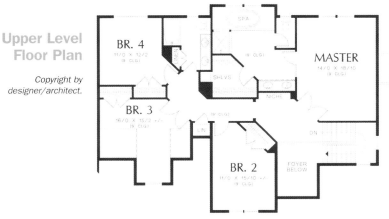

Upper Level Floor Plan

Copyright by designer/architect.

Plan #391056

Dimensions: 73'10" W x 53'4" D
Levels: 2
Square Footage: 2,607
Main Level Sq. Ft.: 1,429
Upper Level Sq. Ft.: 1,178
Bedrooms: 3
Bathrooms: 2½
Foundation: Basement
Materials List Available: No
Price Category: F

Images provided by designer/architect.

The spectacular pavilion front with Palladian window creates a dramatic picture indoors and out.

Features:

- Walk up the steps, onto the porch, and then through the front door with sidelights, this entry opens into a two-story space and feels light and airy. The nearby coat closet is a convenient asset.

- Living Room: This "sunken" room features a cozy fireplace flanked by two doors, allowing access to the wraparound deck. The dining room is open to the area, creating a nice flow between the two spaces.

- Family Room: This casual relaxing area is one step down from the kitchen; it boasts another fireplace and access to the large wraparound deck.

- Kitchen: This island kitchen features plenty of cabinet and counter space and is waiting for the chef in the family to take control. The breakfast area with bay window is the perfect place to start the day.

- Upper Level: This area is dedicated to the master suite with full master bath and two family bedrooms. Enjoy the dramatic view as you look down into the entry.

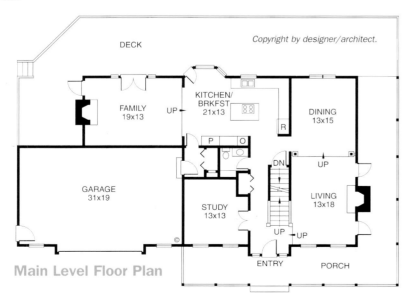

Copyright by designer/architect.

Main Level Floor Plan

Upper Level Floor Plan

Rear View

Kitchen

Living Room

Master Bath

Master Bedroom

Bedroom

Plan #151791

Dimensions: 103'10" W x 68'2" D
Levels: 1.5
Square Footage: 2,660
Main Level Sq. Ft.: 2,360
Upper Level Sq. Ft.: 300
Bedrooms: 3
Bathrooms: 2½
Foundation: Crawl space
CompleteCost List Available: Yes
Price Category: F

A deck adjoins the covered porches of this rustic log home.

Features:

- Great Room: This large open gathering area features a cozy fireplace and access to the covered porch. The two-story wall of windows allows plenty of natural light into the area.

- Kitchen: This large island kitchen is prepared to handle the needs of your family. Its features include the built-in pantry, breakfast nook, and access to the covered porch.

- Master Suite: This retreat has ample closet space and provides access to the covered porch. The master bath boasts a walk-in closet and double vanities.

- Bedrooms: Bedrooms 2 and 3, which have ample closet space, are also located on the main level. Close by is the full bathroom with dual vanities.

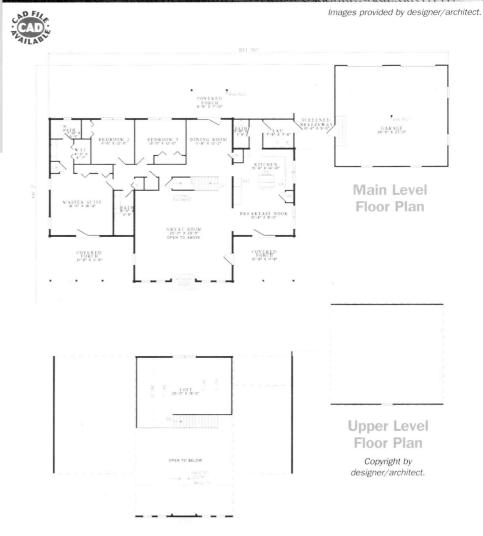

Main Level Floor Plan

Upper Level Floor Plan

Plan #181034

Dimensions: 60' W x 44' D
Levels: 2
Square Footage: 2,687
Main Level Sq. Ft.: 1,297
Upper Level Sq. Ft.: 1,390
Bedrooms: 3
Bathrooms: 2½
Foundation: Full basement
Materials List Available: Yes
Price Category: F

Images provided by designer/architect.

CAD FILE AVAILABLE

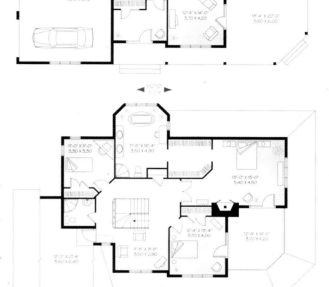

Main Level Floor Plan ▲ ▼

Upper Level Floor Plan

Copyright by designer/architect.

Plan #141021

Dimensions: 70'10" W x 78'9" D
Levels: 1
Square Footage: 2,614
Bedrooms: 3
Bathrooms: 2½
Foundation: Basement
Materials List Available: Yes
Price Category: F

Images provided by designer/architect.

Living Room

Dining Room

Copyright by designer/architect.

Rear View

Plan #321044

Dimensions: 61' W x 49'4" D
Levels: 2
Square Footage: 2,618
Main Level Sq. Ft.: 1,804
Upper Level Sq. Ft.: 814
Bedrooms: 4
Bathrooms: 2½
Foundation: Basement
Materials List Available: Yes
Price Category: F

Images provided by designer/architect.

Copyright by designer/architect.

Upper Level Floor Plan

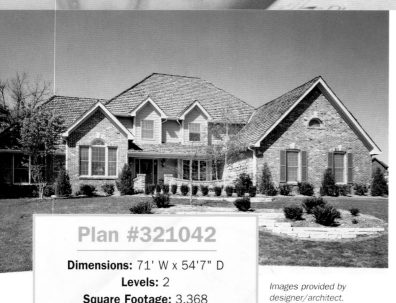

Plan #321042

Dimensions: 71' W x 54'7" D
Levels: 2
Square Footage: 3,368
Main Level Sq. Ft.: 2,150
Upper Level Sq. Ft.: 1,218
Bedrooms: 4
Full Bathrooms: 3
Half Bathrooms: 2
Foundation: Basement
Materials List Available: Yes
Price Category: G

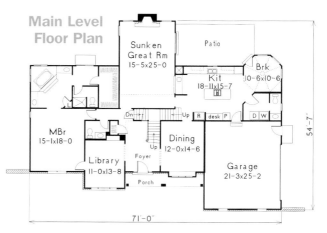

Main Level Floor Plan

Images provided by designer/architect.

Upper Level Floor Plan

Copyright by designer/architect.

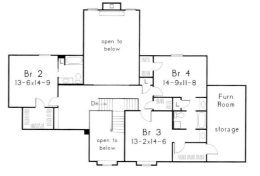

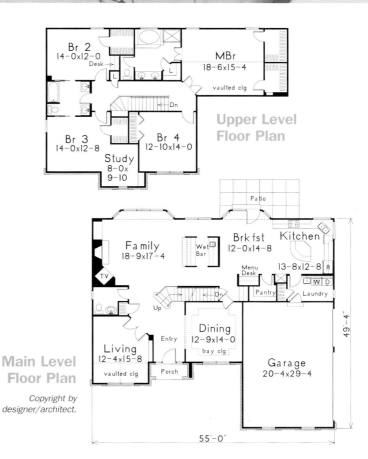

Upper Level Floor Plan

Br 2
14-0x12-0

MBr
18-6x15-4
vaulted clg

Br 3
14-0x12-8

Br 4
12-10x14-0

Study
8-0x
9-10

Family
18-9x17-4

Wet Bar

Brkfst
12-0x14-8

Kitchen
13-8x12-8

TV

Menu Desk

Pantry

Laundry

Up   Dn

Dining
12-9x14-0
tray clg

Living
12-4x15-8
vaulted clg

Entry

Porch

Garage
20-4x29-4

49'-4"

55'-0"

Main Level Floor Plan

Copyright by designer/architect.

Plan #321061

Dimensions: 55' W x 49'4" D
Levels: 2
Square Footage: 3,169
Main Level Sq. Ft.: 1,679
Upper Level Sq. Ft.: 1,490
Bedrooms: 4
Bathrooms: 2½
Foundation: Basement
Materials List Available: Yes
Price Category: G

Images provided by designer/architect.

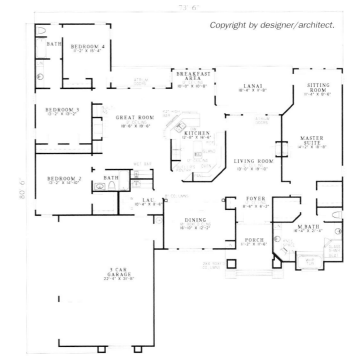

Copyright by designer/architect.

73' 6"

80' 6"

BATH

BEDROOM 4
11'-2" x 15'-4"

BREAKFAST AREA
10'-0" x 10'-8"

LANAI
18'-4" X 11'-8"

SITTING ROOM
11'-4" X 8'-6"

BEDROOM 3
13'-2" X 13'-2"

GREAT ROOM
18'-6" x 19'-6"

KITCHEN
12'-8" X 16'-6"

MASTER SUITE
14'-2" X 18'-8"

LIVING ROOM
13'-0" X 19'-10"

BEDROOM 2
13'-2" X 14'-10"

BATH

WET BAR

LAU.
10'-2" x 8'-6"

FOYER
8'-6" X 6'-2"

DINING
16'-10" X 12'-2"

M.BATH
16'-4" X 2'-4"

PORCH
11'-2" X 11'-6"

3 CAR GARAGE
22'-4" X 31'-8"

Plan #151057

Dimensions: 73'6" W x 80'6" D
Levels: 1
Square Footage: 2,951
Bedrooms: 4
Bathrooms: 3
Foundation: Crawl space, slab, or basement
CompleteCost List Available: Yes
Price Category: F

Images provided by designer/architect.

CAD FILE AVAILABLE

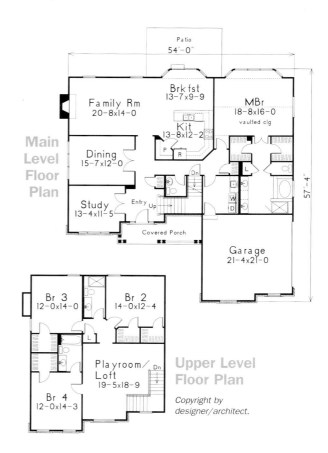

Main Level Floor Plan

Patio 54'-0"

Family Rm 20-8x14-0

Brk fst 13-7x9-9

MBr 18-8x16-0 vaulted clg

Kit 13-8x12-2

Dining 15-7x12-0

Study 13-4x11-5

Entry Up

Covered Porch

Garage 21-4x21-0

57'-4"

Upper Level Floor Plan

Br 3 12-0x14-0

Br 2 14-0x12-4

Playroom/ Loft 19-5x18-9

Br 4 12-0x14-3

Plan #321062

Dimensions: 54' W x 57'4" D
Levels: 2
Square Footage: 3,138
Main Level Sq. Ft.: 1,958
Upper Level Sq. Ft.: 1,180
Bedrooms: 4
Bathrooms: 3½
Foundation: Basement
Materials List Available: Yes
Price Category: G

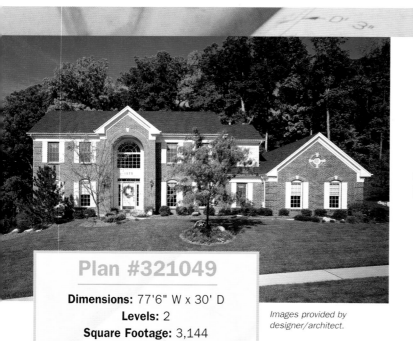

Main Level Floor Plan

Patio

Family 24-4x15-6

Bar

Brk 12-0x14-0

Kitchen 11-0x12-0

Living 17-4x13-6

Foyer

Dining 14-3x13-3

Up

Garage 21-1x31-5

30'-0"

77'-6"

Upper Level Floor Plan

Br 4 12-0x12-0

Br 3 12-0x12-0

MBr 17-4x14-2

open to foyer

Br 2 14-3x13-6

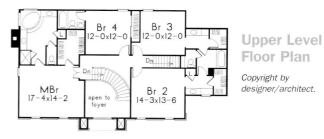

Plan #321049

Dimensions: 77'6" W x 30' D
Levels: 2
Square Footage: 3,144
Main Level Sq. Ft.: 1,724
Upper Level Sq. Ft.: 1,420
Bedrooms: 4
Bathrooms: 4½
Foundation: Basement
Materials List Available: Yes
Price Category: G

Plan #441010

Dimensions: 108' W x 59' D
Levels: 1
Square Footage: 2,973
Bedrooms: 4
Bathrooms: 4½
Foundation: Crawl space;
slab or basement available for fee
Materials List Available: No
Price Category: F

Bordering on estate-sized, this plan borrows elements from Norman, Mediterranean, and English architecture.

CAD FILE AVAILABLE

Images provided by designer/architect.

Features:

- **Great Room:** This gathering area features a large bay window and a fireplace flanked with built-ins. The vaulted ceiling adds to the large feel of the area.

- **Kitchen:** This large island kitchen features a walk-in pantry and a built-in desk. The breakfast nook has access to the patio.

- **Master Suite:** This retreat features a vaulted ceiling in the sleeping area and access to the patio. The master bath boasts dual vanities, a stand-up shower, a spa tub, and a very large walk-in closet.

- **Bedrooms:** Two family bedrooms, each with its own private bathroom, have large closets.

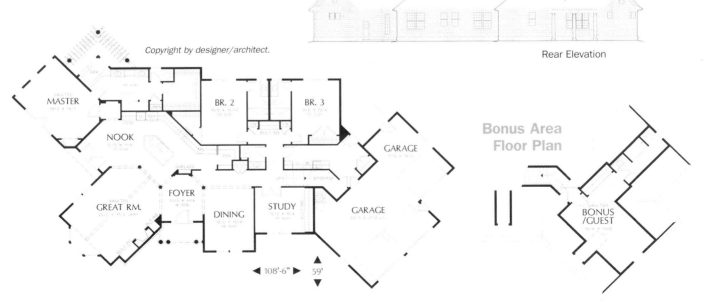

Copyright by designer/architect.

Rear Elevation

Plan #361061

Dimensions: 77'1" W x 80'8" D

Levels: 2

Square Footage: 2,979

Main Level Sq. Ft.: 2,375

Upper Level Sq. Ft.: 604

Bedrooms: 3

Bathrooms: 3

Foundation: Crawl space

Materials List Available: No

Price Category: F

Images provided by designer/architect.

This home, with its slight Southwestern flair, would be perfect for any neighborhood.

Features:

- Kitchen: This peninsula kitchen makes the most of the built-in pantry and raised bar, which adjoins the dining room.

- Entertaining: The dining room, great room, and living room are all open into each other to form one large entertainment area. The living room features a cozy fireplace.

- Master Suite: This private area is located in a wing of its own and features a large sleeping area. The master bath boasts dual vanities, a spa tub, and a separate shower.

- Bedrooms: Located on the opposite side of the home from the master suite for privacy, the two secondary bedrooms share a common bathroom.

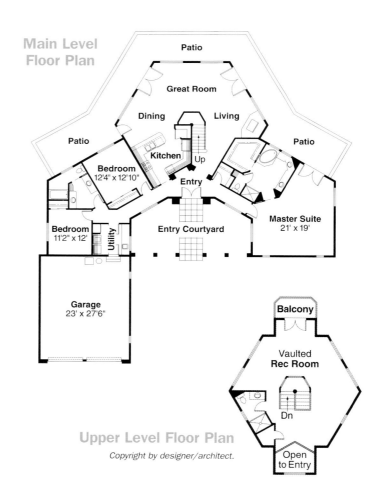

Main Level Floor Plan

Upper Level Floor Plan

Copyright by designer/architect.

Plan #291015

Dimensions: 88'6" W x 58'3" D
Levels: 1.5
Square Footage: 2,901
Main Level Sq. Ft.: 2,078
Upper Level Sq. Ft.: 823
Bedrooms: 3
Bathrooms: 2½
Foundation: Basement
Materials List Available: No
Price Category: F

Images provided by designer/architect.

Upon entering this home, a cathedral-like timber-framed interior fills the eye.

Features:

- **Great Room:** This large gathering area's ceiling rises up two stories and is open to the kitchen. The beautiful fireplace is the focal point of this room.

- **Kitchen:** This island kitchen is open to the great room and the breakfast nook. Warm woods of all species enhance the great room and this space.

- **Master Suite:** This suite has a sloped ceiling and adjoins a luxurious master bath with twin walk-in closets that open to a sunroom with a private balcony.

- **Upper Level:** This upper level has an open lounge that leads to two bedrooms with vaulted ceilings and a generous second bath.

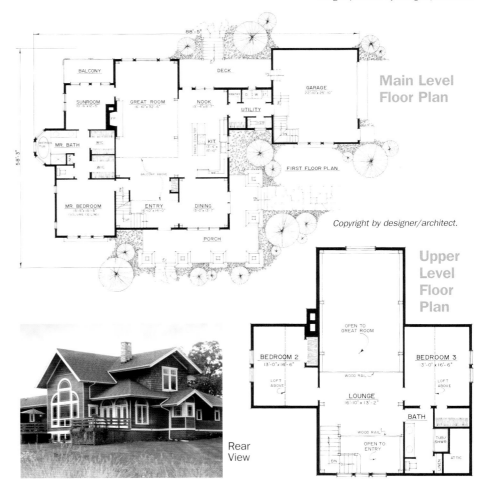

Main Level Floor Plan

Copyright by designer/architect.

Upper Level Floor Plan

Rear View

Plan #101019

Dimensions: 58'4" W x 55'2" D

Levels: 2

Square Footage: 2,954

Main Level Sq. Ft. 2093

Upper Level Sq. Ft. 861

Bedrooms: 4

Bathrooms: 3½

Foundation: Crawl space, slab, or basement

Materials List Available: No

Price Category: F

CAD FILE AVAILABLE

Images provided by designer/architect.

This luxurious home features a spectacular open floor plan and a brick exterior.

Features:

• Ceiling Height: 9 ft. unless otherwise noted.

• Foyer: This inviting two-story foyer, which vaults to 18 ft., will greet guests with an impressive "welcome."

• Dining Room: To the right of the foyer is this spacious dining room surrounded by decorative columns.

• Family Room: There's plenty of room for all kinds of family activities in this enormous room, with its soaring two-story ceiling.

• Master Suite: This sumptuous retreat boasts a tray ceiling. Optional pocket doors provide direct access to the study. The master bath features his and her vanities and a large walk-in closet.

• Breakfast Area: Perfect for informal family meals, this bayed breakfast area has real flair.

• Secondary Bedrooms: Upstairs are three large bedrooms with 8-ft. ceilings. One has a private bath.

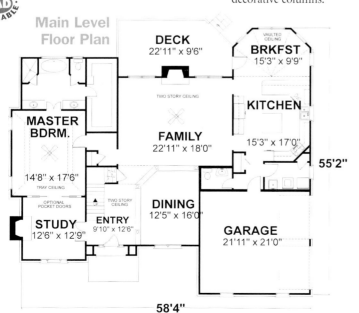

Main Level Floor Plan

Upper Level Floor Plan

Copyright by designer/architect.

Main Level Floor Plan

Family 16-4x19-4 vaulted

Patio

Kitchen 13-0x12-8

Brk 13-2x10-9

Bar

up Dn

Garage 20-4x21-10

Dining 12-2x13-0

Foyer

Study 13-5x13-0

MBr 15-0x16-11 vaulted

Porch Depth 6-0

55'-6"

70'-6"

Plan #321054

Dimensions: 70'6" W x 55'6" D
Levels: 2
Square Footage: 2,828
Main Level Sq. Ft.: 2,006
Upper Level Sq. Ft.: 822
Bedrooms: 5
Bathrooms: 3½
Foundation: Basement
Materials List Available: Yes
Price Category: F

Upper Level Floor Plan

open to below

Br 5 10-7x11-0

Dn

Br 2 10-7x11-0

Br 4 10-7x10-7

open to below

Br 3 10-7x10-7

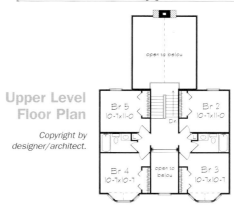

Rear View

Plan #321016

Dimensions: 88' W x 70'8" D
Levels: 1
Square Footage: 3,814
Main Level Sq. Ft.: 3,566
Lower Level Sq. Ft.: 248
Bedrooms: 3
Bathrooms: 2½
Foundation: Daylight basement
Materials List Available: Yes
Price Category: H

Deck

Atrium

Deck

Brk 16-0x14-0 vaulted

plant shelf

Dn

Great Rm 20-0x23-8 vaulted

MBr 14-0x22-0 coffered clg

Dn

Hearth Rm 14-0x26-0

Kitchen 19-4x13-8

plant shelf

Dn

Garage 21-4x29-4

W D

Dining 13-9x12-0 plant shelf

Foyer

Porch

Living 13-9x12-0 plant shelf

Br 2 13-4x11-0

Br 3 17-0x11-0 vaulted

70'-8"

88'-0"

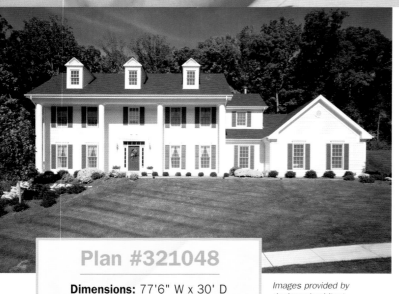

Deck

Hearth
12-5x10-0
vaulted

Family
20-8x15-6

Bar

Brk
12-5x12-0

Kitchen
11-2x12-0

R

Garage
21-1x31-5

30-0"

Living
17-4x13-3

Foyer

Up

Dining
14-6x13-3

Dn

Up

P

W
D

Porch
45-0x6-0

77'-6"

Plan #321048

Dimensions: 77'6" W x 30' D
Levels: 2
Square Footage: 3,216
Main Level Sq. Ft.: 1,834
Upper Level Sq. Ft.: 1,382
Bedrooms: 4
Bathrooms: 4½
Foundation: Basement
Materials List Available: Yes
Price Category: G

Images provided by designer/architect.

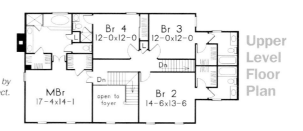

Br 4
12-0x12-0

Br 3
12-0x12-0

L

Dn

**Upper
Level
Floor
Plan**

Copyright by designer/architect.

MBr
17-4x14-1

Dn

open to foyer

Br 2
14-6x13-6

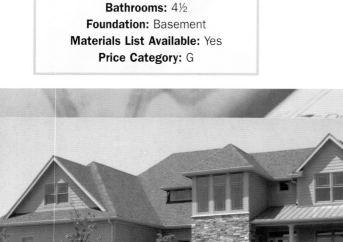

CLOSET
10-4' x 6-10"
9' CH

MASTER
BEDROOM 2
13-0' x 18-2'
9' CH

FAMILY ROOM
16-0' x 15-8'
10-12' CH

BREAKFAST
7-4' x 12'-8"
10-12' CH

MASTER
BATH
9' CH

FP

KITCHEN
18-6' x 12'-10'
9' CH

49'-9 1/2'

PDR
9' CH

R

3 CAR
GARAGE
21'-0' x 29'-8'
8' CH

CLO

SUN ROOM/
DINING ROOM
11'-0 x 13'-0'
9' CH

UTILITY
9' CH

W

D

DN

UP

ENTRY
9' CH

PORCH
9' CH

66'-4 1/2'

Plan #121160

Dimensions: 66'4" W x 49'9" D
Levels: 1.5
Square Footage: 2,188
Main Level Sq. Ft.: 1,531
Upper Level Sq. Ft.: 657
Bedrooms: 3
Bathrooms: 2½
Foundation: Slab; basement for fee
Materials List Available: Yes
Price Category: D

Images provided by designer/architect.

Front View

BEDROOM 3
11'-0' x 14'-0'
8'-10 CH

UNFINISHED
STORAGE
5'-6"-8 CH

CLO

BATH 2
8' CH

CLO

BEDROOM 2
11'-0 x 13'-0'
8'-10 CH

8' CH

DN

Copyright by designer/architect.

Plan #131021

Dimensions: 60' W x 52'4" D
Levels: 2
Square Footage: 3,110
Main Level Sq. Ft.: 1,818
Upper Level Sq. Ft.: 1,292
Bedrooms: 5
Bathrooms: 2½
Foundation: Crawl space, slab, or basement
Materials List Available: Yes
Price Category: H

Images provided by designer/architect.

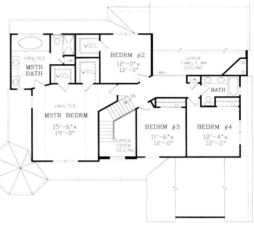

Main Level Floor Plan

Upper Level Floor Plan

Copyright by designer/architect.

Plan #321051

Dimensions: 69'8" W x 46' D
Levels: 2
Square Footage: 2,624
Main Level Sq. Ft.: 1,774
Upper Level Sq. Ft.: 850
Bedrooms: 4
Bathrooms: 2½
Foundation: Basement
Materials List Available: Yes
Price Category: F

Images provided by designer/architect.

This home, as shown in the photograph, may differ from the actual blueprints. For more detailed information, please check the floor plans carefully.

Main Level Floor Plan

Copyright by designer/architect.

Upper Level Floor Plan

Master Bath

Main Level Floor Plan

Plan #121063

Dimensions: 84' W x 52' D
Levels: 2
Square Footage: 3,473
Main Level Sq. Ft.: 2,500
Upper Level Sq. Ft.: 973
Bedrooms: 4
Bathrooms: 3½
Foundation: Basement
Materials List Available: Yes
Price Category: G

Images provided by designer/architect.

Upper Level Floor Plan

Copyright by designer/architect.

Plan #321036

Dimensions: 78'4" W x 68'6" D
Levels: 1
Square Footage: 2,900
Bedrooms: 4
Bathrooms: 2½
Foundation: Basement
Materials List Available: No
Price Category: F

Images provided by designer/architect.

Copyright by designer/architect.

Optional Basement Level Floor Plan

Plan #131029

Dimensions: 56'4" W x 46'6" D
Levels: 2
Square Footage: 2,936
Main Level Sq. Ft.: 1,680
Upper Level Sq. Ft.: 1,256
Bedrooms: 4
Bathrooms: 2½
Foundation: Crawl space, slab, or basement
Materials List Available: Yes
Price Category: G

This home, as shown in the photograph, may differ from the actual blueprints. For more detailed information, please check the floor plans carefully.

This home is ideal if you love the look of a country-style farmhouse.

Features:

- Foyer: Walk across the large wraparound porch that defines this home to enter this two-story foyer.

- Living Room: French doors from the foyer lead into this living room.

- Family Room: The whole family will love this room, with its vaulted ceiling, fireplace, and sliding glass doors that open to the wooden rear deck.

- Kitchen: A beautiful sit-down center island opens to the family room. There's also a breakfast nook with a lovely bay window.

- Master Suite: Luxury abounds with vaulted ceilings, walk-in closets, private bath with whirlpool tub, separate shower, and dual sinks.

- Loft: A special place with vaulted ceiling and view into the family room below.

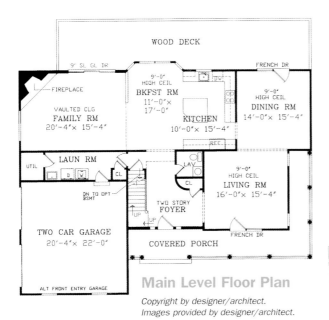

Main Level Floor Plan

Upper Level Floor Plan

Rear Elevation

Copyright by designer/architect.
Images provided by designer/architect.

Plan #441025

Dimensions: 70' W x 101'6" D
Levels: 2
Square Footage: 3,457
Main Level Sq. Ft.: 2,222
Upper Level Sq. Ft.: 1,235
Bedrooms: 4
Bathrooms: 3 full, 2 half
Foundation: Crawl space;
slab or basement available for fee
Materials List Available: No
Price Category: G

Classic Craftsman tradition shines through in this spectacular two-story home.

Features:

- **Great Room:** This open room features two sets of double doors to the rear yard, a fireplace, and a built-in media center.

- **Kitchen:** Casual dining takes place in the breakfast nook, which is open to this island kitchen and leads to a vaulted porch.

- **Master Suites:** One master suite is found on the first floor. It glows with appointments, from double-door access to the rear yard to a fine bath with spa tub, separate shower, and double sinks. The second master suite, on the second floor, holds a window seat and a private bath with spa tub.

- **Bedrooms:** Two additional bedrooms (or a bedroom and a study) share a full compartmented bathroom with private vanities for each room.

- **Garage:** This four-car garage connects to the main house at a laundry/mud room with a half-bath, coat closet, built-in bench, and washer/dryer space. Extra room in the garage can be used as a workshop or for storage space.

Images provided by designer/architect.

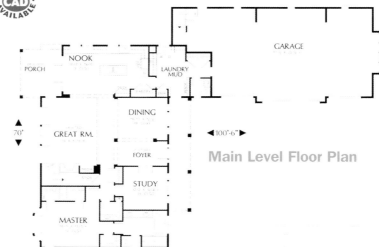

Main Level Floor Plan

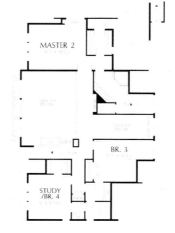

Upper Level Floor Plan

Copyright by designer/architect.

Plan #121082

Dimensions: 68'8" W x 60' D
Levels: 2
Square Footage: 2,932
Main Level Sq. Ft.: 2,084
Upper Level Sq. Ft.: 848
Bedrooms: 4
Bathrooms: 3½
Foundation: Basement
Materials List Available: Yes
Price Category: F

Images provided by designer/architect.

Enjoy the spacious covered veranda that gives this house so much added charm.

Features:

• **Great Room:** A volume ceiling enhances the spacious feeling in this room, making it a natural gathering spot for friends and family. Transom-topped windows look onto the veranda, and French doors open to it.

• **Den:** French doors from the entry lead to this room, with its unusual ceiling detail, gracious fireplace, and transom-topped windows.

• **Hearth Room:** Three skylights punctuate the cathedral ceiling in this room, giving it an extra measure of light and warmth.

• **Kitchen:** This kitchen is a delight, thanks to its generous working and storage space.

Main Level Floor Plan

Upper Level Floor Plan

Copyright by designer/architect.

Plan #441012

Dimensions: 65' W x 55' D
Levels: 1
Square Footage: 3,682
Main Level Sq. Ft.: 2,192
Basement Level Sq. Ft.: 1,490
Bedrooms: 4
Bathrooms: 4
Foundation: Slab
Materials List Available: No
Price Category: H

Images provided by designer/architect.

Accommodating a site that slopes to the rear, this home is not only good-looking but practical.

Features:

• Den: Just off the foyer is this cozy space, complete with built-ins.

• Great Room: This vaulted gathering area features a lovely fireplace, a built-in media center, and a view of the back yard.

• Kitchen: This island kitchen is ready to handle the daily needs of your family or aid in entertaining your guests.

• Lower Level: Adding even more livability to the home, this floor contains the games room with media center and corner fireplace, two more bedrooms (each with a full bathroom), and the wide covered patio.

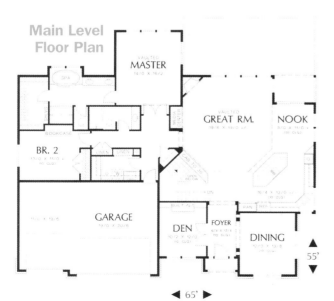

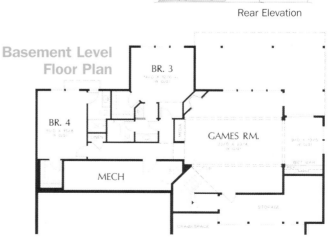

Copyright by designer/architect.

Plan #361062

Dimensions: 86' W x 65' D
Levels: 2
Square Footage: 3,291
Main Level Sq. Ft.: 2,183
Upper Level Sq. Ft.: 1,108
Bedrooms: 4
Bathrooms: 3½
Foundation: Slab or basement
Materials List Available: No
Price Category: G

The wraparound porch gives this home a nice relaxed feeling.

Features:

- **Family Room:** This vaulted gathering area features access to the rear deck. The area is open to the kitchen.

- **Kitchen:** This island kitchen is open to the breakfast nook and has access to the garage through the mudroom. Take note of the pocket door between the kitchen and the dining room.

- **Master Suite:** Located on the first floor for convenience and privacy, this retreat features a sitting area. The master bath boasts a spa tub, large walk-in closet, and dual vanities.

- **Bedrooms:** The two family bedrooms and guest bedroom are located on the upper level. One bedroom shares a common bathroom with the guest room, while the other bedroom has its own bathroom.

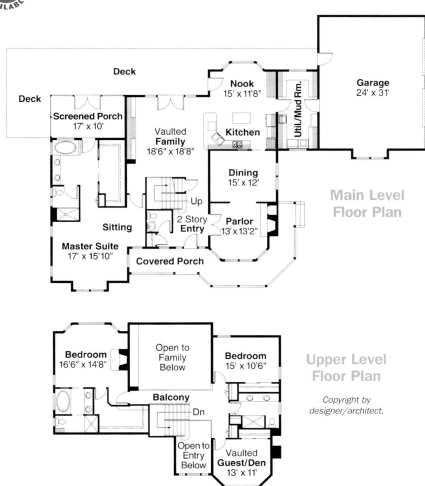

Main Level Floor Plan

Upper Level Floor Plan

Copyright by designer/architect.

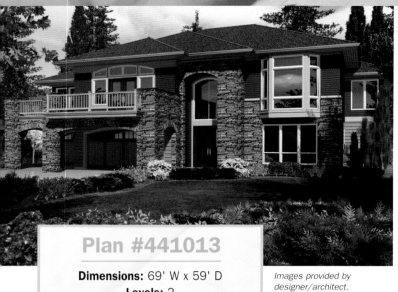

**Main Level
Floor Plan**

Lower Level Floor Plan

*Images provided by
designer/architect.*

CAD FILE AVAILABLE

Copyright by designer/architect.

Plan #441013

Dimensions: 69' W x 59' D
Levels: 2
Square Footage: 3,317
Main Level Sq. Ft.: 2,657
Lower Level Sq. Ft.: 660
Bedrooms: 4
Bathrooms: 3½
Foundation: Slab
Materials List Available: No
Price Category: G

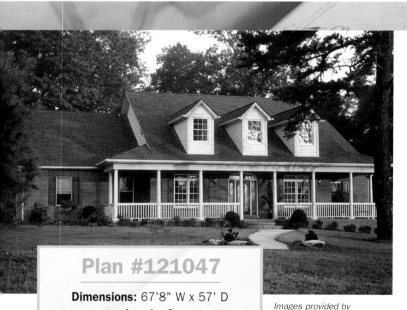

**Main Level
Floor Plan**

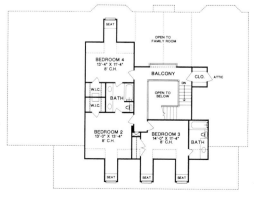

**Upper Level
Floor Plan**

Copyright by designer/architect.

*Images provided by
designer/architect.*

CAD FILE AVAILABLE

Plan #121047

Dimensions: 67'8" W x 57' D
Levels: 2
Square Footage: 3,072
Main Level Sq. Ft.: 2,116
Upper Level Sq. Ft.: 956
Bedrooms: 4
Bathrooms: 3½
Foundation: Slab
Materials List Available: Yes
Price Category: G

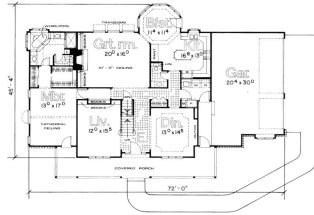

Plan #121083

Dimensions: 72' W x 45'4" D
Levels: 2
Square Footage: 2,695
Main Level Sq. Ft.: 1,881
Upper Level Sq. Ft.: 814
Bedrooms: 4
Bathrooms: 3½
Foundation: Basement
Materials List Available: Yes
Price Category: F

Images provided by designer/architect.

CAD FILE AVAILABLE

Upper Level Floor Plan

Copyright by designer/architect.

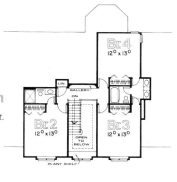

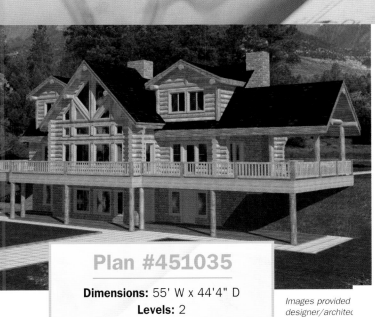

Upper Level Floor Plan

Plan #451035

Dimensions: 55' W x 44'4" D
Levels: 2
Square Footage: 2,883
Main Level Sq. Ft.: 1,622
Upper Level Sq. Ft.: 1,261
Bedrooms: 4
Bathrooms: 3½
Foundation: Walkout basement
Materials List Available: No
Price Category: F

Images provided designer/architec

CAD FILE AVAILABLE

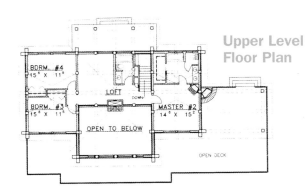

Basement Level Floor Plan

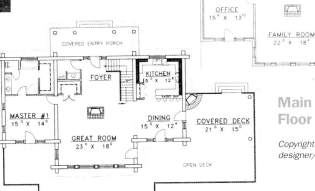

Main Level Floor Plan

Copyright by designer/architect.

Plan #441033

Dimensions: 67' W x 68' D
Levels: 2
Square Footage: 2,986
Main Level Sq. Ft.: 2,162
Upper Level Sq. Ft.: 824
Bedrooms: 3
Bathrooms: 2½
Foundation: Crawl space; slab or basement for fee
Materials List Available: No
Price Category: F

This home, as shown in the photograph, may differ from the actual blueprints. For more detailed information, please check the floor plans carefully.

Images provided by designer/architect.

Dramatic design coupled with elegant architectural detailing brings this comfortable home a lovely facade.

Features:

• Great Room: This room is two stories tall; the fireplace is flanked by built-ins.

• Dining Room: The interior was specifically created for family lifestyles. This formal room, accented with columns, is also graced by the butler's pantry, which connects it to the kitchen for convenience.

• Master Suite: The left wing is dedicated to this suite. The extensive master bath, with spa tub, separate shower, and walk-in closet, complements the master salon, which features a tray ceiling and large window over looking the rear yard.

• Upper Level: The two family bedrooms are on the second floor; they share the full bathroom with double sinks. The games room opens through double doors just off the loft library.

Main Level Floor Plan

Upper Level Floor Plan

Copyright by designer/architect.

Rear Elevation

Front View

Plan #441028

Dimensions: 53'6" W x 73' D
Levels: 2
Square Footage: 3,165
Main Level Sq. Ft.: 1,268
Upper Level Sq. Ft.: 931
Lower Level Sq. Ft.: 966
Bedrooms: 4
Bathrooms: 3½
Foundation: Slab
Materials List Available: No
Price Category: G

Images provided by designer/architect.

Arts and Crafts style meets hillside design. The result is this stunning design, which fits perfectly on a sloped site.

CAD FILE AVAILABLE

Features:

- **Porch:** This covered porch introduces the front entry but also allows access to a mud-room and the three-car garage beyond.

- **Great Room:** This room is vaulted and has a fireplace, media center, and window seat in a corner window area—a cozy place to read or relax.

- **Dining Room:** The recess in this room is ideal for a hutch, and the double French doors open to the wide lower deck.

- **Upper Level:** This floor holds the two family bedrooms with walk-in closets, the shared bathroom, and the master suite. A spa tub and vaulted salon with private deck appoint the suite.

- **Lower Level:** This floor features another bedroom, with its full bathroom; the recreation room, which has a fireplace and wet bar; and the wine cellar.

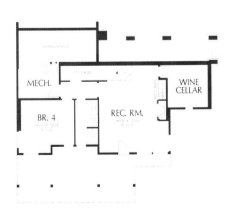

Lower Level Floor Plan
Copyright by designer/architect.

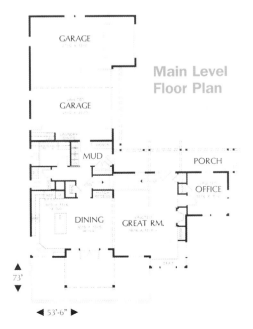

Main Level Floor Plan

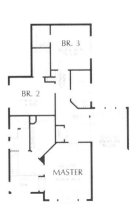

Upper Level Floor Plan

Plan #441036

Dimensions: 60' W x 50' D
Levels: 2
Square Footage: 2,902
Main Level Sq. Ft.: 1,617
Upper Level Sq. Ft.: 1,285
Bedrooms: 3
Bathrooms: 2½
Foundation: Crawl space
Materials List Available: No
Price Category: F

Images provided by designer/architect.

Features:

- **Great Room:** Come in and relax in this room, with its media center and fireplace. Look onto the backyard through the large windows.

- **Kitchen:** This kitchen is wonderfully appointed, containing an island cooktop, walk-in pantry, built-in desk, and corner sink. The laundry room is nearby.

- **Master Suite:** This suite is especially note-worthy, opening from double doors and boasting a walk-in closet and a bath with a spa tub, separate shower, double vanities, and compartmented toilet.

- **Bedrooms:** Two additional bedrooms share the upper level with the master suite. Both bedrooms have large closets and share a Jack-and-Jill bathroom.

It's a natural: a two-story traditional with board-and-batten siding, cedar shingles, stone detail at the foundation and Craftsman-inspired porch columns.

CAD FILE AVAILABLE

Main Level Floor Plan

Upper Level Floor Plan

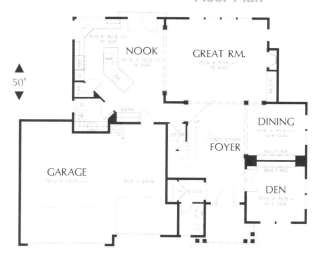

Copyright by designer/architect.

Plan #121067

Dimensions: 56' W x 59'4" D
Levels: 2
Square Footage: 2,708
Main Level Sq. Ft.: 1,860
Upper Level Sq. Ft.: 848
Bedrooms: 4
Bathrooms: 3½
Foundation: Basement
Materials List Available: Yes
Price Category: F

Images provided by designer/architect.

CAD FILE AVAILABLE

Upper Level Floor Plan

Main Level Floor Plan

Copyright by designer/architect.

Plan #141022

Dimensions: 90' W x 93' D
Levels: 1
Square Footage: 2,911
Bedrooms: 3
Bathrooms: 2½
Foundation: Basement
Materials List Available: No
Price Category: F

Images provided by designer/architect.

Copyright by designer/architect.

Rear View

Plan #441011

Dimensions: 67' W x 46' D
Levels: 1
Square Footage: 2,898
Main Level Sq. Ft.: 1,744
Basement Level Sq. Ft.: 1,154
Bedrooms: 3
Bathrooms: 2½
Foundation: Walkout basement
Materials List Available: No
Price Category: F

Think one-story, then think again—it's a hillside home designed to make the best use of a sloping lot. Elegant in exterior appeal, this home uses high arches and a hipped room to promote a sense of style.

Images provided by designer/architect.

Features:

- Dining Room: Box beams and columns define this formal space, which is just off the foyer.

- Kitchen: This fully equipped kitchen has everything the chef in the family could want. Nearby is the breakfast nook with sliding glass doors to the deck, which acts as the roof for the patio below.

- Master Suite: This suite is located on the right side of the main level. The master bath is

replete with a spa tub, compartmented toilet, separate shower, and dual lavatories.

- Lower Level: The two extra bedrooms, full bathroom, and games room are on this lower floor, which adds to the great livability of the home. The wet bar in the games room is a bonus.

Rear Elevation

Main Level Floor Plan

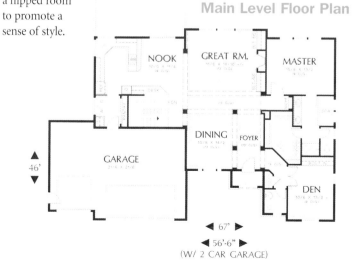

NOOK
GREAT RM.
MASTER
GARAGE
DINING
FOYER
DEN
46'
67'
56'-6"
(W/ 2 CAR GARAGE)

Basement Level Floor Plan

BR. 3
GAMES RM.
BR. 2
STORAGE

Copyright by designer/architect.

Plan #451223

Dimensions: 71'6" W x 87'6" D
Levels: 2
Square Footage: 3,650
Main Level Sq. Ft.: 2,106
Upper Level Sq. Ft.: 272
Lower Level Sq. Ft.: 1,272
Bedrooms: 3
Bathrooms: 3½
Foundation: Crawl space
Materials List Available: No
Price Category: H

This timber-frame log home would look great in a neighborhood or in the backcountry.

Features:

• Great Room: The cozy fireplace, which is flanked by built-ins, makes this two-story gathering area special. The wet bar here features a serving shelf to the rear deck.

• Kitchen: This Island kitchen makes the most of its built-in pantry, and its raised bar is open to the great room and dining area. The utility room with washer and dryer are just a few steps away.

• Master Suite: The romantic fireplace in the bedroom is just the start in this retreat, which also provides access to the rear deck. The master bath features a spa tub, dual vanities, and a separate shower.

• Lower Level: This area offers the option of an additional bedroom, a guest suite, and a recreation room. The mechanical room is also on this level.

Images provided by designer/architect.

**Main Level
Floor Plan**

**Upper Level
Floor Plan**

**Basement Level
Floor Plan**

Copyright by designer/architect.

Plan #221022

Dimensions: 79' W x 55' D
Levels: 2
Square Footage: 3,382
Main Level Sq. Ft.: 2,376
Upper Level Sq. Ft.: 1,006
Bedrooms: 4
Bathrooms: 3½
Foundation: Basement
Materials List Available: No
Price Category: G

Images provided by designer/architect.

The traditional-looking facade of stone, brick, and siding opens into a home you'll love for its spaciousness, comfort, and great natural lighting.

Features:

- Ceiling Height: 9 ft.

- Great Room: The two-story ceiling here emphasizes the dimensions of this large room, and the huge windows make it bright and cheery.

- Sunroom: Use this area as a den or an indoor conservatory where you can relax in the midst of health-promoting and beautiful plants.

- Kitchen: This well-planned kitchen features a snacking island and opens into a generous dining nook where everyone will gather.

- Master Suite: Located on the main floor for privacy, this area includes a walk-in closet and a deluxe full bathroom.

- Upper Level: Look into the great room and entryway as you climb the stairs to the three large bedrooms and full bath on this floor.

Rear View

Main Level Floor Plan

Upper Level Floor Plan

Copyright by designer/architect.

Plan #151759

Dimensions: 70'10" W x 83'8" D
Levels: 1.5
Square Footage: 3,098
Main Level Sq. Ft.: 1,870
Upper Level Sq. Ft.: 1,228
Bedrooms: 4
Bathrooms: 3
Foundation: Crawl space
CompleteCost List Available: Yes
Price Category: G

Images provided by designer/architect.

An impressive 8-ft.-deep covered porch nearly encircles this log home.

Features:

• Great Room: This room with fireplace is open to the loft and has three skylights above.

• Kitchen: This large island kitchen is open to the great room and dining area and has a large walk-in pantry.

• Master Suite: Located on the main level, this suite includes double vanities and a corner whirlpool tub in the bath.

• Bedrooms: Bedroom 2 is located on the main level. Two additional bedrooms with walk-in closets are located on the upper level and share a common bathroom.

Main Level Floor Plan

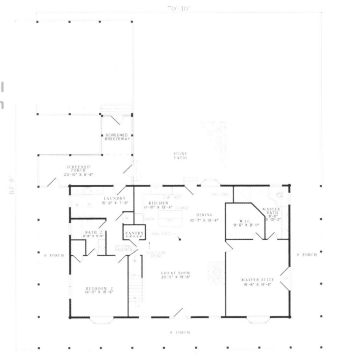

Upper Level Floor Plan

Copyright by designer/architect.

Plan #451217

Dimensions: 103'6" W x 53'11" D
Levels: 1
Square Footage: 4,711
Main Level Sq. Ft.: 2,470
Lower Level Sq. Ft.: 2,241
Bedrooms: 4
Bathrooms: 3
Foundation: Walkout basement
Materials List Available: No
Price Category: I

Images provided by designer/architect.

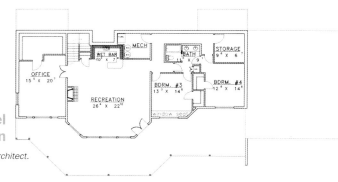

Main Level Floor Plan

Basement Level
Floor Plan

Copyright by designer/architect.

Plan #121100

Dimensions: 100'10" W x 80'5" D
Levels: 2
Square Footage: 3,750
Main Level Sq. Ft.: 2,274
Upper Level Sq. Ft.: 1,476
Bedrooms: 4
Bathrooms: 3½
Foundation: Slab
Materials List Available: No
Price Category: G

Images provided by designer/architect.

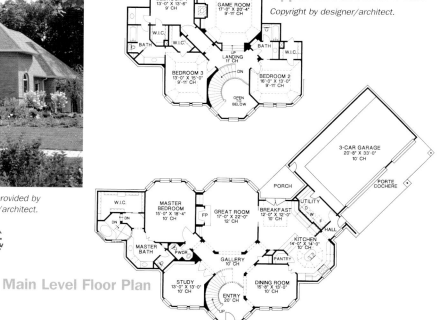

Upper Level Floor Plan
Copyright by designer/architect.

Main Level Floor Plan

Plan #121019

Dimensions: 70' W x 60' D
Levels: 2
Square Footage: 3,775
Main Level Sq. Ft.: 1,923
Upper Level Sq. Ft.: 1,852
Bedrooms: 4
Bathrooms: 3
Foundation: Basement
Materials List Available: Yes
Price Category: H

Images provided by designer/architect.

The grand exterior presence is carried inside, beginning with the dramatic curved staircase.

Features:

- Ceiling Height: 8 ft.
- Den: French doors lead to this sophisticated den, with its bayed windows and wall of bookcases.
- Living Room: A curved wall and a series of arched windows highlight this large space.
- Formal Dining Room: This room shares the curved wall and arched windows found in the living room.

- Screened Porch: This huge space features skylights and is accessible by another French door from the dining room.
- Family Room: Family and guests alike will be drawn to this room, with its trio of arched windows and fireplace flanked by bookcases.
- Kitchen: An island adds convenience and distinction to this large, functional kitchen.
- Garage: This spacious three-bay garage provides plenty of space for cars and storage.

Main Level Floor Plan

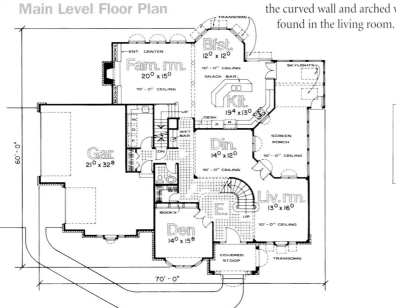

Upper Level Floor Plan

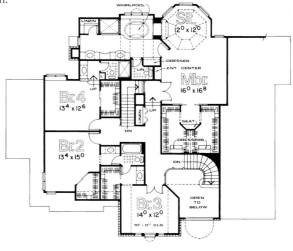

Copyright by designer/architect.

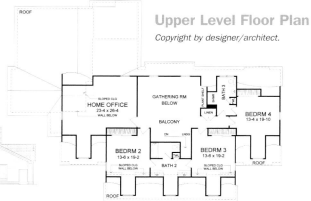

Main Level Floor Plan

SCREENED PORCH 13-8 x 11-8

GARAGE 23-6 x 33-0

WOOD DECK 21-10 x 11-8

DINETTE 13-8 x 12-10

WALL ABV

KITCHEN 11-8 x 14-6

GATHERING RM 20-0 x 16-6

WHIRLPOOL TUB

M BATH

WIC

M BEDRM 13-8 x 17-6

PORCH

ENTRY

HALL

DINING RM 13-6 x 13-6

DEN 13-6 x 13-6

PDR LAUND

FOYER

WINDOW SEAT

WOOD PORCH 41-0 x 8-0

Upper Level Floor Plan

Copyright by designer/architect.

ROOF

HOME OFFICE 23-4 x 26-4
SLOPED CLG
WALL ABV

GATHERING RM BELOW

BATH 3

LINEN

BEDRM 4 13-4 x 19-10

BALCONY

BEDRM 2 13-6 x 19-2
SLOPED CLG
WALL BELOW

BEDRM 3 13-6 x 19-2
SLOPED CLG
WALL BELOW

BATH 2

ROOF

ROOF

Plan #261011

Dimensions: 85' W x 56' D
Levels: 2
Square Footage: 4,042
Main Level Sq. Ft.: 2,492
Upper Level Sq. Ft.: 1,550
Bedrooms: 4
Bathrooms: 3½
Foundation: Walkout basement
Materials List Available: No
Price Category: I

Images provided by designer/architect.

Rear Elevation

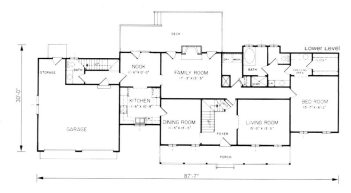

Main Level Floor Plan

STORAGE

BATH

NOOK 11'-6" x 10'-0"

DECK

FAMILY ROOM 17'-3" x 13'-5"

BATH

Lower Level

30'-0"

GARAGE

KITCHEN 11'-6" x 10'-9"

DINING ROOM 11'-5" x 13'-5"

LIVING ROOM 15'-0" x 13'-5"

FOYER

BED ROOM 13'-7" x 16'-2"

PORCH

87'-7"

Plan #341007

Dimensions: 87'7" W x 30' D
Levels: 2
Square Footage: 4,068
Main Level Sq. Ft.: 3,218
Upper Level Sq. Ft.: 850
Bedrooms: 4
Bathrooms: 2½
Foundation: Crawl space, slab, or basement
Materials List Available: Yes
Price Category: I

Images provided by designer/architect.

CAD FILE AVAILABLE

Upper Level Floor Plan

Copyright by designer/architect.

RECREATION 12'-0" x 23'-0"

BED ROOM 12'-0" x 9'-9"

BATH

BED ROOM 11'-5" x 16'-0"

BED ROOM 11'-5" x 16'-2"

BONUS SPACE

Plan #121018

Dimensions: 95'9" W x 70'2" D
Levels: 2
Square Footage: 3,950
Main Level Sq. Ft.: 2,839
Upper Level Sq. Ft.: 1,111
Bedrooms: 4
Bathrooms: 4 full, 2 half
Foundation: Basement
Materials List Available: Yes
Price Category: H

Images provided by designer/architect.

CAD FILE AVAILABLE · CAD ·

Main Level Floor Plan

Upper Level Floor Plan

Copyright by designer/architect.

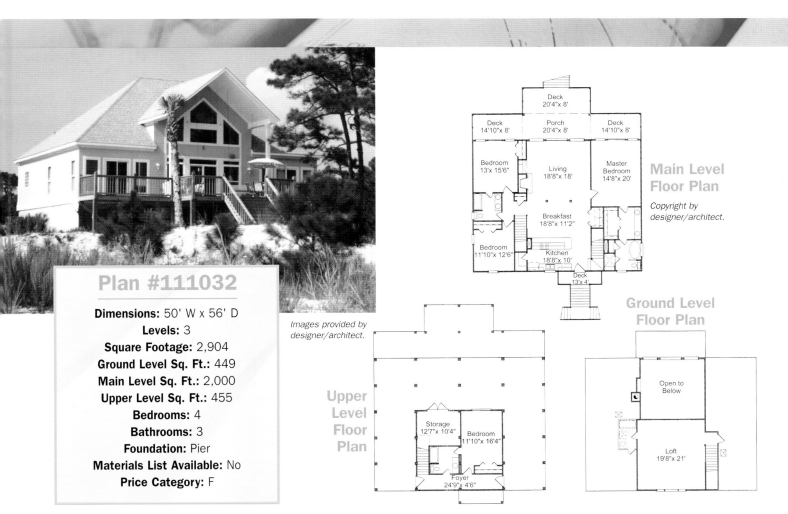

Plan #111032

Dimensions: 50' W x 56' D
Levels: 3
Square Footage: 2,904
Ground Level Sq. Ft.: 449
Main Level Sq. Ft.: 2,000
Upper Level Sq. Ft.: 455
Bedrooms: 4
Bathrooms: 3
Foundation: Pier
Materials List Available: No
Price Category: F

Images provided by designer/architect.

Main Level Floor Plan

Copyright by designer/architect.

Ground Level Floor Plan

Upper Level Floor Plan

Plan #441029

Dimensions: 70' W x 71' D
Levels: 2
Square Footage: 3,217
Main Level Sq. Ft.: 2,292
Upper Level Sq. Ft.: 925
Bedrooms: 3
Bathrooms: 3½
Foundation: Crawl space; slab or basement available for fee
Material List Available: No
Price Category: G

Images provided by designer/architect.

Influenced by the Modernist movement, this California contemporary design is grand in façade and comfortable to live in.

Features:

• **Entry:** The two-story foyer opens to the formal dining room (also two-story) and the great room. Decorative columns help define these spaces. The curved wall of glass overlooking the rear patio brightens the great room.

• **Master Suite:** This suite, which has a salon with curved window wall, features a private bath with spa tub and walk-in closet.

• **Bedrooms:** The two family bedrooms share the upper level with the library, which has built-ins. Each upper-level bedroom has its own bathroom and walk-in closet.

• **Home Office:** The left wing of the main level contains this space, which features a curved window wall.

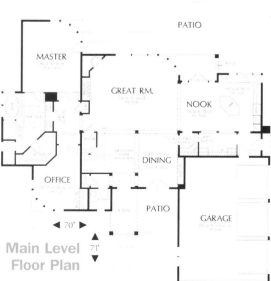

Main Level Floor Plan

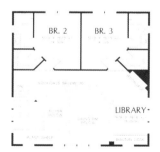

Upper Level Floor Plan

Copyright by designer/architect.

Rear View

Plan #181122

Dimensions: 62' W x 36'4" D
Levels: 2
Square Footage: 3,105
Main Level Sq. Ft.: 1,470
Upper Level Sq. Ft.: 1,635
Bedrooms: 4
Bathrooms: 3
Foundation: Walkout basement
Materials List Available: Yes
Price Category: G

Images provided by designer/architect.

CAD FILE AVAILABLE

Upper Level Floor Plan

Copyright by designer/architect.

Plan #361068

Dimensions: 95'5" W x 73'11" D
Levels: 2
Square Footage: 3,405
Main Level Sq. Ft.: 2,022
Upper Level Sq. Ft.: 1,383
Bedrooms: 3
Bathrooms: 3 full, 3 half
Foundation: Slab
Materials List Available: No
Price Category: G

Images provided by designer/architect.

CAD FILE AVAILABLE

Main Level Floor Plan

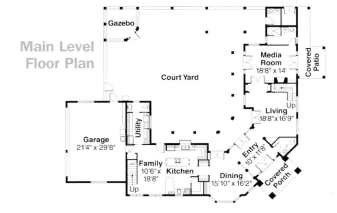

Upper Level Floor Plan

Copyright by designer/architect.

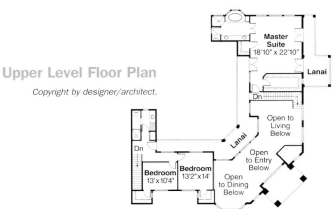

Images provided by designer/architect.

Plan #121023

Dimensions: 85'5" W x 74'8" D
Levels: 2
Square Footage: 3,904
Main Level Sq. Ft.: 2,813
Upper Level Sq. Ft.: 1,091
Bedrooms: 4
Bathrooms: 3½
Foundation: Basement
Materials List Available: Yes
Price Category: H

CAD FILE AVAILABLE

Spacious and gracious, here are all the amenities you expect in a fine home.

Features:

• Ceiling Height: 8 ft. except as noted.

• Foyer: This magnificent entry features a graceful curved staircase with balcony above.

• Sunken Living Room: This sunken room is filled with light from a row of bowed windows. It's the perfect place for social gatherings both large and small.

• Den: French doors open into this truly distinctive den with its 11-ft. ceiling and built-in bookcases.

• Formal Dining Room: Entertain guests with style and grace in this dining room with corner column.

• Master Suite: Another set of French doors leads to this suite that features two walk-in closets, a whirlpool flanked by vanities, and a private sitting room with built-in bookcases.

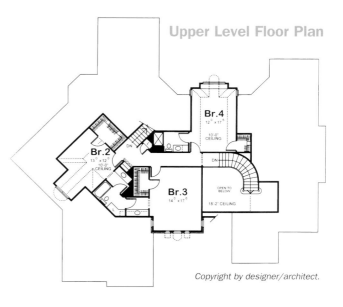

Copyright by designer/architect.

Plan #441030

Dimensions: 117'6" W x 63'6" D
Levels: 2
Square Footage: 5,180
Main Level Sq. Ft.: 3,030
Upper Level Sq. Ft.: 2,150
Bedrooms: 6
Bathrooms: 5
Foundation: Crawl space; slab or basement available for fee
Materials List Available: No
Price Category: J

Images provided by designer/architect.

There's no doubt, this home plan is pure luxury. The plan incorporates a wealth of space on two levels, plus every amenity a family could desire.

CAD FILE AVAILABLE

Features:

- **Great Room:** Defined by columns, this room with fireplace and built-in cabinet has an 11-ft.-high ceiling. There is access to the rear patio through French doors.

- **Kitchen:** Furnished with multiple work-stations, this kitchen can accommodate a cook and helpers. The island is equipped with a sink and dishwasher. The secondary sink occupies the half-wall facing the family room. The walk-in pantry beside the dining room supplements storage.

- **Main Level:** The main level is host to rooms devoted to special interests-the office, complete with storage units and a French door to the front porch, and the crafts or hobby room, furnished with an L-shaped work surface.

- **Upper Level:** The upper level of the home accommodates three bedrooms, two bath rooms, the full-service laundry room, and the master suite, which is a dream come true. The master bedroom is divided into sitting and sleeping areas. French doors open it to a private deck. A two-sided fireplace warms both the sitting area and the master bath. The highlight of the spacious bath is the oval tub, which is tucked beneath a bay window.

Rear View

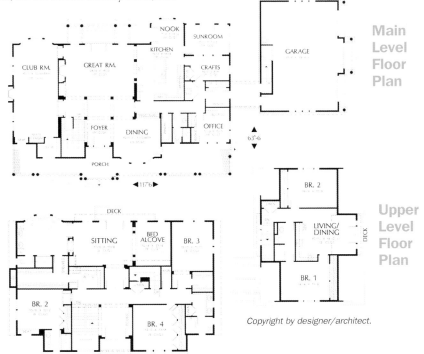

Copyright by designer/architect.

Plan #441024

Dimensions: 90'6" W x 84' D
Levels: 2
Square Footage: 3,517
Main Level Sq. Ft.: 2,698
Upper Level Sq. Ft.: 819
Bedrooms: 3
Bathrooms: 3½
Foundation: Crawl space;
slab or basement available for fee
Materials List Available: No
Price Category: H

You'll feel like royalty every time you pull into the driveway of this European-styled manor house.

Features:

- **Kitchen:** This gourmet chef's center hosts an island with a vegetable sink. The arched opening above the primary sink provides a view of the fireplace and entertainment center in the great room. A walk-in food pantry and a butler's pantry are situated between this space and the dining room.

- **Master Suite:** Located on the main level, this private retreat boasts a large sleeping area and a sitting area. The grand master bath features a large walk-in closet, dual vanities, a large tub, and a shower.

- **Bedrooms:** Two secondary bedrooms are located on the upper level, and each has its own bathroom.

- **Laundry Room:** This utility room houses cabinets, a folding counter, and an ironing board.

Images provided by designer/architect.

- **Garage:** This large three-car garage has room for storage. Family members entering the home from this area will find a coat closet and a place to stash briefcases and backpacks.

Rear View

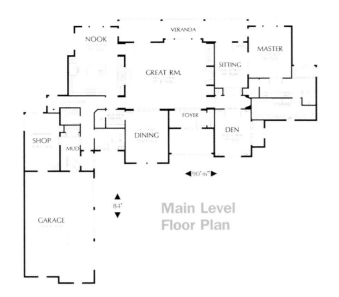

VERANDA

NOOK

MASTER

GREAT RM.

SITTING

SHOP

FOYER

DINING

DEN

MUD

GARAGE

◄90'-6"►

84'

Main Level
Floor Plan

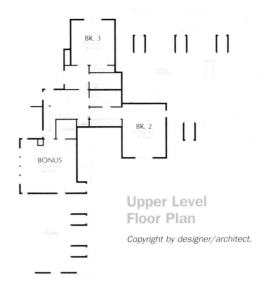

BR. 3

BR. 2

BONUS

Upper Level
Floor Plan

Copyright by designer/architect.

Kitchen

Great Room

Master bath

Master Bedroom

Plan #161028

Dimensions: 84'6" W x 69'4" D
Levels: 1
Square Footage: 3,570
**Optional Finished Basement
Sq. Ft.:** 2,367
Bedrooms: 3
Bathrooms: 3½
Foundation: Basement
Materials List Available: Yes
Price Category: H

Images provided by designer/architect.

From the gabled stone-and-brick exterior to the wide-open view from the foyer, this home will meet your greatest expectations.

Features:

- Great Room/Dining Room: Columns and 13-ft. ceilings add exquisite detailing to the dining room and great room.
- Kitchen: The gourmet-equipped kitchen with an island and a snack bar merges with the cozy breakfast and hearth rooms.
- Master Bedroom: The luxurious master bed room pampers with a separate sitting room with a fireplace and a dressing room boasting a whirlpool tub and two vanities.

- Additional: Two bedrooms upstairs include a private bath and walk-in closet. The optional finished basement solves all your recreational needs: bar, media room, billiards room, exercise room, game room, as well as an office and fourth bedroom.

Rear Elevation

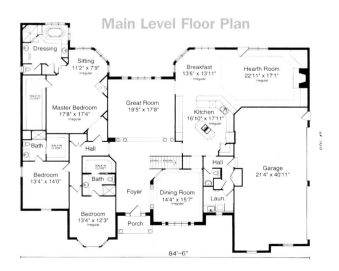

Copyright by designer/architect.

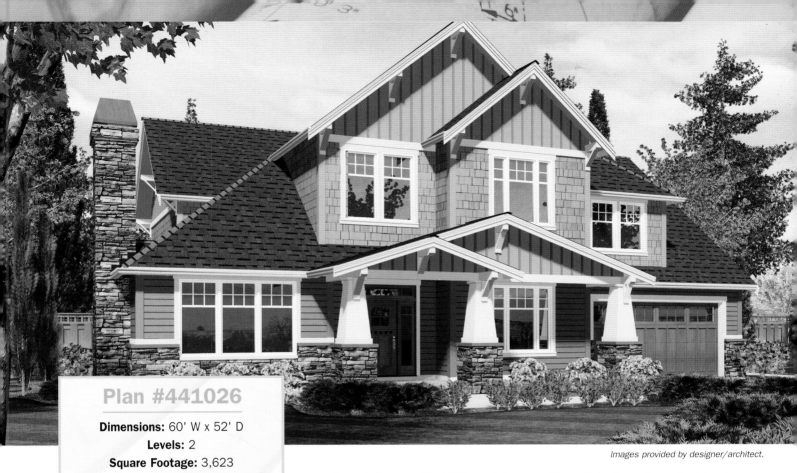

Plan #441026

Dimensions: 60' W x 52' D
Levels: 2
Square Footage: 3,623
Main Level Sq. Ft.: 1,835
Upper Level Sq. Ft.: 1,788
Bedrooms: 4
Bathrooms: 2½
Foundation: Crawl space
Materials List Available: No
Price Category: H

Images provided by designer/architect.

Crazy about Craftsman styling? This exquisite plan has it in abundance and doesn't skimp on the floor plan, either. Massive stone bases support the Arts and Crafts columns at the entry porch.

Features:

- **Living Room:** This large gathering area features a cozy fireplace.
- **Dining Room:** This formal room is connected to the island kitchen via a butler's pantry.

- **Master Suite:** Located upstairs, this suite features a walk-in closet and luxury bath.
- **Bedrooms:** The three family bedrooms share a centrally located compartmented bathroom.

Rear Elevation

CAD FILE AVAILABLE

Main Level Floor Plan

Copyright by designer/architect.

Upper Level Floor Plan

Plan #401049

Dimensions: 77'10" W x 55'8" D
Levels: 2
Square Footage: 4,087
Main Level Sq. Ft.: 2,403
Upper Level Sq. Ft.: 1,684
Bedrooms: 4
Bathrooms: 4½
Foundation: Basement
Materials List Available: Yes
Price Category: I

Images provided by designer/architect.

Finished in stucco, with an elegant entry, this dramatic two-story home is the essence of luxury.

CAD FILE AVAILABLE — CAD

Features:

- Foyer: Double doors open to this foyer, with a sunken living room on the right and a den on the left.

- Dining Room: An archway leads to this formal room, mirroring its own bow window and the curved window in the living room.

- Den: This den and the nearby computer room have use of a full bathroom — making them handy as extra guest rooms when needed.

- Family Room: This room, like the living room, is sunken and warmed by a hearth, but it also has built-in bookcases.

- Kitchen: A snack-bar counter separates this U-shaped kitchen from the light-filled breakfast room.

- Master Suite: This gigantic space has his and her vanities, an oversized shower, a walk-in closet, and a sitting area.

Main Level Floor Plan

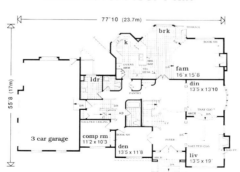

Optional Upper Level Floor Plan

Copyright by designer/architect.

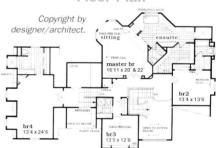

Upper Level Floor Plan

Basement Level Floor Plan

Plan #441031

Dimensions: 78'2" W x 68' D
Levels: 2
Square Footage: 4,150
Main Level Sq. Ft.: 2,572
Upper Level Sq. Ft.: 1,578
Bedrooms: 4
Bathrooms: 4½
Foundation: Crawl space;
slab or basement available for fee
Materials List Available: No
Price Category: I

Images provided by designer/architect.

Features:

- **Great Room:** The main level offers this commodious room, with its beamed ceiling, alcove, fireplace, and built-ins.

- **Kitchen:** Go up a few steps to the dining nook and this kitchen, and you'll find a baking center, walk-in pantry, and access to a covered side porch.

- **Formal Dining Room:** This formal room lies a few steps up from the foyer and sports a bay window and hutch space.

- **Guest Suite:** This suite, which is located at the end of the hall, features a private bathroom and walk-in closet.

- **Master Suite:** A fireplace flanked by built-ins warms this suite. Its bath contains a spa tub, compartmented toilet, and huge shower.

Graceful and gracious, this superb shingle design delights with handsome exterior elements. A whimsical turret, covered entry, upper-level balcony, and bay window all bring their charm to the facade.

CAD FILE AVAILABLE CAD

Main Level Floor Plan

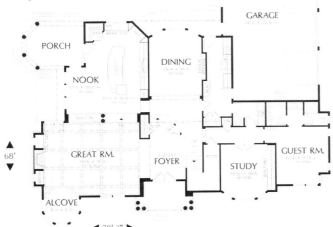

Upper Level Floor Plan

Copyright by designer/architect.

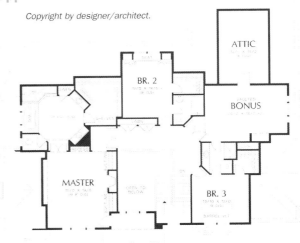

Plan #271087

Dimensions: 43'5½" W x 43'5½" D
Levels: 2
Square Footage: 2,734
Main Level Sq. Ft.: 1,564
Basement Level Sq. Ft.: 1,170
Bedrooms: 4
Bathrooms: 3
Foundation: Crawl space
or daylight basement
Materials List Available: No
Price Category: F

Images provided by designer/architect.

This octagonal home offers a choice of exterior finish: wood or stucco.

Features:

• Entry: A seemingly endless deck leads to the main entry, which includes a coat closet.

• Living Room: A fireplace enhances this spacious room, which offers great outdoor views, plus deck access via sliding glass doors.

• Master Suite: At the end of a hallway, the quiet master bedroom boasts a private bath.

• Lower Level: The basement includes a versatile general area, which could be a nice playroom. A handy den, an extra bedroom and a two-car garage round out this level.

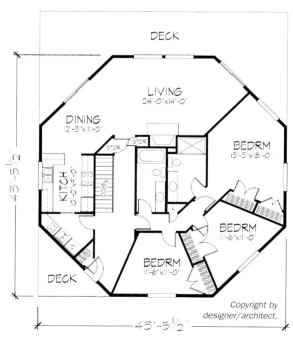

Main Level Floor Plan

Basement Level Floor Plan

Plan #131033

Dimensions: 84'10" W x 48' D
Levels: 2
Square Footage: 2,813
Main Level Sq. Ft.: 1,890
Upper Level Sq. Ft.: 923
Bedrooms: 5
Bathrooms: 3½
Foundation: Crawl space, slab, or basement
Materials List Available: Yes
Price Category: G

Images provided by designer/architect.

Contemporary styling, luxurious amenities, and the classics that make a house a home are all available here.

Features:

- Family Room: A sloped ceiling with skylight and a railed overlook to make this large space totally up to date.

- Living Room: Sunken for comfort and with a cathedral ceiling for style, this room features a fireplace flanked by windows and sliding glass doors.

- Master Suite: Unwind in this room, with its cathedral ceiling, with a skylight, walk-in closet, and private access to the den.

- Upper Level: A bridge overlooks the living room and foyer and leads through the family room to three bedrooms and a bath.

- Optional Guest Suite: 500 sq. ft. above the master suite and den provides total comfort.

Main Level Floor Plan

Copyright by designer/architect.

Upper Level Floor Plan

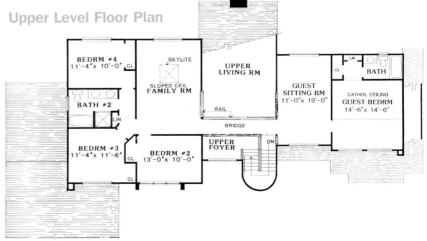

Plan #441009

Dimensions: 94' W x 53' D
Levels: 1
Square Footage: 2,650
Bedrooms: 4
Bathrooms: 2½
Foundation: Crawl space;
slab or basement available for fee
Materials List Available: No
Price Category: F

Images provided by designer/architect.

You'll love to call this plan home. It's large enough for the whole family and has a façade that will make you the envy of the neighborhood.

Features:

- Foyer: The covered porch protects the entry, which has a transom and sidelights to brighten this space.

- Great Room: To the left of the foyer, beyond decorative columns, lies this vaulted room, with its fireplace and media center. Additional columns separate the room from the vaulted formal dining room.

- Kitchen: A casual nook and this island work center are just around the corner from the great room. The second covered porch can be reached via a door in the nook.

- Master Suite: This luxurious space boasts a vaulted salon, a private niche that could be a small study, and a view of the front yard. The master bath features a spa tub, separate shower, compartmented toilet, huge walk-in closet, and access to the laundry room.

- Bedrooms: The two additional bedrooms are located at the back of the plan and share the Jack-and-Jill bathroom.

Copyright by designer/architect.

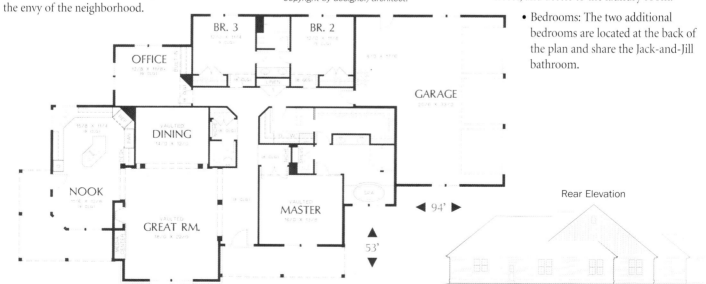

Plan #151753

Dimensions: 68' W x 45'5" D
Levels: 2
Square Footage: 3,341
Main Level Sq. Ft.: 2,126
Upper Level Sq. Ft.: 1,215
Bedrooms: 3
Bathrooms: 2½
Foundation: Crawl space
CompleteCost List Available: Yes
Price Category: G

Images provided by designer/architect.

This charming log home features dormers with upper balconies.

Features:

- Great Room: This two-story gathering area boasts a wall of windows and a fireplace. There is access to the front deck from this area.

- Kitchen: This Island kitchen features a walk-in pantry and is open into the dining room.

- Master Suite: Located on the first floor for convenience, this retreat has access to the rear deck. The master bath boasts a spa tub and separate shower.

- Bedrooms: The two large secondary bedrooms located on the upper level share a common bathroom.

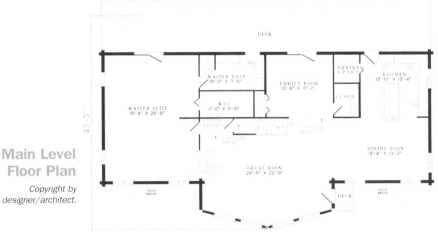

Main Level Floor Plan

Copyright by designer/architect.

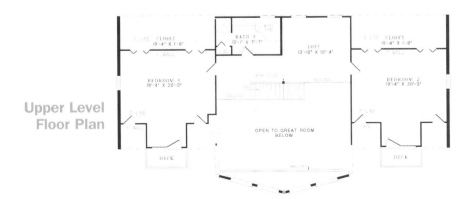

Upper Level Floor Plan

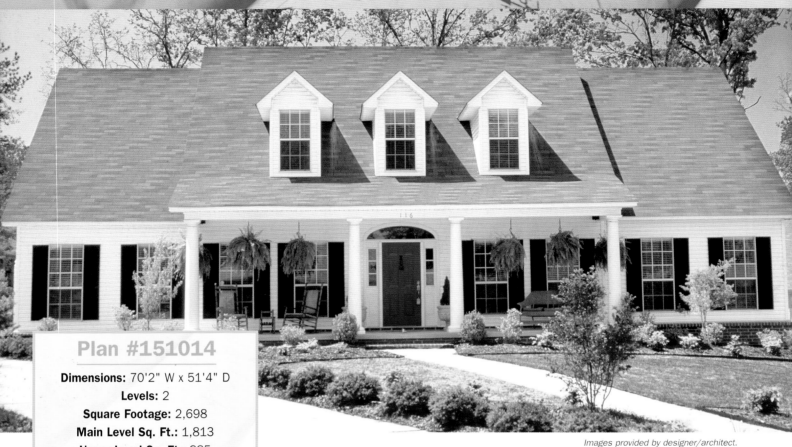

Plan #151014

Dimensions: 70'2" W x 51'4" D
Levels: 2
Square Footage: 2,698
Main Level Sq. Ft.: 1,813
Upper Level Sq. Ft.: 885
Bedrooms: 5
Bathrooms: 3
Foundation: Crawl space, slab; basement option for fee
CompleteCost List Available: Yes
Price Category: F

Images provided by designer/architect.

A comfortable front porch welcomes you into this home that features a balcony over the great room, a study, and a kitchen designed for gourmet cooks.

CAD FILE AVAILABLE CAD

Features:

- Ceiling Height: 9 ft.
- Front Porch: Stately 12-in.-wide pillars form the entryway.
- Foyer: Open to upper story.
- Great Room: A fireplace, vaulted 9-ft. ceiling, and balcony from the second floor add character to this lovely room.
- Dining Room: Open to the kitchen for convenience.
- Kitchen: A large walk-in pantry, well-designed work areas, and eat-in bar make this room a treasure.
- Breakfast Room: Enjoy this spot that opens to both the kitchen and a large covered porch at the rear of the house.
- Study: This quiet room has French doors leading to the yard.
- Master Suite: This spacious area has cozy window seats as well as his and her walk-in closets. The master bathroom is fitted with a whirlpool tub, a glass shower, and his and her sinks.

Upper Level Floor Plan

Main Level Floor Plan

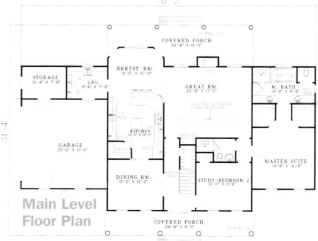

Copyright by designer/architect.

Plan #401048

Dimensions: 57'8" W x 103'6" D
Levels: 2
Square Footage: 5,159
Main Level Sq. Ft.: 2,473
Upper Level Sq. Ft.: 2,686
Bedrooms: 4
Bathrooms: 4½
Foundation: Basement
Materials List Available: Yes
Price Category: I

Images provided by designer/architect.

This unusual stucco-and-siding design opens with a grand portico to a foyer that extends to the living room with fireplace.

CAD FILE AVAILABLE

Features:

- **Dining Room:** Step up a few steps to this dining room, with its coffered ceiling and butler's pantry, which connects to the gourmet kitchen.

- **Hearth Room:** Attached to the kitchen, this hearth room has the requisite fireplace and three sets of French doors that lead to the covered porch.

- **Family Room:** This room features a coffered ceiling and a fireplace flanked by French doors.

- **Master Suite:** This area includes a tray ceiling, covered deck, and lavish bath.

- **Bedrooms:** All bedrooms are located on the second floor. Two full bathrooms serve the family bedrooms and a bonus room that might be used as an additional bedroom or hobby space.

Main Level Floor Plan

Copyright by designer/architect.

103'6 (31.5m) · 57'8 (17.6m)

three-car garage 34' x 27' & 23'
study 12' x 12'2
ldr
K 21' x 15'4
hearth rm 10'6 x 13'6
WET BAR
din 13'2 x 17'2 — COFFERED CEILING
FOYER
fam 15' x 19'10
liv 18' x 15'

Upper Level Floor Plan

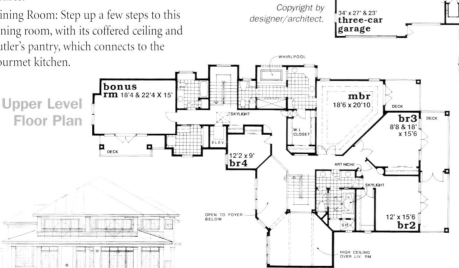

bonus rm 18'4 & 22'4 X 15'
WHIRLPOOL
SKYLIGHT
ELEV.
DECK
br4 12'2 x 9'
W.I. CLOSET
mbr 18'6 x 20'10
DECK
br3 8'8 & 18' x 15'6
ART NICHE
SKYLIGHT
OPEN TO FOYER BELOW
SH.
br2 12' x 15'6
HIGH CEILING OVER LIV. RM

Rear Elevation

Rear View

Plan #441015

Dimensions: 130'3" W x 79'3" D
Levels: 1
Square Footage: 4,732
Bedrooms: 4
Bathrooms: 3 full, 2 half
Foundation: Walkout basement
Materials List Available: No
Price Category: I

An artful use of stone was employed on the exterior of this rustic hillside home to complement other architectural elements, such as the angled, oversize four-car garage and the substantial roofline.

CAD FILE AVAILABLE

Features:

- **Great Room:** This massive vaulted room features a large stone fireplace at one end and a formal dining area at the other. A built-in media center and double doors separate the great room from a home office with its own hearth and built-ins.

- **Kitchen:** This kitchen features a walk-in pantry and snack counter and opens to a skylighted outdoor kitchen. Its appointments include a cooktop and a corner fireplace.

- **Home Theatre:** This space has a built-in viewing screen, a fireplace, and double terrace access.

- **Master Suite:** This private space is found at the other side of the home. Look closely for expansive his and her walk-in closets, a spa tub, a skylighted double vanity area, and a corner fireplace in the salon.

- **Bedrooms:** Three family bedrooms are on the lower level; bedroom 4 has a private bathroom and walk-in closet.

- **Garage:** This large garage has room for four cars; don't miss the dog shower and grooming station just off the garage.

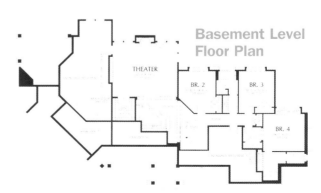

Main Level Floor Plan

Copyright by designer/architect.

Entry

Basement Level Floor Plan

Master Bath

Rear View

Foyer

Dining Room

Great Room

Images provided by designer/architect.

Plan #151253

Dimensions: 61'8" W x 75' D
Levels: 2
Square Footage: 4,882
Main Level Sq. Ft.: 2,583
Upper Level Sq. Ft.: 2,299
Bedrooms: 6
Bathrooms: 6½
Foundation: Slab
CompleteCost List Available: Yes
Price Category: I

Luxury abounds in this six-bedroom home for larger families. You'll find lavish comforts throughout the design.

Features:

- **Living Room:** This open room hosts a bar and wine storage for entertaining family and friends. The two-story space boasts a dramatic fireplace and access to the rear covered porch.

- **Family Room:** An open snack bar faces this room, which will become a favorite for the family to enjoy a movie and popcorn. On nice days or evenings you can step out the double doors and onto the rear covered porch.

- **Master Suite:** This private oasis features a large sleeping area, a sitting area, and an exercise room complete with a sauna and steam room. The large master bath features a spa tub, dual vanities, a separate shower, and a private lavatory area.

- **Bedrooms:** Five additional bedrooms, each with a private full bathroom, complete the floor plan. Two bedrooms are located on the first level, with the remaining three on the upper level with the master suite.

Rear View.

Main Level Floor Plan

Copyright by designer/architect.

Upper Level Floor Plan

Let Us Help You
Plan Your
Dream Home

Whether you've always dreamed of building your own home or you can't find the right house from among the dozens you've toured, our collection of ultimate home plans can help you achieve the home of your dreams. You could have an architect create a one-of-a-kind home for you, but the design services alone could end up costing up to 15 percent of the cost of construction—a hefty premium for any building project. Isn't it a better idea to select from among the hundreds of unique designs shown in our collection for a fraction of the cost?

What does Creative Homeowner® Offer?

In this book, Creative Homeowner® provides hundreds of home plans from the country's best architects and designers. Our designs are among the most popular available. Whether your taste runs from traditional to contemporary, Victorian to early American, you are sure to find the best house design for you and your family. Our plans packages include detailed drawings to help you or your builder construct your dream house. **(See page 278.)**

Can I Make Changes to the Plans?

Creative Homeowner® offers three ways to help you achieve a truly unique home design. Our customizing service allows for extensive changes to our designs. **(See page 279.)** We also provide reverse images of our plans, or we can give you and your builder the tools for making minor changes on your own. **(See page 280.)**

Can You Help Me Stay on Budget?

Building a house is a large financial investment. To help you stay within your budget, Creative Homeowner® can provide you with general construction costs based on your zip code. **(See page 280.)** Also, many of our plans come with the option of buying detailed materials lists to help you price out construction costs.

Is There Anything I Missed?

A typical construction crew consists of a number of skilled professionals. If you plan on doing all or part of the work yourself, or you want to keep tabs on your builder, we offer best-selling building and design books at attractive prices. (See our company Web site at www.creativehomeowner.com.) Our home-building book package covers all phases of home construction, from framing and drywalling to wiring and plumbing. **(See page 288.)**

Our Plans Packages Offer:

All of our home plans are the result of many hours of work by leading architects and professional designers. Most of our home plans include each of the following.

Frontal Sheet

This artist's rendering of the front of the house gives you an idea of how the house will look once it is completed and the property landscaped.

Detailed Floor Plans

These plans show the size and layout of the rooms. They also provide the locations of doors, windows, fireplaces, closets, stairs, and electrical outlets and switches.

Foundation Plan

A foundation plan gives the dimensions of basements, walk-out basements, crawl spaces, pier foundations, and slab construction. Each house design lists the type of foundation included. If the plan you choose does not have the foundation type you require, our customer service department can help you customize the plan to meet your needs.

Roof Plan

In addition to providing the pitch of the roof, these plans also show the locations of dormers, skylights, and other elements.

Exterior Elevations

These drawings show the front, rear, and sides of the house as if you were looking at it head on. Elevations also provide information about architectural features and finish materials.

Interior Elevations and Details

Interior elevations show specific details of such elements as fireplaces, kitchen and bathroom cabinets, built-ins, and other unique features of the design.

Cross Sections

These show the structure as if it were sliced to reveal construction requirements, such as insulation, flooring, and roofing details.

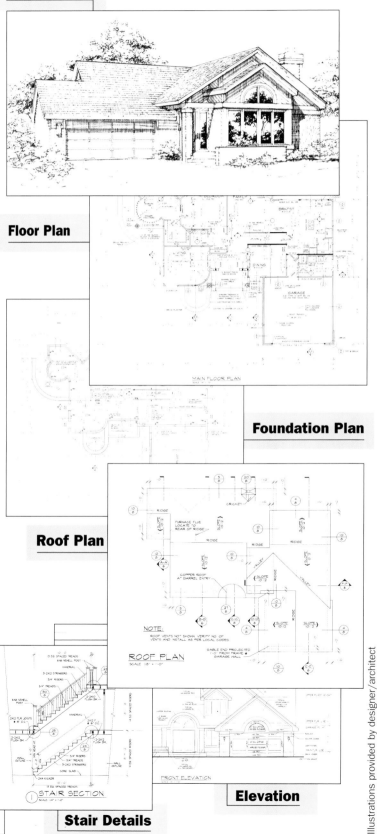

Frontal Sheet

Floor Plan

Foundation Plan

Roof Plan

Cross Sections

Stair Details

Elevation

Illustrations provided by designer/architect

Customize Your Plans in 4 Easy Steps

1 **Select the home plan** that most closely meets your needs. Purchase of a reproducible master is necessary in order to make changes to a plan.

2 **Call 1-800-523-6789 to place your order.** Tell our sales representative you are interested in customizing your plan. To receive your customization cost estimate, we will send you a checklist (via fax or email) for you to complete indicating the changes you would like to make to your plan. There is a $50 nonrefundable consultation fee for this service. If you decide to continue with the custom changes, the $50 fee is credited to the total amount charged.

3 **Fax the completed checklist** to 1-201-760-2431 or email it to us at customize@creativehomeowner.com. Within three business days of receipt of your checklist, a detailed cost estimate will be provided to you.

4 **Once you approve the estimate,** a 75% retainer fee is collected and customization work begins. Preliminary drawings typically take 10 to 15 business days. After approval, we will collect the balance of your customization order cost before shipping the completed plans. You will receive five sets of blueprints or a reproducible master, plus a customized materials list if desired.

Modification Pricing Guide

Categories	Average Cost For Modification
Add or remove living space	Quote required
Bathroom layout redesign	Starting at $120
Kitchen layout redesign	Starting at $120
Garage: add or remove	Starting at $400
Garage: front entry to side load or vice versa	Starting at $300
Foundation changes	Starting at $220
Exterior building materials change	Starting at $200
Exterior openings: add, move, or remove	$65 per opening
Roof line changes	Starting at $360
Ceiling height adjustments	Starting at $280
Fireplace: add or remove	Starting at $90
Screened porch: add	Starting at $280
Wall framing change from 2x4 to 2x6	Starting at $200
Bearing and/or exterior walls changes	Quote required
Non-bearing wall or room changes	$65 per room
Metric conversion of home plan	Starting at $400
Adjust plan for handicapped accessibility	Quote required
Adapt plans for local building code requirements	Quote required
Engineering stamping only	Quote required
Any other engineering services	Quote required
Interactive illustrations (choices of exterior materials)	Quote required

Note: *Any home plan can be customized to accommodate your desired changes. The average prices above are provided only as examples of the most commonly requested changes, and are subject to change without notice. Prices for changes will vary according to the number of modifications requested, plan size, style, and method of design used by the original designer. To obtain a detailed cost estimate, please contact us.*

Terms & Copyright

These home plans are protected under the terms of United States Copyright Law and may not be copied or reproduced in any way, by any means, unless you have purchased reproducible masters, which clearly indicate your right to copy or reproduce. We authorize the use of your chosen home plan as an aid in the construction of one single-family home only. You may not use this home plan to build a second or multiple dwellings without purchasing another blueprint or blueprints, or paying additional home plan fees.

Architectural Seals

Because of differences in building codes, some cities and states now require an architect or engineer licensed in that state to review and "seal" a blueprint, or officially approve it, prior to construction. Delaware, Nevada, New Jersey, and New York require that all plans for houses built in those states be redrawn by an architect licensed in the state in which the home will be built. We strongly advise you to consult with your local building official for information regarding architectural seals.

Before Customization

After

Decide What Type of Plan Package You Need

How many Plans Should You Order?

Standard 8-Set Package. We've found that our 8-set package is the best value for someone who is ready to start building. Once the process begins, a number of people will require their own set of blueprints. The 8-set package provides plans for you, your builder, the subcontractors, mortgage lender, and the building department.

Minimum 5-Set Package. If you are in the bidding process, you may want to order only four sets for the bidding round and reorder additional sets as needed.

1-Set Study Package. The 1-set package allows you to review your home plan in detail. The plan will be marked as a study print, and it is illegal to build a house from a study print alone. It is a violation of copyright law to reproduce a blueprint without permission.

Buying Additional Sets

If you require additional copies of blueprints for your home construction, you can order additional sets within 60 days of the original order date at a reduced price. The cost is $45.00 for each additional set. For more information, contact customer service.

Reproducible Masters

If you plan to make minor changes to one of our home plans, you can purchase reproducible masters. Printed on vellum paper, an erasable paper that you can reproduce in a copying machine, reproducible masters allow an architect, designer, or builder to alter our plans to give you a customized home design. This package also allows you to print as many copies of the modified plans as you need for construction.

CAD Files

CAD files are the complete set of home plans in an electronic file format. Choose this option if there are multiple changes you wish made to the home plans and you have a local design professional able to make the changes. Not available for all plans. Please contact our order department or visit our website to check the availability of CAD files for your plan.

Mirror-Reverse Sets/Right-Reading Reverse

Plans can be printed in mirror-reverse—we can "flip" plans to create a mirror image of the design. This is useful when the house would fit your site or personal preferences if all the rooms were on the opposite side than shown. As the image is reversed, the lettering and dimensions will also be reversed, meaning they will read backwards. Therefore, when ordering mirror-reverse drawings, you must order at least one set of right-reading plans. A $50.00 fee per plan order will be charged for mirror-reverse (regardless of the number of mirror-reverse sets ordered). Some plans are available in right-reading reverse, this feature will show the plan in reverse, but the writing on the plan will be readable. A $150.00 fee per plan order will be charged for right-reading reverse (regardless of the number of right-reading reverse sets ordered). Please contact our order department at or visit our website to check the availibility of this feature for your chosen plan.

EZ Quote: Home Cost Estimator

EZ Quote is our response to one of the most frequently asked questions we hear from customers: "How much will the house cost me to build?" EZ Quote: Home Cost Estimator will enable you to obtain a calculated building cost to construct your home, based on labor rates and building material costs within your zip code area. This summary is useful for those who want to know the total construction costs before purchasing sets of home plans. It will also provide a level of comfort when you begin soliciting bids. The cost is $29.95 for the first EZ Quote and $14.95 for each additional one. Available only in the U.S. and Canada.

CompleteCost Estimator

CompleteCost Estimator is a valuable tool for use in planning and constructing your new home. It combines the detail of a materials list with line-by-line cost estimating. The result is a complete, detailed estimate—similar to a bid. CompleteCost Estimator is only available for certain plans (please see Plan Index) and may only be ordered with the purchase of at least five sets of home plans. The cost is $125.00 for CompleteCost Estimator.

Materials List

Available for most of our plans, the Materials List provides you an invaluable resource in planning and estimating the cost of your home. Each Materials List outlines the quantity, dimensions, and type of materials needed to build your home (with the exception of mechanical systems). You will get faster, more-accurate bids from your contractors and building suppliers. A Materials List may only be ordered with the purchase of at least five sets of home plans.

Order Toll Free by Phone
1-800-523-6789
By Fax: 201-760-2431

Regular office hours are
8:30AM–7:30PM ET, Mon–Fri
Orders received 3PM ET, will be processed and
shipped within two business days.

Order Online
www.ultimateplans.com

Mail Your Order
Creative Homeowner
Attn: Home Plans
24 Park Way
Upper Saddle River, NJ 07458

Canadian Customers
Order Toll Free 1-800-393-1883

Mail Your Order (Canada)
Creative Homeowner Canada
Attn: Home Plans
113-437 Martin St., Ste. 215
Penticton, BC V2A 5L1

Before You Order

Our Exchange Policy

Blueprints are nonrefundable. However, should you find that the plan you have purchased does not fit your needs, you may exchange that plan for another plan in our collection within 60 days from the date of your original order. The entire content of your original order must be returned before an exchange will be processed. You will be charged a processing fee of 20% of the amount of the original order, the cost difference between the new plan set and the original plan set (if applicable), and all related shipping costs for the new plans. Contact our order department for more information. Please note: reproducible masters may only be exchanged if the package is unopened.

Building Codes and Requirements

At the time of creation, our plans meet the bulding code requirements published by the Building Officials and Code Administrators International, the Southern Building Code Congress International, the International Conference of Building Officials, or the Council of American Building Officials. Because building codes vary from area to area, some drawing modifications and/or the assistance of a professional designer or architect may be necessary to comply with your local codes or to accommodate specific building site conditions. We strongly advise you to consult with your local building official for information regarding codes governing your area.

Blueprint Price Schedule

Price Code	1 Set	5 Sets	8 Sets	Reproducible Masters	CAD	Materials List
A	$300	$345	$395	$530	$950	$85
B	$375	$435	$480	$600	$1,100	$85
C	$435	$500	$550	$650	$1,200	$85
D	$490	$560	$610	$710	$1,300	$95
E	$550	$620	$660	$770	$1,400	$95
F	$610	$680	$720	$830	$1,500	$95
G	$670	$740	$780	$890	$1,600	$95
H	$760	$830	$870	$980	$1,700	$95
I	$860	$930	$970	$1,080	$1,800	$105
J	$960	$1,030	$1,070	$1,190	$1,900	$105
K	$1,070	$1,150	$1,190	$1,320	$2,030	$105
L	$1,180	$1,270	$1,310	$1,460	$2,170	$105

Note: All prices subject to change

Shipping & Handling

	1-4 Sets	5-7 Sets	8+ Sets or Reproducibles	CAD
US Regular (7–10 business days)	$18	$20	$25	$25
US Priority (3–5 business days)	$25	$30	$35	$35
US Express (1–2 business days)	$40	$45	$50	$50
Canada Express (1–2 business days)	$60	$70	$80	$80
Worldwide Express (3–5 business days)	$80	$80	$80	$80

Note: All delivery times are from date the blueprint package is shipped (typically within 1-2 days of placing order).

Order Form
Please send me the following:

Plan Number: _____ **Price Code:** _____ (See Plan Index.)

Indicate Foundation Type: (Select ONE. See plan page for availability.)

❏ Slab ❏ Crawl space ❏ Basement ❏ Walk-out basement

❏ Optional Foundation for Fee _____ $_____

(Please enter foundation here)

*Please call all our order department or visit our website for optional foundation fee

Basic Blueprint Package   Cost
❏ CAD File $_____
❏ Reproducible Masters $_____
❏ 8-Set Plan Package $_____
❏ 5-Set Plan Package $_____
❏ 1-Set Study Package $_____
❏ Additional plan sets:
   __ sets at $45.00 per set $_____
❏ Print in mirror-reverse: $50.00 per order $_____
   *Please call all our order department
   or visit our website for availibility
❏ Print in right-reading reverse: $150.00 per order $_____
   *Please call all our order department
   or visit our website for availibility

Important Extras
❏ Materials List $_____
❏ CompleteCost Materials Report at $125.00 $_____
   Zip Code of Home/Building Site _____
❏ EZ Quote for Plan #_____ at $29.95 $_____
❏ Additional EZ Quotes for Plan #s_____ $_____
   at $14.95 each
Shipping (see chart above) $_____
SUBTOTAL $_____
Sales Tax (NJ residents only, add 6%) $_____
TOTAL $_____

Order Toll Free: 1-800-523-6789   By Fax: 201-760-2431
Creative Homeowner
24 Park Way
Upper Saddle River, NJ 07458

Name _____
(Please print or type)

Street _____
(Please do not use a P.O. Box)

City _____ State _____

Country _____ Zip _____

Daytime telephone (___)_____

Fax (___)_____
(Required for reproducible orders)

E-Mail _____

Payment ❏ Check/money order *Make checks payable to Creative Homeowner*

❏ VISA   ❏ MasterCard   ❏ American Express Cards   ❏ Discover

Credit card number _____

Expiration date (mm/yy) _____

Signature _____

Please check the appropriate box:
❏ Licensed builder/contractor   ❏ Homeowner   ❏ Renter

SOURCE CODE | CA625   www.ultimateplans.com   281

Copyright Notice

Index

For pricing, see page 281.

Index

For pricing, see page 281.

Plan #	Price Code	Page	Total Finished Sq. Ft.	Materials List	CompleteCost
181003	A	55	958	Y	N
181005	A	19	869	Y	N
181006	A	56	972	Y	N
181010	A	22	947	Y	N
181011	B	44	1,347	Y	N
181012	B	31	1,079	Y	N
181013	B	28	1,147	Y	N
181014	A	18	784	Y	N
181016	B	32	1,080	Y	N
181017	C	101	1,736	Y	N
181019	B	86	1,494	Y	N
181022	B	56	1,098	Y	N
181025	A	46	975	N	N
181034	F	227	2,687	Y	N
181041	C	81	1,556	Y	N
181053	E	184	2,353	Y	N
181062	D	145	1,953	Y	N
181063	D	159	2,037	Y	N
181081	E	212	2,350	Y	N
181085	D	195	2,183	Y	N
181106	E	185	2,361	Y	N
181109	B	35	1,295	Y	N
181110	E	219	2,526	N	N
181111	B	37	1,304	Y	N
181112	B	60	1,148	Y	N
181114	A	46	992	Y	N
181116	C	102	1,737	Y	N
181117	B	43	1,325	Y	N
181120	B	85	1,480	Y	N
181122	G	259	3,105	Y	N
181125	E	185	2,392	Y	N
181126	B	20	1,486	Y	N
181126	B	21	1,486	Y	N
181128	C	94	1,634	Y	N
181131	B	73	1,442	Y	N
181132	B	79	1,437	Y	N
181133	D	138	1,832	Y	N
181145	A	18	840	Y	N
181151	E	182	2,283	Y	N
181151	E	183	2,283	Y	N
181163	D	167	2,117	Y	N
181245	C	101	1,707	Y	N
191001	D	160	2,156	N	N
191014	E	186	2,435	N	N
191016	E	176	2,421	N	N
191022	B	45	1,377	N	N
191032	D	168	2,091	N	N
191034	E	165	2,259	N	N
191036	B	79	1,438	N	N
191037	C	82	1,575	N	N
211002	C	140	1,792	Y	N
211006	D	164	2,177	Y	N
211013	A	70	998	Y	N
211039	D	137	1,868	Y	N
211069	C	83	1,600	Y	N
211081	B	60	1,110	N	N
221022	G	252	3,382	N	N
241017	E	219	2,431	N	N
251001	B	87	1,253	Y	N
251008	D	138	1,808	Y	N
251014	E	166	2,210	Y	N
261011	I	256	4,042	N	N
271011	B	29	1,296	Y	N
271013	B	31	1,498	Y	N
271023	D	122	1,993	Y	N
271025	E	166	2,223	Y	N
271033	C	61	1,516	Y	N
271034	C	72	1,531	Y	N
271050	B	37	1,188	Y	N
271051	D	120	1,920	Y	N
271052	C	126	1,779	Y	N
271053	E	10	1,413	N	N
271063	E	214	2,572	N	N
271085	C	80	1,541	N	N
271086	D	158	1,910	Y	N
271087	F	268	2,734	N	N
281002	D	136	1,859	Y	N
281004	B	33	1,426	Y	N
281005	B	44	1,362	Y	N
281006	C	96	1,702	Y	N
281010	A	19	884	Y	N
281023	B	30	1,011	Y	N
281027	C	92	1,626	Y	N
281028	F	220	2,643	Y	N
281029	D	128	1,833	Y	N
291005	A	39	896	N	N
291006	A	28	965	N	N
291007	B	22	1,065	N	N
291008	B	65	1,183	N	N
291015	F	233	2,901	N	N
321006	D	152	1,977	Y	N
321009	E	178	2,295	Y	N
321016	H	235	3,814	Y	N
321019	E	187	2,452	Y	N
321020	D	157	1,882	Y	N
321025	A	58	914	Y	N
321035	B	81	1,384	Y	N
321036	F	238	2,900	Y	N
321037	E	177	2,397	Y	N
321038	B	47	1,452	Y	N
321040	B	64	1,084	Y	N
321041	E	190	2,286	Y	N
321042	G	228	3,368	Y	N
321044	F	228	2,618	Y	N
321045	D	159	2,058	Y	N
321046	E	198	2,411	Y	N
321048	G	236	3,216	Y	N
321049	G	230	3,144	Y	N
321051	F	237	2,624	Y	N
321053	D	135	1,985	Y	N
321054	F	235	2,828	Y	N
321055	E	201	2,505	Y	N
321057	C	61	1,524	Y	N
321058	C	96	1,700	Y	N
321060	C	65	1,575	Y	N
321061	G	229	3,169	Y	N
321062	G	230	3,138	Y	N

Index

For pricing, see page 281.

Plan #	Price Code	Page	Total Finished Sq. Ft.	Materials List	CompleteCost
321064	C	132	1,769	Y	N
341007	I	256	4,068	Y	N
341010	B	34	1,261	Y	N
341022	B	88	1,281	Y	N
341029	C	105	1,737	Y	N
341035	C	89	1,680	Y	N
341038	C	82	1,560	Y	N
341044	C	120	1,704	Y	N
341045	B	73	1,440	Y	N
341057	C	99	1,642	Y	N
361029	A	29	960	N	N
361035	B	23	1,384	N	N
361061	F	232	2,979	N	N
361062	G	243	3,291	N	N
361068	G	259	3,405	N	N
361104	D	177	2,094	N	N
371007	D	121	1,944	N	N
371033	C	119	1,724	N	N
371033	C	124	1,724	N	N
371042	D	139	1,999	N	N
371053	C	112	1,654	N	N
371071	C	131	1,729	N	N
371072	C	104	1,772	N	N
371094	D	135	1,875	N	N
381017	C	88	1,540	Y	N
381019	E	201	2,535	Y	N
381021	B	33	1,425	Y	N
391001	D	193	2,015	Y	N
391026	B	13	1,470	Y	N
391027	B	78	1,434	Y	N
391036	B	11	1,301	Y	N
391042	B	32	1,307	Y	N
391056	F	224	2,607	Y	N
391056	F	225	2,607	Y	N
391058	E	212	2,477	Y	N
391068	D	155	1,855	Y	N
391069	B	43	1,492	Y	N
391070	D	145	1,960	Y	N
401005	B	26	1,073	Y	N

Plan #	Price Code	Page	Total Finished Sq. Ft.	Materials List	CompleteCost
401006	C	115	1,670	Y	N
401007	B	80	1,286	Y	N
401019	B	24	1,256	Y	N
401020	B	66	1,230	Y	N
401021	C	74	1,543	Y	N
401027	C	98	1,634	Y	N
401030	C	142	1,795	Y	N
401033	B	63	1,405	Y	N
401035	C	114	1,659	Y	N
401036	C	71	1,583	Y	N
401047	B	42	1,064	Y	N
401048	J	273	5,159	Y	N
401049	I	266	4,087	Y	N
431003	B	71	1,030	Y	N
431004	B	72	1,156	Y	N
441001	D	154	1,850	N	N
441006	D	153	1,891	N	N
441009	F	270	2,650	N	N
441010	F	231	2,973	N	N
441011	F	250	2,898	N	N
441012	F	242	3,682	N	N
441013	H	244	3,317	N	N
441015	I	274	4,732	N	N
441015	I	275	4,732	N	N
441016	D	156	1,893	N	N
441017	C	118	1,707	N	N
441017	C	127	1,707	N	N
441021	C	130	1,760	N	N
441024	H	262	3,517	N	N
441024	H	263	3,517	N	N
441025	G	240	3,757	N	N
441026	H	265	3,623	N	N
441028	G	247	3,165	N	N
441029	G	258	3,217	N	N
441030	J	261	5,180	N	N
441031	I	267	4,150	N	N
441032	D	144	1,944	N	N
441033	F	246	2,986	N	N
441034	E	163	2,262	N	N

Plan #	Price Code	Page	Total Finished Sq. Ft.	Materials List	CompleteCost
441035	E	189	2,196	N	N
441036	F	248	2,902	N	N
441037	E	193	2,237	N	N
441038	E	217	2,518	N	N
441039	D	180	2,120	N	N
441040	D	188	2,079	N	N
441041	D	161	2,164	N	N
441042	E	211	2,538	N	N
441046	F	223	2,606	N	N
441047	F	222	2,605	N	N
441048	E	199	2,453	N	N
441049	D	181	2,124	N	N
451035	F	245	2,883	N	N
451052	D	122	1,895	N	N
451165	D	121	1,933	N	N
451185	D	128	1,804	N	N
451217	I	254	4,711	N	N
451223	H	251	3,650	N	N
451231	E	197	2,281	N	N
451249	E	198	2,281	N	N

Plan #291015

Dimensions: 88'6" W x 58'3" D
Levels: 1.5
Square Footage: 2,901
Main Level Sq. Ft.: 2,078
Upper Level Sq. Ft.: 823
Bedrooms: 3
Bathrooms: 2½
Foundation: Basement
Materials List Available: No
Price Category: F

Upon entering this home, a cathedral-like timber-framed interior fills the eye.

Features:

- Great Room: This large gathering area's ceiling rises up two stories and is open to the kitchen. The beautiful fireplace is the focal point of this room.

- Kitchen: This island kitchen is open to the great room and the breakfast nook. Warm woods of all species enhance the great room and this space.

- Master Suite: This suite has a sloped ceiling and adjoins a luxurious master bath with twin walk-in closets that open to a sunroom with a private balcony.

- Upper Level: This upper level has an open lounge that leads to two bedrooms with vaulted ceilings and a generous second bath.

Images provided by designer/architect.

Main Level Floor Plan

Copyright by designer/architect.

Upper Level Floor Plan

Rear View

Featured House Plan
See page 233

Master Bath

Kitchen

Rear Porch

Dining Room

Complete Your Home Plans Library with these Great Books from Creative Homeowner

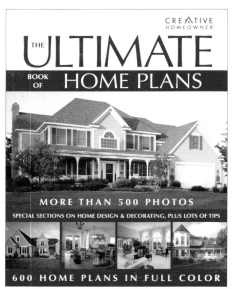

528 pages
Book # 277039

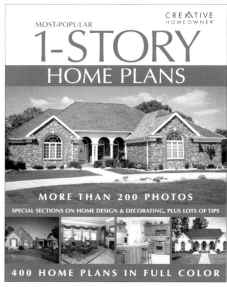

352 pages
Book # 277020

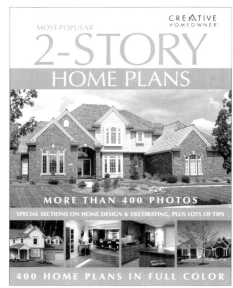

352 pages
Book # 277028

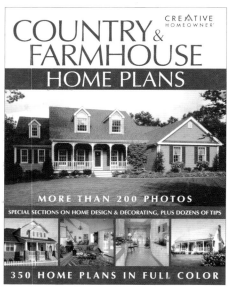

320 pages
Book # 277027

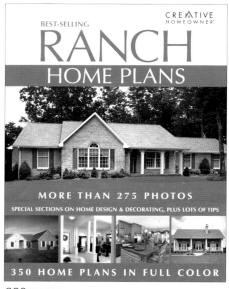

320 pages
Book # 277005

The Best Home Plan Books You Can Find

- Hundreds of home designs from top residential architects and designers

- Hundreds of full-color photographs of actual home that have been built. Many of the homes also include beautiful interior photographs

- Up to 1,000 or more drawings of floor plans, side views and rear views

- Dozens of informative pages containing design and decorating ideas and tips, from working with builders to designing kitchens and installing trimwork and landscaping

---

Books To Help You Build

Creative Homeowner offers an extensive selection of leading how-to books.

Home Building Package

Build and repair your home—inside and out—with these essential titles.

Retail Price: $74.80
Your Price: $65.95
Order #: 267095

Wiring: Complete Projects for the Home
Provides comprehensive information about the home electrical system. Over 750 color photos and 100 illustrations. 288 pages.

Plumbing: Basic, Intermediate & Advanced Projects
An overview of the plumbing system with code-compliant, step-by-step projects. Over 750 full-color photos, illustrations. 272 pages.

House Framing
Walks you through the framing basics, from assembling simple partitions to cutting compound angles for dormers. 650 full-color illustrations and photos. 240 pages.

Drywall: Pro Tips for Hanging and Finishing
Covers tools and materials, estimating, cutting, hanging, and finishing gypsum wallboard. 250 color photos and illustrations. 160 pages.

Look for these and other fine **Creative Homeowner books** wherever books are sold
For more information and to place an order, go to **www.creativehomeowner.com**